Changing Times

Changing Times

Transforming Culture and Behaviors for Law Enforcement

Edited by
Frank Mielke and Charles Kocher

ROWMAN & LITTLEFIELD
Lanham • Boulder • New York • London

Published by Rowman & Littlefield
An imprint of The Rowman & Littlefield Publishing Group, Inc.
4501 Forbes Boulevard, Suite 200, Lanham, Maryland 20706
www.rowman.com

6 Tinworth Street, London SE11 5AL, United Kingdom

British Library Cataloguing in Publication Information Available

Library of Congress Cataloging-in-Publication Data

Names: Mielke, Frank, 1944– editor. | Kocher, Charles, 1950– editor.
Title: Changing times : transforming culture and behaviors for law
    enforcement / edited by Frank Mielke and Charles Kocher.
Description: Lanham, Maryland : Rowman & Littlefield, [2020] | Includes
    bibliographical references and index.
Identifiers: LCCN 2019057227 (print) | LCCN 2019057228 (ebook) | ISBN
    9781538127612 (cloth) | ISBN 9781538127629 (epub)
    ISBN 9781538164556 (pbk)
Subjects: LCSH: Police social work. | Crisis intervention (Mental health
    services) | Assistance in emergencies.
Classification: LCC HV8079.2 .C43 2020 (print) | LCC HV8079.2 (ebook) |
    DDC 361.3—dc23
LC record available at https://lccn.loc.gov/2019057227
LC ebook record available at https://lccn.loc.gov/2019057228

Contents

v

PART III: COMMUNITY

Preface

This book identifies the components necessary to transform attitudes, behaviors, and culture in the interest of diverting the mentally ill out of the criminal justice system and into treatment, where appropriate. Times are changing with an increasing awareness of the financial, regulatory, public safety, and moral imperatives related to diversion.

Change requires a systemic shift in a very diverse landscape, with sometimes competing entities, necessitating a carefully orchestrated strategy. We propose that law enforcement should be at the forefront. This requires an appreciation of the current environment, a realistic appraisal of their organization, and the recognition of the power of the community.

In addition, throughout the book, we weave the results of a recently completed survey of more than eight hundred police officers to provide additional perspective.

PARTS

The chapters in this book are divided into three parts:

Environment

In the first three chapters, we identify the imperatives for change and provide a useful reference of illnesses and syndromes that guide law enforcement officers when encountering someone in crisis. Understanding the history of the interaction between law enforcement and the mentally ill identifies how we have progressed but also underscores the need for change.

Organization

Among the many forces of change is the organization, specifically law enforcement. For law enforcement to be effective in matters of diversion, they must be a force multiplier as a change agent. The transition from an old to a new way of thinking requires alignment within the organization so that all are behaving in a consistent manner, with everyone conforming to both the letter and the spirit of the change as presented in chapter 4. In chapter 5, we recognize that law enforcement must be aligned with the mental health landscape. This necessitates breaking down silos that currently inhibit meaningful change regarding diversion. Chapters 6 digs deeper into organizational considerations by recognizing that those in law enforcement are subject to trauma and the ensuing impact on their professional and personal life. In chapter 7, we present the response to trauma, which is resiliency.

If diversion is to be effective and in recognition of the silos that plague the effort, it's important to acknowledge the four faces of mental health to law enforcement officers: First, the quality and responsiveness of a mobile crisis unit. Second, availability of a transfer facility. Third, crisis training. And fourth, counseling offered to police officers who are subject to enormous stress and trauma.

Community

Our editors, authors, and coauthors, who represent law enforcement, crisis trainers and responders, academicians, leaders in primary and secondary education, community leaders, and researchers, all embrace the power of the community. Chapter 8 profiles one such community, and chapter 9 provides examples of effective intervention programs. The book concludes with an in-depth analysis of a program designed to address diversion at its core, our children.

Part I

ENVIRONMENT

Chapter One

Response to a Need

Frank Mielke and Charles Kocher

INTRODUCTION

Today, leaders in law enforcement face unprecedent challenges. Among them is the appropriate interaction with the mentally ill. Mishandling results in unwanted headlines, unnecessary expenditures of taxpayer money, and heightened public safety risks. Perhaps the most compelling reason to respond to this challenge is the moral imperative. It's the right thing to do.

This book provides a pathway to change for leaders in law enforcement. This chapter presents the foundation for change and the need for a response to this need.

BEFORE WE BEGIN

You know someone with a mental illness.

According to the Centers for Disease Control and Prevention, about 25 percent of all U.S. adults have a mental illness and nearly 50 percent of U.S. adults will develop at least one mental illness during their lifetime.[1] The illness may not be obvious, due to some combination of medication, therapy, support, self-discipline, and persistence that enables these individuals dealing with mental illness to lead productive lives.

Unfortunately, unlike those suffering from a heart condition, diabetes, or cancer, some with mental illness find themselves in jail—not because of some criminal intent, but because their illness may cause behaviors that are unusual, annoying, or threatening. We opine that arrest is counterproductive, ineffective, and inefficient.

The compilation of chapters is designed to accelerate the effort to divert those in crisis away from the criminal justice system and into treatment, which we call diversion. To initiate or accelerate a diversion effort, we propose a twofold strategy that will unfold in this and future chapters:

1. *Start Locally*—Leaders have the power to influence change within their sphere of influence, limited only by their energy and imagination. Change is most effective when it's bottom up. In other words, local leaders working in collaboration with their peer organizations bring about a fundamental change in attitudes, culture, and behaviors. A "bottom-up strategy" enhances ownership because it is a product of local leaders. In addition, collaborators build in community nuances state and federal regulations often miss.
2. *Think Systemically*—The nature of a diversion strategy requires cross-functional thinking and action. The strategy lends itself to systems thinking that may require a fundamental adjustment in thought processes. This change begs the question: As a leader, are you willing to move out of your comfort zone? Are you willing to entertain practices not aligned with your own? Critical "out-of-the-box" thinking and leadership are required ingredients. We emphasize that change must take place within the parameters of existing laws and reflect good judgment in the interest of the individual in crisis and the community. Thinking systemically leads to a simple formula: information leads to collaboration, which, in turn, leads to innovation—a formula explored in greater detail throughout this book.

Law enforcement is in a pivotal position to undertake a significant portion of the responsibility to bring about a required paradigm shift. Often, a police officer is an initial responder or an integral part of a crisis intervention team. Although law enforcement is often at the forefront, the application of systems thinking recognizes that they are not alone.

We wrote this book to help you understand the forces that drive attitudes, culture, and behavior and how to shift direction in the interest of diversion. More important, and where appropriate, the chapters in this book will link theory to application, bolstering the confidence of the reader to initiate meaningful change.

You will understand the dynamics of a highly interdependent landscape of systems. We call this the "network," in which participants have common goals but execute them with different and sometimes conflicting agendas. Further, we suggest how to overcome blockages to change while leveraging the strengths within the network.

As a result, you will:

- develop an appreciation for the compelling reasons to change;
- obtain a working knowledge of the various types of illnesses and disorders;
- recognize alignment issues within and among organizations in the criminal justice, behavioral health, and education systems, among others;
- learn more about police officers' exposure to trauma as a platform for understanding the emotional challenges leading to destructive behaviors such as addiction and suicide;
- assess emerging theories and practices; and
- articulate a proactive position to change and engage the community in diversion efforts.

THE CRIMINAL JUSTICE/BEHAVIORAL HEALTH NETWORK

Developing a response to the need to accelerate diversion requires an understanding of the environment within which the criminal justice and behavioral health systems reside. These systems reside in a network of other systems characterized as large, complex, underfunded, and controlled through myriad cumbersome regulations. Organizations participating in the network often are driven by conflicting agendas and find difficulty in acclimating to a new way of thinking. Those suffering mental illness live with a stigma imposed by society and linked to an apathetic public. Finally, the mentally ill suffer the consequences of a dysfunctional system.

SYSTEMS THEORY

Understanding the network requires an understanding of systems theory. Although it is beyond the scope of this book to delve into this complicated and abstract theory, it is useful to identify some basic concepts,[2] including:

A system contains a structure of organized components of similar and/or different types.
   The effectiveness of a diversion effort stems from different components, ideally working in a collaborative manner. When the components work at cross-purposes, as is sometimes the case, the result is dysfunction, such as a person in crisis facing unwarranted incarceration rather than treatment.

No system exists in isolation. A system interfaces with other systems that may be of a similar or different type.

Some have a misconception that responsibility for diversion rests solely with law enforcement or solely with the behavioral health system. At times, organizational behaviors are driven by such thinking bolstered by attitudes and culture. The pathway to diversion is a function of collaboration and synergy. The purpose of this book is to propose means to change the paradigm of culture and attitudes, thereby changing behaviors.

The functioning of a system affects multiple other systems and is affected by multiple other systems.

This element of interconnectivity and the resulting impact are evident in the behavioral health system. If the police exacerbate the condition of a patient in crisis, attending to that patient is more difficult for those who follow, be it a crisis worker or someone in an emergency room.

On a larger scale, if a behavioral health system in a jurisdiction, usually at a county level, decides to be less or more aggressive pursuing involuntary commitments, the impact can be felt throughout the network. For example, an overly aggressive strategy in pursuit of involuntary commitments may tax the capacity of facilities that provide beds for crisis patients. A less-aggressive strategy suggests that crisis patients may be released prematurely back to the community and prove that they are, in fact, a danger to themselves or others.

The constant interaction between systems results in a constant state of change.

The network is in a constant state of flux. Changes include new or different regulations; shifting insurance provisions that impact the availability and type of coverage; new leadership in any of the organizations that may result in a change of attitudes, culture, and behaviors.

The mental health network is large, comprised of entities that touch those in crisis. Table 1.1 provides some of the major participants in the behavioral health system and briefly describes each entity.

SYSTEMS AND SILOS

Often, the term silo is used to identify isolated components in a system or network. As a result of silos, dysfunction ensues. Each entity in the network is a stand-alone organization with the potential of becoming isolated and thereby a silo. Further, siloed organizations, operating at cross-purposes

Table 1.1. Providers and Union Representatives

Entity	Description
Funders	Includes insurance companies and state and local agencies that provide funds for services for the mentally ill.
General Public	There are various aspects of the general public: • Attitudes are shaped by their experiences or perceptions or those of others; • Influences public policy through their elected officials; • A stigma of mental illness is that prevalent; and • They are often the first with the ability to react to a mental illness crisis.
Providers	Includes hospitals, crisis centers, for- and not-for-profit agencies and other organizations that deliver services to the mentally ill.
Advocacy Groups	Groups that promote a behavioral health agenda to address the needs of the mentally ill. The National Alliance on Mental Illness (NAMI) is one of the better-known advocacy groups.
Law Enforcement	Operates at the pivotal point that significantly influences the path toward incarceration or treatment. This occurs when law enforcement intervenes during a crisis.
Judicial System	Makes the ultimate decision on the involuntary commitment process; some jurisdictions have promoted mental health courts in the interest of the patient. Although this approach enjoys wide acceptance, it should be pointed out that the patient is already in the judicial system.
Health System	Hospitals may or may not have behavioral health or crisis intervention units. Those that don't are required to attend to those in crisis. Some abuse what a hospital emergency room (ER) is required to offer. ER personnel complain about the "frequent fliers"—those who frequently present themselves at an ER looking for a warm bed or a hot meal by claiming they have suicidal thoughts.
Education System	Mental illness can start at an early age caused by trauma from a variety of sources. Chapter 10 covers a program initiated by a very enterprising school district in response to the alarming statistics about children experiencing mental illness.
Faith-Based Systems	In a time of crisis, an individual may turn to his priest, minister, rabbi, or imam for help. They can be instrumental in a crisis situation working with the police and others.
Business Community	Unfortunately, the workplace is a target for violence, at times from those in crisis. Also, consider that businesses provide insurance and wellness programs, both supportive of mental health.
Labor Unions	A Columbia University study indicates that in the face of "new interests and directions in relation to people with mental health conditions, they (labor unions) will want to take a leading role in forging a path of fairness in employment and access to jobs for mental health service recipients."[1]

1. Sheila Akabas, Lauren Gates, and Lori Bikson, "Unions Helping Workers with Mental Health Conditions: A Guide for Consumers," Columbia University, September 30, 2002.

because of different policies and procedures, deter efforts to divert. Silos are characterized by:

- failure to recognize and respect the overall goals of the network and the need to place the goals of the network ahead of theirs where legally and morally allowable;
- interest in the individual organization over the interest of the network as a whole;
- breakdown in communication;
- problem-solving processes that are self-serving and solutions that may create problems for others; and
- adversarial relationships.

Law enforcement needs to understand each of the organizations in table 1.1 and how all relate to law enforcement and their interactions with those in crisis. This takes some effort because different organizations in the network have different policies and procedures steeped in long-standing cultures.

A silo between or among organizations can vary in rigidity. At one level, there is agreement on an ultimate goal. There is also a level of respect and acknowledgment of differences. This respect leads to compromise and reconciliation. On another level, organizations become blinded by their own prejudices and fail even to consider an alternative point of view. At this level, the relationship becomes adversarial, significantly compromising the ability to achieve the ultimate goal.

An example of organizations driven by different philosophies that contribute to silos is evident when an individual in crisis is taken into custody. Police transport the individual handcuffed in the backseat of a cruiser. This practice, which operates without exception, flies in the face of the "least-restrictive alternative" practice of mental health practitioners. Within their individual organizations, both are correct. The problem occurs because both parties demonstrate a failure to recognize and respect the underlying reasons supporting the practices of the other. When this happens, both organizations operate with a siloed mentality.

Perhaps the most tragic example of a siloed network is the mass killings at Virginia Tech on April 16, 2007, which left thirty-two students and faculty dead at the hands of a mentally deranged individual. This individual interacted with various entities in the network including the university, the judicial system, and several mental health professionals, among others. A key finding in a report to the governor was: "No one knew all the information and no one connected all the dots"[3]—a clear sign that Cho, the perpetrator of the violence, fell through the cracks in a siloed network.

HIPAA[4] often is cited as a contributor to a siloed environment where communications may be reduced to a trickle or may even shut down completely. We suggest that readers understand what can and cannot be shared as recommended by a National Alliance on Mental Illness (NAMI) publication, *Understanding What HIPAA Means for Mental Illness.*[5]

Consider the following question and answer from this publication:

Can health-care providers share protected mental health information with law enforcement officials?

Yes, in certain circumstances, particularly if the person living with mental illness poses a danger to self or others; then health-care providers may disclose necessary information.[6]

Interactions among the entities within the network vary by frequency and circumstance. For example, the level of interaction is high between a funder, such as an insurance company, and a provider, such as a hospital, for the proper distribution of funds and treatment. Interactions between law enforcement and other entities in the network occur during a period of crisis where response times are limited and the consequences of decisions often are significant. An individual in crisis needs help now. The level of interaction will be an important consideration as we proceed to test levels of alignment between and among various network entities, addressed in chapter 5.

Consider the following *select* participants within the system and the roles they play:

General Public

At times, behaviors that pose a threat to self or others take place in a public forum where police respond to calls from concerned citizens about an individual's disturbing behaviors. Often, they are alerted by citizens who have no personal ties to the individual. At other times, these behaviors may take place in the home, workplace, or school where personal ties or fear of embarrassment may deter concerned individuals from alerting officials.

Although some members of the general public react in a timely manner, too often people don't respond and lament that they should have recognized the signals. The lack of a response may be a result of:

- Ignorance (they had no idea)
- Priority (it just wasn't that important)
- Perspective (don't make a mountain out of molehill)
- Denial (understands but fails to face reality)
- Fear (retribution)

At a micro level, the general public may trigger involvement by law enforcement or others. At a macro level, they influence critical decisions on funding and legislative initiatives.

AFFIRMING THE NEED—GENERAL PUBLIC

At a micro level, the general public may trigger involvement by law enforcement or others. At a macro level, they influence critical decisions on funding and legislative initiatives.

Law Enforcement

The police are often the first responders to someone with a suspected mental illness. The behavior of the individual may range from violence to himself/herself or others to antisocial behaviors that make him/her different. In other words, the behaviors may constitute nothing other than a public nuisance, or, in the extreme, may lead to violence.

Dealing with those in crisis is materially different from dealing with a felon. In Montreal, Canada, the police learn to improve their interactions with people who suffer from mental illness from social workers and psychiatrists.[7]

Popular training programs, in the United States and elsewhere, include:

- CIS training (Montgomery County Emergency Services)
- CIT training (University of Memphis)
- Mental health first aid
- ACEs training

There are always potential issues once the individual is detained. Before a final resolution is reached, at times the police have to detain the individual in a facility not designed for someone exhibiting self-destructive behaviors. The inadequacy of their jail prompted the Phoenixville, Pennsylvania, Police Department to secure a grant from the Phoenixville Community Health Foundation to build a more compassionate detention area where padded walls replace concrete, as shown below.

This interaction between the Phoenixville Police Department and the Phoenixville Community Health Foundation demonstrates positive synergy and how the potential of the local community can address critical issues. This is a topic covered, and examples included, in chapters 8 to 10.

One may reasonably question how a more compassionate detention facility contributes to diversion. A less compassionate facility may have consequences, including criminal charges. Here is an example:

A warrant for an involuntary commitment was issued to an individual well known through prior interactions with the local police. Prior to this incident, in midwinter, a corporal had arrested the individual on criminal charges. The corporal ultimately had to dive into an icy stream to make the arrest. Now, that same corporal had to respond to execute a warrant for an involuntary commitment.

Upon arriving at his residence, the corporal found the individual barricaded in his basement. Instead of breaking down the door, he enlisted the help of the patient's father; they were successful in coaxing him out so they could deliver him to the local hospital to begin the commitment process. There, the process continued without incident. They fed him. He even engaged the staff in friendly conversation about the hospital's computer system. But things started to deteriorate after several hours in a padded locked room with a camera so hospital personnel could monitor his behavior. Finally, he snapped. He used his bed as a battering ram and tore the sprinkler system out of the ceiling, causing thousands of dollars in damages. The police were called, resulting in criminal charges.

AFFIRMING THE NEED—LAW ENFORCEMENT

Before encountering an individual in crisis, the police must be trained and provided resources to protect the public, the patient, and themselves. Training strategies must move from the intuitively obvious to a rigorous, evidence-based program evaluation.

Health System

The Phoenixville case, cited above, demonstrates how the interaction between entities in the network can break down. However, weakness in one entity of the network reverberates through the entire system.

Because of the scarcity of resources, it's unfair to lay blame solely at the feet of either the medical or behavioral health system.

For the medical system, some hospitals are equipped, by virtue of service offerings, facilities, or training, to treat mentally ill patients adequately whether their presence is voluntary or involuntary. Others, without such resources and training, particularly those in the emergency room, struggle. The problem is becoming more severe. According to a survey by the Robert Wood Johnson Foundation, more than 68 percent of adults with a mental disorder (diagnosed through a structured clinical interview) reported having at least one general medical disorder, and 29 percent of those with a medical disorder had a comorbid mental health condition.[8]

At times, emergency room personnel must diagnose and treat a multitude of illnesses and disorders the patient presents, including:

• medical disorders
• mental health disorders
• conditions involving drugs and alcohol
• combinations of all of the above

In the face of growing demand, capacity problems are surfacing. Community hospitals[9] were characterized as the "front door to the mental health system for Washington State residents who are committed involuntarily."[10] A report contains dire predictions:

> Low hospital payments and inadequate post-discharge community resources are resulting in financial losses, forcing community hospitals to question their ability to continue providing inpatient mental health care. More and more hospitals are concluding they must downsize or close their inpatient mental health units because the financial drain they pose threatens their entire facilities.[11]

The situation within the health system does not bode well for the police. As systems theory tells us, weaken one link in the chain, and the chain becomes weaker.

AFFIRMING THE NEED—HEALTH SYSTEM

Hospitals rely on law enforcement for protection when crisis patients pose a threat to themselves or others and neutralizing the threat exceeds the capacity of the hospital. In turn, the police rely on hospitals and others in the response chain to handle those in crisis.

Behavioral Health System

After an individual in crisis is taken into custody, an array of entities have wide-ranging roles to assess and deliver behavioral health interventions and to accommodate a variety of everyday needs including, but not limited, to transportation, housing, and socialization. Based on a 2013 study,[12] researchers found that characterizations of the mental health system vary, usually against a backdrop of pessimism and despair. On more than one occasion, the researchers encountered the comment, "The system is dead." Dr. Caroline Smith, then deputy mental health director, Chester County, Pennsylvania, offered a more balanced opinion. She cited successes but admitted that the system is "complex with lots of gaps and difficult to navigate." Further, the funding mechanisms are complex.

High-profile incidents such as the one in December 2012 at the Sandy Hook Elementary School, where twenty schoolchildren and six staff members were murdered, raises the concern of the adequacy of the response of the behavioral health system. Following the Sandy Hook incident, the Senate Health, Education, Labor, and Pensions Committee commenced hearings in January 2013 to examine the state of America's behavioral health system. According to C-SPAN, "The hearing discusses ways to improve access to services for those who need them, the need to focus on prevention and early intervention and will include a review of issues related to mental health and gun violence."[13]

All these years later, no meaningful change is evident. Events such as Sandy Hook highlight the challenges law enforcement faces to protect our children. As a result, heightened security measures at our schools serve as a reminder of the environment in which we live. Our faith in government diminishes with each day of inactivity.

Systems thinking guides the recognition and understanding of entities in the network and provides a starting point for a more precise assessment to bring about meaningful change.

AFFIRMING THE NEED—BEHAVIORAL HEALTH SYSTEM

Responding to an individual in crisis often requires individuals from law enforcement and the behavioral health system to execute an effective crisis intervention. On a local basis, leaders in both systems must act synergistically to ensure that all members in their respective departments respect others' culture, attitudes, and behaviors to resolve any point-of-contact issues in the best interest of the patient. At all times, communication lines must be open.

WHERE ARE WE?

We provide an array of U.S. data and indicators of the current state of affairs. This data should serve as a reference for those at the local level. In other words, what is the local data that can and should be compared to U.S. results?

Consider national statistics. According to the National Alliance on Mental Illness, some two million people in the United States are booked into jail each year. Of those, nearly 15 percent of men and 30 percent of women have a serious mental condition.[14] Further, according to a 2006 Bureau of Justice statistics report, approximately 74 percent of state prisoners, 63 percent of federal prisoners, and 76 percent of jail inmates met the criteria for a mental health disorder.[15]

In the face of such need, it's widely recognized that the three largest mental health facilities in the United States are Los Angeles County Jail, Cook County (Illinois) Jail, and Rikers Island Jail in New York City.[16] Relying on prisons and jails is an embarrassing response to a critical problem. Our jails and prisons are ill equipped to treat those with a mental illness. In fact, according to NAMI, many in jail don't receive necessary treatment and end up getting worse instead of better.[17] Often, while incarcerated, the mental illness patient is essentially a target of abuse, thereby exacerbating the problem. Upon release, and back in the community, the patient may continue to find himself without medical coverage, access to needed professional attention, or a support group to provide guidance. Too often, the patient again finds himself interacting with law enforcement, so the vicious cycle starts anew.

The concluding comments of a three-year study in Virginia, which studied mental illness and recidivism, reflect key insights on the subject:

> The "revolving door" between incarceration and the community for individuals with mental health issues are propelled largely by untreated mental illness and co-occurring substance abuse disorders among returning citizens. As predicted, the decreased availability of hospital and training center beds without a congruent increase in community services has increased the "criminalization" of the mentally ill in Virginia.[18]

There is no single solution. As with any complex problem, myriad components are interconnected; and, as we learn from the study of systems theory, a change in one part can impact other components and the systems as a whole. Sometimes the change is immediate and visible. At other times, the impact of the change takes considerable time to manifest itself. Changes, both immediate and long term, can be either positive or negative.

This issue is not new. As early as the 1960s, deinstitutionalization was viewed as an appropriate strategy for the mentally ill. It was a movement in response to recognized abuse of the mentally ill in state facilities. The idea was to move the patient from an institution to a community-based facility. However, funding did not follow the patient to the community. The unfortunate legacy from this change in strategy exists even today.

Approximately forty years later, the problem persists. On July 12, 1999, New York Senator Patrick Moynihan read the following into the *Congressional Record*:

> Over the past 45 years, we have emptied state mental hospitals, but we have not provided commensurate outpatient treatment. Increasingly, individuals with mental illnesses are left to fend for themselves on the streets, where they vic-

timize others or, more frequently, are victimized themselves. Eventually, many wind up in prison, where the likelihood of treatment is nearly as remote.[19]

The conditions Moynihan cited are still true, and they demonstrate the consequences of how a shift in a system can have unintended consequences. We eliminated the abuses in our institutions but are left with far too many who suffer from mental illness without homes and on the street, who often wind up in our jails and prisons.

Although the data reveals disturbing results in the United States as a whole, local law enforcement agencies confront the challenge every day. Consider the 2016 shooting in El Cajon, California. Police responded to calls about a man acting erratically who refused to follow their orders. The incident escalated until police shot and killed the suspect. According to newspaper reports, "The shooting sparked protests in the San Diego County city, with friends of the man's family saying he suffers from a mental illness and did not pose a threat to the officers."[20]

This incident has multiple facets, not the least of which is the community response to the police shooting of a minority. We offer this observation without judgment. Another facet of this encounter is the mental condition of the victim. The question we pose, without judgment, is: Might the police have handled this situation differently?

The mentally ill are not the only victims in an encounter with the police. Consider the case of a forty-eight-year-old New York City police officer. Miosotis Familia was sitting alone in a police vehicle when she was approached by a lone gunman who shot her at point-blank range. It was later determined that the shooter, Alexander Bonds, suffered from mental illness. At her funeral, the New York City police commissioner said in frustration, "I don't know how else to say it. This was an act of hate, in this case against police officers. The very people who stepped forward and made a promise to protect you, day and night."[21]

Whether it's in El Cajon or New York City, leaders in law enforcement at the local level need a framework to begin the process of changing attitudes, culture, and behaviors.

IMPERATIVES FOR CHANGE

The response to the issues presented can be reduced to four imperatives (see figure 1.1):

1. Financial
2. Regulatory
3. Public Safety
4. Moral

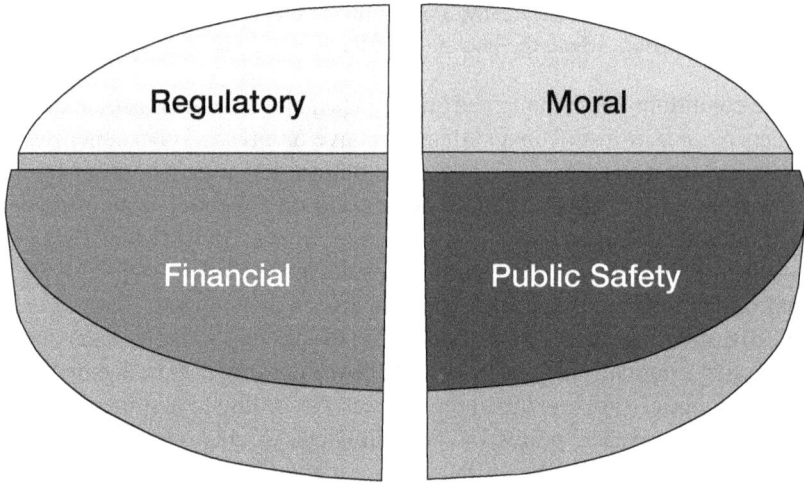

Figure 1.1.

Financial Imperative

At times, countrywide statistics lose their relevancy. It's difficult to put hundreds of millions or billions of dollars in perspective for leaders in law enforcement when their budgets are significantly less. Regardless, local law enforcement leaders feel the pinch when officers are required to attend a hearing or watch over a crisis patient in an emergency room. Another perspective relayed to us on multiple occasions when an officer is responding to an individual in crisis is, "We are not arresting the bad guys."

The community covers the cost of law enforcement, related to mental illness or not. But costs related to mental illness not directly associated with law enforcement are exacerbated by the failure to divert those in crisis appropriately.

Consider the following cost categories; this is not an exhaustive list but rather items for consideration. We suggest positioning the cost of mental illness within the following framework:

The list is not complete. Costs, both direct and indirect, vary based on the community profile.

Another facet of cost is homelessness. According to the National Coalition for the Homeless, "Serious mental illnesses disrupt people's ability to carry out essential aspects of daily life, such as self-care and household management."[22] A connection exists between mental illness and homelessness, and homelessness presents a cost to the community.

The failure to divert the homeless/mentally ill contributes to a destructive cycle of events as indicated in figure 1.2. Send the mentally ill/homeless person to jail, and her condition most certainly will deteriorate, creating a cycle of recidivism.

Table 1.2.

	Agency	Community
Direct	• Manpower to respond to those in crisis; directly correlated to volume of crisis calls. • Cost of crisis training, including tuition, travel, and meals where necessary. • Overtime where such expenses emanate from involvement in crisis situations.	• The community, at a local, regional, state, or federal level, underwrites the cost of providing the mentally ill prisoner appropriate psychiatric treatment. Diverting the crisis patient into treatment provides more cost-effective interventions and reduces the very costly expense of recidivism.
Indirect	• When the police take time to address an individual in crisis, they are not taking drugs off the street or pursuing the priorities of their agency. • The police accept the responsibility to address dangerous or potentially dangerous situations in a timely fashion but bristle when the behavioral health agencies are slow to respond to a crisis. Poor attitudes have consequences.	• It may seem insensitive or callous to link public image and mental illness as a cost consideration. But consider a parent reluctant to patronize "main street" merchants because the children are exposed to those who look, behave, or smell funny. The business community cites a loss of revenue because the law enforcement or the mental health system, or both, fails to respond adequately.

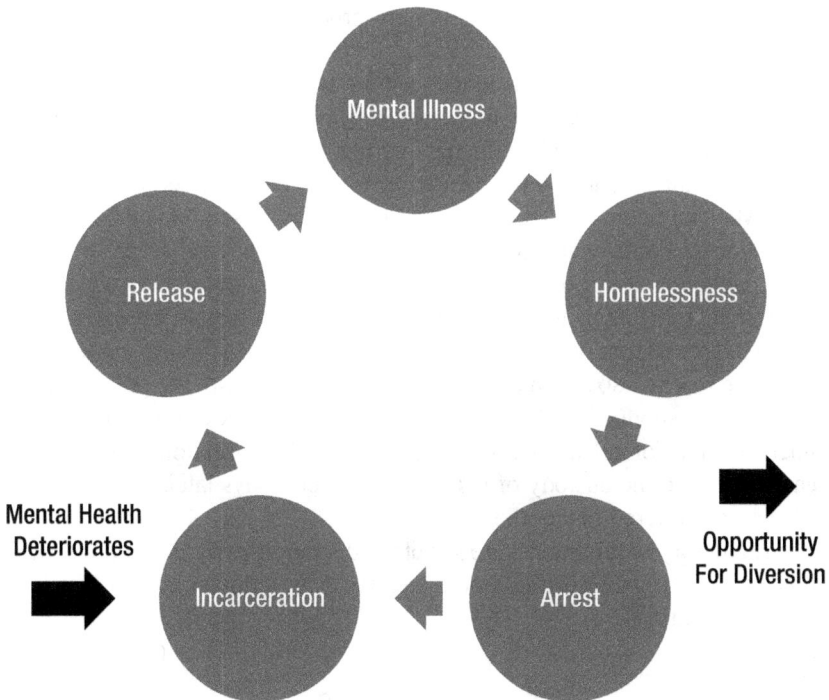

Figure 1.2.

Regardless of how the costs are identified, leaders in law enforcement must take the initiative to identify them to establish the foundation for meaningful change.

Regulatory Imperative

States have regulations addressing the involuntary commitment of the mentally ill. Under defined protocols, law enforcement, among others, initiates involuntary commitment procedures, but the effectiveness of these regulations is, at times, disappointing.

The Treatment Advocacy Center, in an evaluation of the quality of involuntary treatment (civil commitment) laws in forty-five states, found that seventeen of them earned a cumulative grade of "D" or "F"; no state earned a grade of "A."[23] The grading was determined, in part, on the:

- adequacy of its statute to facilitate emergency hospitalization for evaluation in a psychiatric emergency;
- commitment to a psychiatric facility for treatment; and
- commitment to the less-restrictive option of a court order to remain in treatment as a condition of living in the community.

The failure of the involuntary commitment process has a real face. Consider the following example.

The regulation governing involuntary commitments in Pennsylvania is called a "302." According to Pennsylvania Code Title 50 that governs an involuntary commitment, the person who initiates the action must have direct firsthand knowledge of the person and the danger posed to himself/herself or others.

Sean Michael Scott was known in the community as someone dealing with mental illness. Those who knew him from the convenience store where he worked, including police officers who frequented this establishment, knew him as an affable young man, and they appreciated that he was gainfully employed.

The 302 regulation was put to a test when Scott threw a cinderblock through the rear window of a police cruiser and fought with the police officer before he was subdued and taken to the local emergency room. There, his mother pleaded for release over a commitment. The decision was made to release Sean into the custody of his mother. Several days later, on March 16, 2014, Scott murdered his mother.

The regulatory requirements are simple and straightforward, but the execution is immersed in confusion, ignorance, and conflicting cultures of participating organizations.

The background for Scott's case emanates from news accounts[24] and interviews associated with the publication of a report on response times for the mentally ill.[25]

A retrospective view and knowledge of the outcome shapes opinions about what should have been done. The police could have initiated the 302 but delivered the patient to the emergency room and left, believing the county's crisis provider or the emergency room personnel would process the 302. The nursing director, in an interview, believes the correct decision was made to release custody to the mother, and she would make the same decision today.

Perhaps the factor triggering the incident was the mother having to cut the necessary pills in half for economic reasons. Should someone have intervened earlier? Clearly, we should not spend law enforcement resources on what is, perhaps, a social services responsibility. But this is one of numerous societal failures whose consequences require a law enforcement response.

Public Safety Imperative

High-profile incidents such as Virginia Tech contribute to the *impression* of correlation between violence and mental illness. This perception is reinforced following other high-profile incidents. Consider a presidential tweet following the tragic shooting at the Marjory Stoneman Douglas High School in Parkland, Florida, where a gunman killed seventeen people.

"So many signs that the Florida shooter was mentally disturbed, even expelled from school for bad and erratic behavior," Mr. Trump said in a tweet hours before he addressed the public. "Neighbors and classmates knew he was a big problem. Must always report such instances to authorities, again and again!"

These incidents contribute to distorted public opinions about the mentally ill.

As recently as 2013, almost forty-six per cent of respondents to a national survey said that people with mental illness were more dangerous than other people. According to two recent Gallup polls, from 2011 and 2013, more people believe that mass shootings result from a failure of the mental-health system than from easy access to guns. Eighty per cent of the population believes that mental illness is at least partially to blame for such incidents.[26]

The data suggests otherwise. According to the *New England Journal of Medicine*, mental illness contributes very little to the overall rate of violence. The risk has been estimated to be between 3 and 5 percent.[27]

Another important perspective relates to the issue of public safety. Results from a survey of the mentally ill published by the University of North

Carolina in 2014 "found that a significantly higher percentage of partici-pants—30.9 percent—had been victims of violence in the same time period. And of those who said they were victimized, 43.7 percent said they'd been victimized on multiple occasions."[28]

The data should compel leaders in law enforcement to recognize the need to protect all citizens regardless of their mental state, and leads to a discussion of the moral imperative.

Moral Imperative

It is widely known but not fully appreciated that mental illness is a disease. The understanding and appreciation are blurred due to co-occurring depen-dencies when the patient presents herself with symptoms of mental illness and substance abuse.

According to the Substance Abuse and Mental Health Services Administra-tion (SAMHSA), "People with mental health disorders are more likely than people without mental health disorders to experience an alcohol or substance use disorder."[29] The diagnosis of co-occurring disorders can be difficult to diagnose due to the complexity of symptoms and the fact that resulting be-haviors may vary in severity.

The presence of co-occurring disorders raises a question about the link between alcoholism/substance abuse and mental illness. Does the abuse stem from mental illness, or does mental illness cause or contribute to abuse? The blurry line around co-occurring disorders influences individual attitudes and the placement of an individual in crisis.

The challenge for a first responder—such as a police officer—or an inter-ventionist—such as an emergency room nurse—is to differentiate between mental illness and substance abuse when both symptoms are present. To the interventionist, the odor of alcoholic beverages may signal a moral failure. No empirical evidence suggests that treatment is compromised in such situa-tions, but it causes one to wonder in the face of an emergency room director's statement, "I have no use for drunks." In some instances, might a police of-ficer of like attitude opt for an arrest over treatment?

In 1956, the American Medical Association declared alcoholism an illness. Consider also that overprescribing pain-killing medication contributes to the current opioid crisis.

The placement of patients with co-occurring disorders is challenging. Intake facilities are selective about which patients they accept, and they are leery of those with co-occurring disorders. At times, such patients are com-bative, and diagnosis and treatment are difficult. It's a common practice for the intake facility not to accept such a patient until they first "dry out" or come down from their high. This places a burden on emergency rooms that are not equipped to handle the crisis patient.

The perception of a moral failure adversely influences efforts to treat rather than incarcerate.

Advances in medicine, psychiatry, and related fields are providing a clearer understanding of mental illness and addiction. Although the contributors are clear in some cases, in others cases the exact causes are unknown. So, the dilemma continues: Does mental illness cause addiction, or does addiction cause mental illness? The answer resides with the scientists. And in the midst of this scientific debate stands the police officer or others who make the critical decision: Arrest or seek treatment?

The moral imperative also extends to post-traumatic stress disorder (PTSD) and related disorders. This condition crosses all demographic boundaries, but by virtue of the nature of their work, the military and first responders are particularly susceptible. Sadly, in the United States, we are confronted with the disturbing data that suicides for combat veterans are occurring at the rate of twenty-two per day. Confronting the combat veteran in crisis is particularly problematic. According to some police observers, the veteran may be proficient in the use of weapons and adept in hand-to-hand combat. Concern for personal safety may motivate the officer to be more aggressive, thereby exacerbating an already dangerous situation.

Although the exact cause of most of the conditions we mentioned is not known, it is becoming clear through research that many of these conditions are caused by a combination of genetic, biological, psychological, and environmental factors—not personal weakness or a character defect—and recovery from a mental illness is simply not a matter of will and self-discipline. Understanding disorders becomes more confused when we introduce conditions such as intellectual disabilities or dementia.

As previously noted, the root of the moral dilemma goes back to the 1960s. Those with severe mental illness residing in state institutions were subject to deplorable conditions. Influenced by the civil rights movement, the introduction of new medications, and the need to save money, patients were mainstreamed into communities.

The American Medical Association notes, "People with severe mental illness can still be found in deplorable environments, medications have not successfully improved function in all patients even when they improve symptoms, and the institutional closings have deluged underfunded community services with new populations they were ill-equipped to handle."[30]

Those who understand the need for diversion, who frequently face life-altering decisions, are impatient for change. Our politicians in Washington, D.C., and in our state capitals are slow to act. In chapter 8 we set the stage and demonstrate how the community can be a conduit for change. An effective proactive strategy starts locally where the problems are understood and solutions are customized to needs.

ACCOMPANYING RESEARCH

A survey, titled *Assessing the Climate, Diverting the Mentally Ill away from the Criminal Justice System and into Treatment*, was conducted for select law enforcement agencies in Camden County, New Jersey; and Chester, Montgomery, and Philadelphia Counties in Pennsylvania. It was conducted to support various chapters in this book.

The survey team consisted of:

- Frank Mielke, Audubon Management Consultants (AMC)
- Michelle Monzo, Montgomery County Emergency Service (MCES)
- William Mossman, East Coventry Police Department and Audubon Management Consultants

Survey participants responded to mostly declarative statements with both a positive and negative orientation, using a seven-point Likert scale (levels of agreement and disagreement).

The project team followed two strict protocols:

1. Confidentiality was assured in every communication.
2. Only the project team viewed individual responses.

The survey, as a basis to support future research, consists of twenty-six core statements that draw on social science and management theories and research. The assessment is a product of more than twenty years of research based in large part on the people-centered organization theory[31] developed by Dr. Miles Overholt. In addition, we draw on the work of the American Institute of Chemical Engineers,[32] which identified a series of systemic or underlying problems that contributed to the outcomes of a series of catastrophic events.

The police chiefs and department coordinators were advised to communicate that participation was not mandatory, but to encourage participation in the interest of improving the law enforcement/mental health climate. Participants were asked to identify a series of demographic factors, including age, years of experience, and military experience, among others.

The ability to analyze responses to the statements by demographic factor provides the opportunity to identify underlying systemic differences and the resulting influence on behaviors.

The process of analyzing data is driven by a series of scales, aggregate measures of responses around a common theme. Scales facilitates analysis and communication. The process provides the opportunity to dig down to individual statements, and, if necessary, potential uniqueness by demographics.

The 829 responses from this survey, coupled with data from other surveys, allow the team to do additional in-depth research. The result will be a series of white papers, with no references to specific departments, that will be in the public domain. The results from this survey are interspersed in several chapters in this book.

FINAL THOUGHTS

The authors of this book are police officers, crisis workers, educators, community leaders, and researchers. Often, we hear the comment "it's a shame" from a police officer involved with an incident with someone in crisis regarding our inability to respond.

Today, two questions resonate:

1. Does law enforcement have the required mind-set and behaviors to deal with the resulting challenges?
2. Will law enforcement assume a position of leadership in changing the paradigm for both their department and the community at large?

CONCLUDING COMMENTS

The criminal justice/behavioral health network is large and complex. The effort to divert those in crisis does not fall solely in the domain of a single entity but rather a confluence of different organizations with different cultures, attitudes, and behaviors united in a common goal.

The dilemma is multifaceted. Each chapter in this book discusses segments of the dilemma. It is up to those in law enforcement to decide whether they are to assume a position of leadership and a proactive, thoughtful approach to the subject of diversion.

Chapter Two

Framing the Environment, Understanding Behavioral Health Crises

Tony Salvatore and Patricia Griffin

INTRODUCTION

Generally, the police contact with a person with serious mental illness, intellectual disability, or other behavioral or cognitive vulnerability occurs when the person is experiencing some type of crisis related to his illness or disability or an exacerbation of symptoms. The person's behavior in such situations may conflict with local ordinances or statutes and put the person at risk of arrest. Therefore, it is imperative that the police officer on the scene be able to identify such crises, safely intervene, and, as appropriate, divert the individual away from the criminal justice system and possible incarceration, and toward the behavioral health system—and help.

For this to occur, the officer must not only be familiar with signs of possible mental illness or developmental disability, but also be able to assist the individual to accept the necessary services. In many instances, the available services will be of a crisis intervention or emergency mental health nature such as a crisis center or a mobile crisis team. In this chapter we discuss the types of crises that police officers may encounter and the range of crisis intervention and emergency mental health services that may—or should—be available in the community to assist and facilitate with diverting at-risk individuals away from the criminal justice system when indicated.

This chapter describes what is meant by the "recovery model," recovery concepts, and crisis services. The recovery model has increasingly shaped county, state, and federal community mental health policy making for the past decade. Recovery concepts enhance crisis prevention and resolution. Recovery is an essential component of a diversion strategy, and it is promoted by diverting a person in crisis to assessment and treatment. We will consider elements of the recovery model that relate most closely to adult crisis intervention, and present a continuum of discrete crisis behaviors staged in terms of potential impact for an individual's mental health and wellness. We also will indicate the opportunities for diversion at various points in the continuum. We will outline the continuum of crisis situations that arise for individuals with behavioral health and/or developmental disabilities and describe crisis response resources that relate appropriately to these behaviors.

We also will present an overview of crisis diversion practices in terms of their appropriateness as a response to each type of crisis behavior in our proposed continuum. *We will discuss how each type of crisis relates to the risk of incarceration and how different crisis intervention resources may be mobilized by police to avert arrest and charges.* Finally, we will present the Crisis Diversion Sequential Intercept Model[1] as a tool to show where and how individuals may enter the crisis response system, indicate points for intervention, and outline how the various services should operate within the community mental health system. Inasmuch as crises associated with serious mental illness and developmental disability are complex and have distinct features requiring specific forms of crisis response, police and behavioral health providers in a community should know what is available and what unmet needs may exist. The proposed model is an aid to accomplish this.

BACKGROUND

Evidence shows that the number of individuals with a behavioral or mental disorder being hospitalized and incarcerated in our nation's jails and prisons is increasing disproportionately. The National Alliance on Mental Illness (NAMI, nami.org), Mental Health America (MHA, www.mhanational.org), Substance Abuse and Mental Health Services Administration (SAMHSA, www.samhsa.gov), the National Council for Behavioral Health (www.the nationalcouncil.org*)*, the Council of State Governments (www.csg.org), and the American Psychiatric Association (www.psychiatry.org) are among the professional organizations seeking to reverse and reduce this trend.

During a ten-year period, 2005–2014, overall hospitalization stays decreased approximately 13 percent nationally, whereas, the number of hospital stays for those with mental health/substance abuse diagnoses increased 44.1 percent. A large percentage of the hospital stays are through the emergency department (ED). The ED visit rate among mental health/substance abuse diagnoses that resulted in a hospital admission increased 31.8 percent. Further, while the overall ED treat-and-release rate decreased 13.1 percent, the rate for mental health/substance abuse diagnoses increased 48.1 percent. The majority of individuals were eighteen to forty-four years of age.

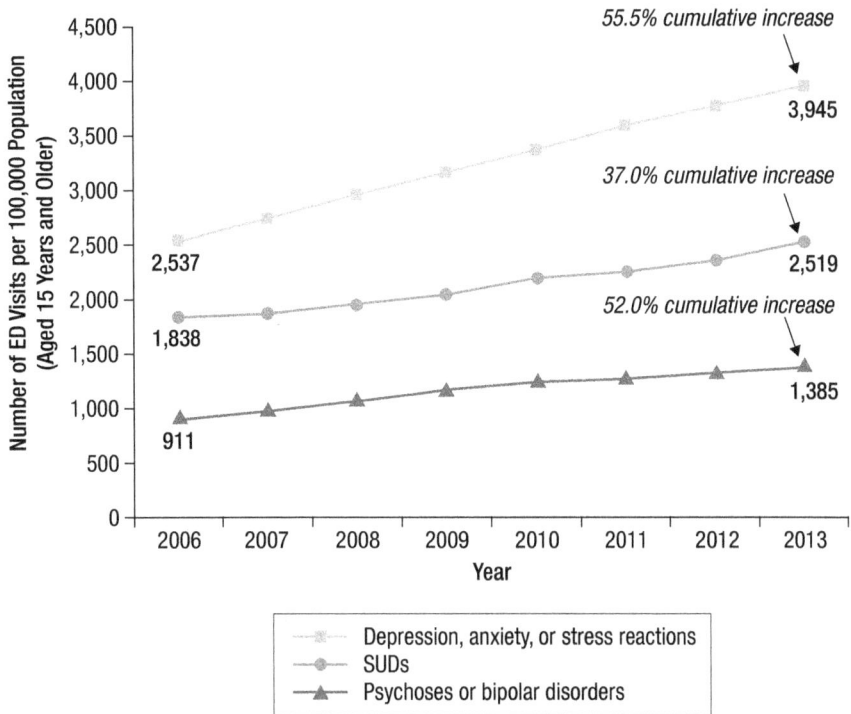

Figure 2.1. Trends in Emergency Department Visits (2006–2014)
Source: Agency for Healthcare Research and Quality, 2017

Figure 2.1 presents the distribution of ED visits by primary diagnosis. Individuals with a mood disorder diagnosis (anxiety, depression) saw the greatest increase of 55.5 percent, followed by a 52.0 percent increase for individuals with a diagnosis of schizophrenia and psychosis.[2]

Overall, the number of persons under correctional supervision in the United States has more than quadrupled from 1980 through 2016 (see figure 2.1). Against this backdrop, the disproportionate representation of people with serious mental illnesses, co-occurring disorders, and substance use disorder in American jails and prisons has led to their use as de facto mental health facilities. The most current data available, 2011–2012, indicates that approximately 50 percent of all state and federal prisoners and 66 percent of jail inmates meet this threshold.

Steadman et al. report that over the course of the year, two million Americans with a serious mental illness will spend time incarcerated.[3] Further, when individuals with a serious mental illness are incarcerated, they spend almost double the time of other individuals facing similar charges.

Although clearly many factors contribute to the prevalence of individuals with a mental illness disorder entering the criminal justice system, the

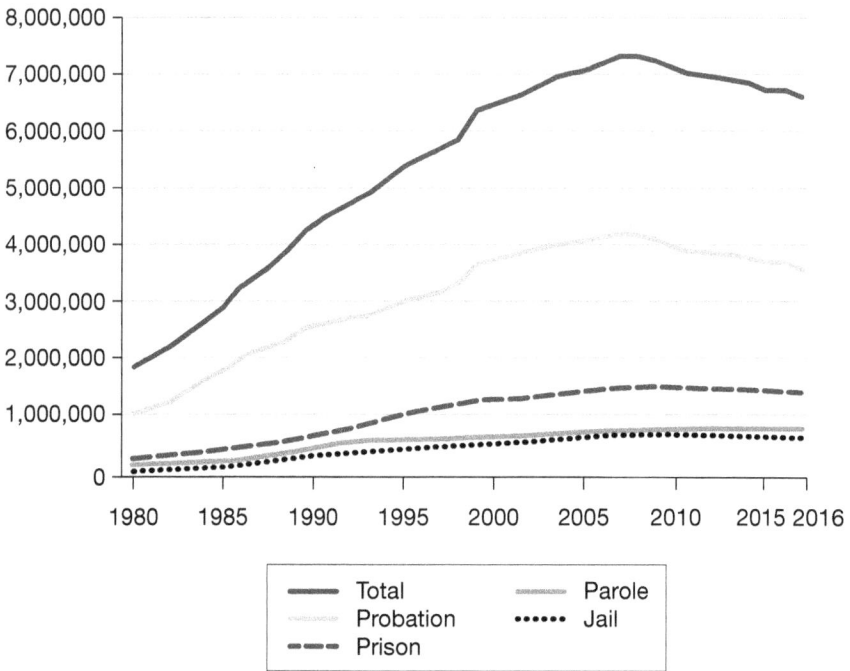

Figure 2.2. Total U.S. adult correctional population, 1980–2016

Source: Bureau of Justice Statistics, Annual Survey of Jails, Annual Survey of Parole, Annual Survey of Probation, Census of Jail Inmates, and National Prisoner Statistics, 1980-2016

deinstitutionalization of state mental hospitals and a corresponding lack of resources for community-based alternatives are recognized as being among the main reasons (see chapter 3). Frequently, the individual's symptomatic behavior results in a family member taking the individual to the emergency department. Others may call 911, which is routinely routed to the police. Officers have the power to restrain and control but not necessarily the skills or resources to provide the most effective response for an individual experiencing a mental health crisis.

When someone with serious mental illness or other behavioral health problem is inappropriately incarcerated, treatment needs go unmet and ties to providers and community supports are severed. Often this increases risk for both the individual and the community. If diversion resources are in place, this need not be the case.

OVERVIEW

Crisis services play a vital role in the community behavioral health system and are a critical support to any community's public safety and emergency services systems. Crisis services are where the behavioral health and criminal justice systems interface. They are the portal to both emergency care and ongoing outpatient care. Crisis services are a critical part of a community's jail diversion strategy, where police officers refer or transport persons in crisis who have criminal justice contact that may put them at risk of incarceration.

The problem-solving capacity of crisis services is well recognized, but they also contribute to system transformation and recovery. This latter role has not been widely explored. That task requires clear understanding of crisis situations, the continuum of crisis services, and how both relate to recovery, from pre-recovery to long-term recovery. We will use this model to outline a framework for employing crisis services as diversion assets.

One suggestion is a typology of crisis situations: precrisis, crisis, mental health crisis, and psychiatric emergency. Each of these may be aligned to an appropriate crisis service response. This typology can be used to map the availability of existing crisis services in a community, identify gaps, and designate resources to which police officers can divert persons in crisis for help and assessment as necessary.

Crisis services can be staged to sustain recovery and community tenure and prevent individuals from moving to a higher level of severity. We use the Sequential Intercept Model to map the community crisis response system to identify where individuals enter the system and the points for intervention at the least restrictive level. We propose a different perspective, the Sequential Diversion Intercept Model, where ten intercepts are proposed: individual and family, peer-operated services, noncrisis providers, mobile crisis, crisis center/hot line, hospital emergency department, police, twenty-three-hour bed programs, crisis stabilization units, and inpatient psychiatric care. The intent here is not to prescribe a model for adoption for all communities but to offer a tool to identify the types of crisis services available as well as possible gaps in the local crisis service system and describe how each service contributes to police officers' use of a jail diversion strategy.

THE RECOVERY MODEL AND CRISIS SERVICES

Adaptability, positiveness, autonomy, empowerment, confidence, self-help, and support are key attributes of recovery that facilitate crisis intervention. At the same time, crisis services directly contribute to maintaining or regaining recovery.

Anthony sees crisis intervention as "an essential client service in a caring system," supporting recovery that assures individual safety by "resolving critical or dangerous problems."[4] Mead and Hilton see crisis services as a buffer between recovery and involuntary care: "Psychiatric interventions for crisis care lie at the center of the conflict between forced treatment and recovery wellness systems in mental health services."[5] Copeland includes a personal crisis plan as part of a Wellness Recovery Action Plan ® (W.R.A.P.), a self-help strategy for managing mental illness symptoms.[6]

Crisis services support recovery by helping to:

- Restore functioning and normality
- Return self-control and self-reliance
- Enhance and expand natural and peer supports
- Maintain or reengage outpatient providers
- Minimize the effects of symptoms and illness
- Prevent future crises

From a recovery perspective, crises are perceived nonjudgmentally as opportunities for growth. They are not seen as "problems" or "negative experiences." Recovery involves a change in self-perception as well as a sense of hopefulness and optimism.

The potential impact of personal beliefs about recovery is evident in Kanel's observation that a crisis involves a subjective perception of a precipitating event believed to be distressful and perceptual redefinition of the precipitating event as part of the crisis resolution process.[7] This echoes Parad's comment that the crisis is not the situation, but the individual's perception of it and response to it.[8]

THE CRISIS RESPONSE SYSTEM CONCEPT

The Technical Assistance Collaborative issued a blueprint for a crisis service delivery system to produce recovery-oriented outcomes.[9] The service array ranges from a warm line to inpatient psychiatric care. The system has an inherent crisis prevention and diversion capability. It should be able to keep situations from becoming crises, build supports, and employ these supports in crisis prevention.

A crisis response system must have four dimensions:

1. crisis prevention;
2. crisis diversion;
3. crisis intervention; and
4. crisis postvention.

Crisis prevention maintains wellness and recovery by averting crisis. Crisis diversion deters crisis progression to more serious situations by enhancing the individual's coping skills and supports. Crisis intervention attempts to alleviate the potentially debilitating effects of a crisis by stabilizing distress and restoring personal control. Postvention attempts to mitigate chronic effects resulting from the crisis episode and promotes post-crisis stability, recovery, and wellness.

Crisis postvention is probably the most neglected. The crisis episode itself may be short-lived, but its effects, especially upon recovery, may last much longer. This is especially true of serious mental health crises and psychiatric emergencies that may produce "transcrisis states" with long-term illness-related consequences.[10] Poor postvention may contribute to someone becoming "crisis-prone," losing the capacity to cope with new stressors, and negatively affect recovery. Crisis services must not lead to "learned helplessness."

Caplan cited the need for prevention at the crisis level.[11] The "course of pathological developments" occurs "in a series of steps, each of which is preceded by a short period of upset to which we have given the term 'crisis.'"[12] Community-based early intervention encompassing crisis diversion has been shown to be feasible in managing serious mental health crises.[13] Crisis services must "complement and augment natural recovery and restorative mechanisms" and not interfere with or replace these resources.[14] This requires a means of positioning specific crisis services for intervention when they can benefit the individual at risk most effectively in terms of strengths and supports.

THE CRISIS SITUATION CONTINUUM

Mental illness crises, and to some degree those experienced by persons with developmental disabilities, tend to follow similar trajectories and may move to higher levels of risk without being recognized.[15] Crisis situations may be triggered by life events that produce emotional discomfort or the recurrence of psychiatric symptoms. Missing or not addressing such precipitants may significantly worsen the individual's situation and put recovery at risk. Classifications of crises by type or severity have been put forth.[16] We distinguish four levels of crisis situations:

Precrisis

This is a noncrisis episode characterized by some disturbance of the psychosocial equilibrium. Such episodes may become the initial developmental phase of a subsequent crisis when the precipitant has become a stressful life event. This stage is characterized by rising stress driven by a precipitant, threatening the individual's psychosocial equilibrium. Relief is sought through customary problem-solving methods. If these are not effective, a "crisis" or a "mental health crisis" may follow.

Generally speaking, this stage includes little need for police involvement. However, some individuals may attract police attention by turning to 911 because of their mounting emotional discomfort and anxiety.

Crisis

This is a brief, temporary non-illness response to severe stress typically related to a life event that the individual perceives as problematic. It may overwhelm coping skills and supports but not involve relapse or recurrence. It does not require clinical intervention but may lead to a mental health crisis if not resolved.

As with the precrisis stage, this level of crisis should, in most cases, be addressed without any need for police presence. But as in precrisis situations, some individuals may experience an "anxiety attack" or panic when their resilience and supports are insufficient to enable them to deal with the situation independently or with the aid of available services. In such circumstances, some individuals may bypass the crisis response system and turn quickly to 911.

Mental Health Crisis

This is a temporary illness-related response to severe stress that ensues if coping efforts are overcome. It usually is recognized by the individual and has potential for either a positive or negative outcome. It may require clinical intervention if it involves recurrence but is not imminently life threatening. Common triggers are trauma, substance misuse, conflict, income or housing issues, and criminal justice contact. Retraumatization may occur at this stage. A mental health crisis may lead to a psychiatric emergency. A mental health crisis is a "complex crisis" that can lead to "episodes of mental illness in those already vulnerable."[17] Individuals with intellectual disability or another developmental disability may become frustrated and agitated and be unable to calm down or be redirected.

Individuals experiencing a mental health crisis are much more likely to have an interaction with police than at earlier stages in the crisis continuum. When the possible basis in mental illness or developmental disability is not recognized, vulnerability to a criminal justice rather that crisis intervention response increases significantly. With proper training or behavioral health support, police officers can opt for a noncustodial response and get the individual to a source of assessment and treatment.

Psychiatric Emergency

This is a potentially life-threatening situation involving an acute disturbance of thought, mood, and/or behavior.[18] It may be situational or illness-based and is generally not recognized by the individual. It involves behavior with the potential to rapidly lead to self-harm or harm to others. An immediate clinical intervention is indicated. Common psychiatric emergencies are exacerbations of psychosis, a suicide attempt or voicing serious intent and a specific plan, uncontrollable anxiety or panic, or homicidality. Psychiatric emergencies engender trauma that persists beyond the episode and heightens the risk of future episodes.

By their very nature, psychiatric emergencies are fraught with high risk of serious physical harm or death. Depending on the symptoms (e.g., paranoid psychosis) or behaviors (e.g., destroying property mistakenly thought to be causing harm) manifested, police intervention may be necessary and unavoidable. If such encounters reoccur with frequency and seem beyond the control of community services, police may fall back on law enforcement tactics. It is imperative that crisis services relieve police officers of responsibility for individuals in psychiatric emergencies as soon as practically and safely possible.

In the absence of crisis intervention skills, basic knowledge of the signs and symptoms of mental illness and developmental disability, and responsive and reliable community crisis services, police will very likely view the person as a dangerous felon. This perspective may precipitate a self-fulfilling prophecy in which injury or worse is experienced by the at-risk individual, the police officers, or both.[19]

These episodes may emerge in sequence or independently. An individual may experience a more serious crisis-related event without immediately experiencing a less serious preceding situation. However, crisis situations do not lend themselves to tidy classification and are not necessarily linear. Nonetheless, such a typology is useful for planning purposes.

Crisis episodes can be matched to potential sources of assistance and target the points at which specific services could be most beneficial. Figure 2.3 illustrates the approximate relative frequency of the crisis situations comprising our typology and their rising severity. Table 2.1 aligns each individual situation to the crisis-related services that should be available to address the situation.

CRISIS SITUATIONS AND CRISIS DIVERSION

The *precrisis* stage is the optimal time to avert an individual from a crisis. Peer support, family, case management, and in-home supports can be effec-

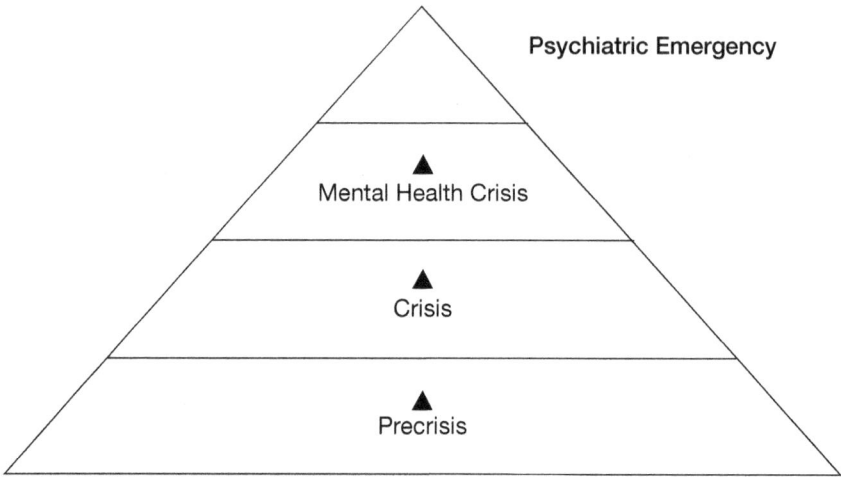

Figrue 2.3.   The Crisis Behavior Pyramid

tive in forestalling the onset of crisis situations. Most individuals resolve precrisis situations on their own, but some lack resources or resilience. Stress may increase and raise the risk of a mental health crisis or psychiatric emergency and jeopardize recovery.

The *crisis stage* presents an opportunity to mobilize the support system to manage a situation provoked by a stressful life event before it affects wellness and recovery. Most individuals deal effectively with crises by using their recovery-based strengths and supports. Conceptually, in a recovery-oriented crisis response system, provider-based resources would be used sparingly at this stage. Self-help and/or peer-based responses would be sufficient to assure that basic crises do not become mental health crises.

Table 2.1.   Crisis Situations and Appropriate Crisis System Resources

Crisis Situation	Crisis Response Resources
Precrisis	• Warm Line
	• Living Room
Crisis	• Warm Line
	• Mobile Crisis Service
	• Crisis Respite, Crisis Hostel
Mental Health Crisis	• Mobile Crisis Service
	• Hot Line/Crisis Center
	• Short-Stay Crisis Residential Program
Psychiatric Emergency	• Hot Line/Crisis Center
	• Twenty-three-Hour Bed; Crisis Stabilization Unit
	• Psychiatric Evaluation (Voluntary/Involuntary)

A *mental health crisis* calls for a response to prevent the situation from rising to the level of a psychiatric emergency. A mental health crisis threatens one's sense of control because symptoms may be exacerbated and recurrence may follow.[20] This may happen even when the individual is in recovery and adherent to treatment. Crisis services must help individuals from experiencing these situations and stabilize them promptly when they arise. Crisis services must work with other providers to prevent mental health crisis recidivism.

A *psychiatric emergency* requires an emergency response by the crisis response system and often other community resources such as the police and hospital emergency departments. It may overtake an individual despite his best efforts and those of the support system. Some psychiatric emergencies are rooted in less serious situations, so every effort must be made to leverage their prevention at the earliest stage possible. A psychiatric emergency is a traumatic event that may threaten recovery. Police contact, ambulance transport, hospital emergency department (ED) treatment, and involuntary psychiatric evaluation are not only traumatic, but they impact self-worth, engender fear, diminish control, and disrupt community living. This is why such episodes may recur.

CLARIFYING THE PEER-LED CRISIS SERVICE ROLE

Peer-led services play an essential role in a crisis response system. They deter unnecessary psychiatric hospitalizations by providing empathy, hope, peer support, choice, and other aspects of the recovery model. By keeping crises from escalating into more serious situations, they prevent mental health crises and psychiatric emergencies. Peer-led crisis services may be optimally effective in precrisis and crisis situations, which do not evoke illness symptoms and do not require a provider-based response.

This is not to suggest that peer-led services have no role in dealing with mental health crises and psychiatric emergencies. In these situations, they complement and supplement the provider-based crisis services that are engaged primarily in clinical assessment, stabilization, and treatment. In addition, peer-led services can significantly extend postvention resources for individuals seeking to recover from severe episodes of depression, suicide attempts, losing friends or family members to suicide, or psychosis.

THE SEQUENTIAL INTERCEPT MODEL

The Sequential Intercept Model is a tool for charting points for diversion within and between systems.[21] It has been proposed for use in developing programs to divert individuals with mental illness from the criminal justice system and lends itself to use in understanding diversion in a crisis response system. Table 2.2 employs the sequential intercept concept as the basis for the Crisis Diversion Intercept Model (CDIM) to show where and how individuals may enter the crisis response system, indicate points for intervention, and outline how the various services should operate within the system. The specific resources comprising any given crisis response system will vary by the area served. Each of the "intercepts" may not be available (or needed)

Table 2.2. The Crisis Diversion Intercept Model

Intercept	Resources	Outcomes
1. Individual/Family	• Use of natural supports • W.R.A.P. • Personal Safety Plan	• Use of self-help to identify/resolve crisis at earliest possible stage
2. Peer-Operated Services	• Warm Line • Living Room • Other Peer-Led Resource	• Use peer support to contain crisis or promote other services
3. Outpatient/Residential Services	• Case Manager • Crisis Respite • Crisis Residences	• Basic crisis intervention to sustain recovery and community tenure
4. Mobile Crisis Service; Police Crisis Team	• Intervention in home, other community setting • Interface with ERs, police	• Resolve crisis in least-restrictive setting as safe • Reduce use of intercepts below
5. Crisis Center/Hot Line	• 24/7 Walk-in Service • 24/7 Call-in Service	• Screen/assess crisis severity; refer to Nos. 1–4 as appropriate
6. Emergency Room (ER)	• Treatment of medical issues related to crisis • Refer to crisis center	• Promote diversion of appropriate cases to Nos. 4–5
7. Police	• Response to potentially life-threatening psychiatric emergencies	• Case finding; referrals to ER, crisis center, mobile crisis as needed
8. Twenty-Three-Hour Bed Program	• Extended evaluation to determine care needs • Brief treatment	• Assist return to home/community care setting • Arrange crisis postvention
9. Crisis Stabilization Unit/Extended Observation	• Brief psychiatric care • Inpatient not indicated	• Assist return to home/community care setting • Arrange postvention
10. Voluntary/Involuntary Psychiatric Evaluation	• Risk assessment and diagnosis • Brief treatment and referral	• Provide for crisis treatment, stabilization, and postvention

in every community. The intercepts are broad benchmarks for outlining the crisis response system in a particular locale in terms of what is present and what gaps may exist. This model posits resolution of individual crises at the earliest point in their emergence, in the home or other community setting, or under auspices of the most suitable community-based provider.

The diversion intercept points in the crisis response system in ascending order of complexity, intensity, and cost are as follows:

Intercept 1: Individual/Family

Whenever feasible and safe, situations should be ameliorated at the level of the individual to best build or preserve recovery. The individual should be aided in employing his coping and problem-solving skills. In addition to "taking charge" when the warning signs of a crisis are seen, self-help can take the form of self-advocacy in terms of possible treatment options. This may involve anticipating crises and putting tools such as Wellness Recovery Action Plan® (W.R.A.P.),[22] personal crisis plans, crisis cards,[23] and psychiatric advanced directives in place to assure some measure of control over care choices even when the individuals may be unable to voice their preferences.

Intercept 2: Peer-Operated Services

Peers are past or current users of mental health services who disclose their mental illness in mutual self-help.[24] Peer-based services must be part of a recovery-focused crisis response system. Examples are a peer-operated non-crisis warm line or a peer-run "Living Room." The latter is a non-cliniclike site where individuals can interact with peer specialists or family members.[25] A peer-run crisis hostel or crisis respite would also fall at this intercept. These are home-like settings where individuals use self-help and peer-support to deal with stressors and augment recovery.[26]

Intercept 3: Outpatient/Residential Services

Provider-based services deal with more complex needs. Crisis prevention should be available from community-based services (recovery coaches, case managers, or assertive community treatment programs). When appropriate, residents of community rehabilitative residences should receive aid without having to leave their living community and supports. Individuals should have access to a provider-sponsored crisis respite, crisis residential programs, and crisis apartments for stays of a few days or more. These offer a structured "time out" for regrouping, rebuilding supports, and preserving recovery.

Intercept 4: Mobile Crisis Service; Police Crisis Team

These programs focus on crisis-related needs at Intercepts 1–3 and on diverting individuals from Intercepts 5–10. Mobile crisis service varies widely. Most are community based and have demonstrated a capacity for hospital diversion.[27] This intercept is where the various models of mental health and law enforcement collaboration (e.g., crisis intervention teams) fit into the crisis service response system.

Intercept 5: Crisis Center/Hot Line

Crisis hot lines are the most common, and often, the only crisis service in some areas. They are an important crisis prevention resource as well as a resource for police officers trying to resolve a crisis in the field. A follow-up study of hot-line callers found telephone intervention decreases suicidality, hopelessness, and psychological pain in the following weeks.[28] Ideally, crisis centers will only help with crises that cannot be addressed by earlier intercepts. They are the entry point for screening and evaluation of mental health crises and psychiatric emergencies. They should attempt to obviate the need for Intercepts 6–8. Crisis centers can serve as "drop offs" for police who encounter an individual willing to accept help and whose condition does not warrant civil commitment and involuntary care.

Intercept 6: Emergency Room (ER)

ERs are often the only 24/7 emergency facility in an area, but they are not always well suited for a mental health "gatekeeper" role.[29] ERs can address serious medical needs associated with a crisis and identify underlying medical conditions, then direct the individual to a crisis center. Some ERs host hospital-based crisis services that triage, evaluate and assess, stabilize, briefly treat, and refer.[30] Police will bring at-risk individuals to ERs for treatment when a medical issue is known or suspected.

Intercept 7: Police

Police are an inextricable part of the crisis response system. Like ERs, police serve as an external gatekeeper to the behavioral health system as first responders to situations involving mental illness. This intercept is where jail diversion takes place. In some areas, the crisis response system provides training for local police (see chapter 3) and offers a "central drop off" for evaluation and treatment.[31] Police may also refer to mobile crisis, a crisis center, or other resources. Some police departments have mental health professionals on staff who respond to mental health calls with officers.

Intercept 8: Twenty-Three-Hour Bed Program

This level of care usually is accessed through a crisis center or a mobile crisis team. It may be located in an inpatient facility, a crisis stabilization unit, or be freestanding. It permits ongoing psychiatric evaluation, clarification of diagnosis, and brief treatment of individuals whose needs may be resolved or clarified within twenty-four hours. Police may use this type of service for individuals awaiting placement or referral.

Intercept 9: Crisis Stabilization Unit/Extended Observation

These programs provide a safe environment to observe, assess, diagnose, treat, and develop plans for ongoing care in the community or other setting. This service is for individuals in a mental health crisis who do not require acute inpatient psychiatric care, but where less intensive residential services, such as a crisis residential program, are not appropriate. Stays usually are short, typically less than five days.

Intercept 10: Voluntary/Involuntary Psychiatric Evaluation

Voluntary and involuntary evaluations and inpatient admissions are indicated for serious mental health crises and psychiatric emergencies. They should be reserved for individuals with an acute loss of behavioral control or potential for imminent danger to self or others. When other intercepts are absent or ineffective, hospitalization may be misused and overused. The psychiatric evaluation is the last point for diversion from hospitalization, and, in some cases, incarceration. Police may hold charges in abeyance until a psychiatric evaluation is completed. Charges may be dropped where serious mental illness or other impairment is found that may account for the offending behavior.

This continuum is meant to be more suggestive than exhaustive in regard to the range of crisis service programs included. In some communities, services associated with a specific intercept (e.g., crisis hot line, crisis center, and mobile crisis) may be offered by a single provider.

INVOLUNTARY EVALUATIONS AS A DIVERSION TOOL

When criminality is not involved, the principal reason for persons with serious mental illness, a developmental disability, or other special need being taken into police custody is to keep them safe from possible self-harm or from possibly harming others. Civil commitment provides an alternative to criminal justice involvement.[32] It is a process to secure an involuntary psychiatric evaluation to determine the basis for the individual's behavior. If the evaluation indicates potential danger and the need for immediate psychiatric care, an involuntary hospitalization can follow.

In this way, civil commitment can divert an at-risk person from criminal charges and possible imprisonment, prevent possible harm, lessen trauma, and assure care of persons who need treatment but who cannot or will not accept it voluntarily. This enables the state through police power to keep at-risk persons from endangering themselves or others. It also satisfies the state's *parens patriae*[33] power to act as caretaker for those who are unable to care for themselves. As such, it is a crisis intervention of the last resort to be used judiciously in cases that meet the criteria for such action established by state mental health law.

CONCLUDING COMMENTS

The crisis response service system links individuals at risk and community-based resources. The system has been shown to be as effective at improving or resolving psychological symptoms of distress as longer inpatient hospitalization, and patients report a more positive experience than those receiving inpatient hospitalization.[34] The significance of this latter fact cannot be underestimated. Evidence points to the fact that consistent and ongoing engagement between a patient/client and behavioral mental health providers reduces the incidence of a psychological crisis. The continuum of crisis services further offers cost-effective alternatives to lengthy in-patient hospital stays when this level of care is not needed.

Crisis services must be capable of identifying and resolving emerging crisis situations and connecting individuals to services that can safely address more serious crises and psychiatric emergencies. The system must have a preventive element to deter crisis situations from becoming critical incidents. It must assure that users access the services that best fit their crisis needs.

This necessitates a holistic view of the crisis response system, showing each crisis service component in a given area. The Sequential Intercept Model lends itself to this purpose when used with a sequential model of crisis situations. This permits the crisis response service system to be mapped and the crisis resources at each intercept identified as to availability, accessibility, appropriateness, and coordination with other services.

Crisis services support recovery and community integration facilitates diversion from the criminal justice system. The proposed Crisis Diversion Intercept Model brings system transformation to the crisis services sector. The model lends itself to planning and evaluating crisis services, setting priorities for adding or modifying services, and serving as a guide for mental health consumers, family members, behavioral health providers, public safety agencies, and others in understanding the nature, scope, and best way to use the crisis services in a community. It also can serve as a companion process for criminal justice system mapping, which is used to inform community planning for diversion of justice-involved individuals from incarceration.[35]

SUGGESTED READINGS

Agency for Healthcare Research and Quality (AHRQ), Center for Delivery, Organization, and Markets, Healthcare Cost and Utilization Project (HCUP). National Inpatient Sample (NIS), 2012.

Allen, M., P. Forster, J. Zealberg, and G. Currier. *Report and Recommendations Regarding Psychiatric Emergency and Crisis Services.* Arlington, VA: American Psychiatric Association, 2002, 12.

Anthony, W. "Recovery from Mental Illness: The Guiding Vision of the Mental Health Service System in the 1990s." *Psychosocial Rehabilitation Journal* 16, no. 6 (1993): 11–23.

Ashcroft, L. *Peer Services in a Crisis Setting: The Living Room* (Phoenix, AZ: Meta Services, 2006).

Baldwin, B., "A Paradigm for the Classification of Emotional Crises: Implications for Crisis Intervention." *American Journal of Orthopsychiatry* 48, no. 3 (1978): 538–51.

Ball, J., P. Links, C. Strike, and K. Boydell. "It's Overwhelming . . . Everything Seems to Be Too Much: A Theory of Crisis for Individuals with Severe Persistent Mental Illness." *Psychiatric Rehabilitation Journal* 29, no. 1 (2005): 10–17.

Boes, M., and B. McDermott. "Crisis Intervention in the Emergency Room," 543–68, in A. Roberts, ed., *Crisis Intervention Handbook: Assessment, Treatment, and Research*, 3rd ed. (New York: Oxford University Press, 2005).

Bureau of Justice Statistics. "Key Statistics, Annual Survey of Jails, Annual Survey of Parole, Annual Survey of Probation, Census of Jail Inmates, and National Prisoner Statistics, 1980–2016" (accessed February 4, 2019).

Caplan, G. *Principles of Preventative Psychiatry.* New York: Basic Books, 1964.

Caplan, G., and R. Caplan. "The Future of Primary Prevention." *Journal of Primary Prevention* (2000): 31–136.

Center for Mental Health Services. *Practice Guidelines: Core Elements for Responding to Mental Health Crises*, HHS Pub. No. SMA-09-4427. Rockville, MD: Substance Abuse and Mental Health Services Administration, 2009.

Copeland, M. *Wellness Recovery Action Plan.* Brattleboro, VT: Peachtree Press, 1997.

———. *Action Planning for Prevention and Recovery, Consumer Information Series, 10*, HHS Pub. No.SMA-3720. Rockville, MD: Substance Abuse and Mental Health Services Administration, 2002.

Crisis Services: Effectiveness, Cost-Effectiveness, and Funding Strategies, HHS Publication No. (SMA)-14-4848. Rockville, MD: Substance Abuse and Mental Health Services Administration, 2014.

Everly, G. "Five Principles of Crisis Intervention: Reducing the Risk of Premature Crisis Intervention." *International Journal of Emergency Mental Health* 2, no. 1 (2000): 1–4.

Glick, R., J. Berlin, A. Fishkind, and S. Zeller. *Emergency Psychiatry: Principles and Practice*. Philadelphia: Lippincott Williams & Wilkins, 2008.

Gould, M., J. Kalafat, J. Munfakh, and M. Kleinman. "An Evaluation of Crisis Hotline Outcomes Part 2: Suicidal Callers." *Suicide and Life-Threatening Behavior*, 37 (2007): 338–52.

Guo, S., D. Biegel, J. Johnsen, and H. Dyches. "Assessing the Impact of Community-Based Mobile Crisis Services on Preventing Hospitalization." *Psychiatric Services* 52, no. 2 (2001): 223–28.

James, R. *Crisis Intervention Strategies*. Belmont, CA: Thomson Brooks, Cole, 2008.

Kanel, K. *A Guide to Crisis Intervention*, 4th ed. Belmont, CA: Thomson Brooks, Cole, 2012.

McDermott, K.W., et al. "Trends in Hospital Inpatient Stays in the United States, 2005–2014." Agency for Healthcare Research and Quality, June 2017.

Mead, S., and D. Hilton. "Crisis and Connection," www.mentalhealthpeers.com/ (accessed March 27, 2012).

Merson, S., P. Tyrer, S. Onyett, S. Lack, P. Birkett, S. Lynch, and T. Johnson. "Early Intervention in Psychiatric Emergencies: A Controlled Clinical Trial." *Lancet* (1992): 311–14.

Moore, B. J. (IBM Watson Health), C. Stocks (AHRQ), and P. L. Owens (AHRQ). *Trends in Emergency Department Visits, 2006–2014*. HCUP Statistical Brief #227. Rockville, MD: Agency for Healthcare Research and Quality, September 2017.

Munetz, M., and P. Griffin. "Use of the Sequential Intercept Model as an Approach to Decriminalization of People with Serious Mental Illness." *Psychiatric Services* 57, no. 4 (2006): 544–49.

Ostrow, L., and D. Fisher. *Peer-Run Crisis Respites*. Washington, DC: National Coalition for Mental Health Recovery, 2011.

Parad, H. "Crisis Intervention," 196–202, in R. Morris, ed., *Encyclopedia of Social Work*, 16th ed. (New York: National Association of Social Work, 1971).

Rosen, A. "Crisis Management in the Community." *Medical Journal of Australia*, 167 (1997): 633–38.

Solomon, P. "Peer Support/Peer Provided Services Underlying Processes, Benefits, and Critical Ingredients." *Psychiatric Rehabilitation Journal* 27, no. 4 (2004): 392–401.

Steadman, H., et al. "Prevalence of Serious Mental Illness among Jail Inmates." *Psychiatric Services*, 60 (2009): 761, 764.

Steadman, H., K. Stainbrook, P. Griffin, J. Draine, R. Dupont, and C. Horey. "A Specialized Crisis Response Site as a Core Element of Police-Based Diversion Programs." *Psychiatric Services* 52, no. 2 (2001): 219–22.

Technical Assistance Collaborative, Inc., Boston, MA: Community-Based Comprehensive Crisis Response Service, 2005.

Chapter Three

Diverting Special Needs Persons from Inappropriate Incarceration

The Role of Police Mental Health Training

Tony Salvatore and Michelle Monzo

INTRODUCTION

Consider the following quote from John Snook of the Treatment Advocacy Center:

> When someone has a heart attack, an ambulance takes them to an emergency room. When someone is in the depths of psychosis, however, police are called and frequently cart that person off to jail.[1]

Carting people with serious mental illness to jail after police contact used to happen much more often than it does now. Police officers may lack the skills, perspective, or experience to deal with "mental health calls." One in ten police calls in the United States involves mental illness to some degree.[2] We will discuss why this side of policing has grown in recent decades, the challenges it presents, why some individuals are disadvantaged in relating to police officers, and why police officers need mental health crisis intervention training.

In this chapter we describe deinstitutionalization, transinstitutionalization, and criminalization as processes putting persons with serious mental illness and other disabilities at risk of contact with the criminal justice system. We provide an overview of the need for diversion of individuals with behavioral health and/or developmental disabilities from criminal justice involvement related to their disability. We also identify selected behavioral health and developmental disabilities that involve symptoms or behaviors that may bring an individual with these conditions into contact with the criminal justice system. Last, we present practices for police officers to use to relate safely and effectively to individuals with behavioral health and developmental disabilities and minimize inappropriate criminal justice system involvement.

43

DEINSTITUTIONALIZATION AS BACKGROUND

Police officers always have had contact with persons manifesting disruptive or potentially harmful behaviors. The frequency of such encounters increased significantly in the United States as state psychiatric hospitals housing individuals with chronic severe mental illness were substantially downsized or shuttered.[3] A similar process took place with state institutions caring for intellectually disabled persons.[4]

The pace of the displacement of individuals from state psychiatric hospitals in the United States is staggering. The populations of such facilities peaked in 1955 at 559,000 patients; by the end of 1998, just over 57,000 patients remained in the state hospitals that were still open.[5] Four years later, in 2002, 49,443 patients were in long-term psychiatric hospitals run by states and some counties.[6] State psychiatric hospitals numbered 322 in 1950; by 2005, their numbers had declined to 204—a 63.3 percent drop—and the state hospital patient population had experienced a 90 percent decrease.[7]

The shift from state hospitals had three drivers:

1. the belief that institutionalization was inhumane;
2. faith in the promise of new antipsychotic medications; and
3. the desire of state governments to save money.[8]

Deinstitutionalization rested on three assumptions:

1. community-based care is inherently preferable to institutional care;
2. communities were capable and willing to offer such care; and
3. mental health services would be "humanized" as the result of this shift of settings.[9]

The deinstitutionalization movement took it as a given that persons manageable in restrictive settings could now be cared for in the community.

Those reentering the community met hostility and discrimination affecting their readjustment to community living and their self-image.[10] Self-stigma often set in.[11] Community response kept many from maintaining aftercare arrangements or developing social supports. This brought on decompensation and a re-manifestation of symptoms and behaviors that had led to their state hospital admission and often found them being involuntarily committed to short-stay psychiatric facilities.[12] No state hospitals were there to provide care, or the length of stay at the dwindling number of remaining facilities was very short.

A cycle of "revolving-door" hospitalizations heightened maladjustment to independent living.[13] Those unable to secure help disrupted the community with bizarre behaviors essential to survival on the street such as trespassing, loitering, panhandling, picking through trash for discarded food, and petty thievery.[14] They also were subject to arrest for shoplifting, engaging in lewd behavior, and not paying for restaurant meals.[15] These often are referred to as "nuisance crimes." Other adversities included addiction, abuse, and other forms of victimization, self-injury, and suicidality. The inability to blend into the community positioned them for police response.

As the number of state hospitals shrank, the need they met did not. More than 70 percent of psychiatric hospital readmissions within thirty days are for patients with a diagnosis of schizophrenia.[16] Such recidivism may be due to poor access to outpatient care or noncompliance with treatment. Whatever the reason, readmissions to the remaining state hospitals are rising as more former patients vie for shorter stays in fewer beds.[17] The severity of symptoms of these recycling patients puts a strain on police, emergency departments, and short-stay psychiatric hospitals.

A pattern of long institutionalization in state hospitals has been replaced by what may be termed "serial institutionalization." This refers to frequent admissions to short-stay psychiatric hospitals interspersed with periods of imprisonment for individuals whose severity of psychiatric or developmental disorders makes community living difficult or impossible without significant support not available in most places. Police officers may have contact with such at-risk persons when their ability to manage independently breaks down and placement in a safer setting becomes necessary.

CRIMINALIZATION OF PERSONS WITH SERIOUS MENTAL ILLNESS AND OTHER DISABILITIES

Criminalization is the process by which individuals previously not regarded as criminals come to be seen as offenders. It occurs when a behavior is redefined by statute as unlawful. Criminalization of persons with serious mental illness manifests itself when members of this population are treated punitively because of their mental illness, regardless of the nature of the offense.[18]

Criminalization of mental illness resulted from the state-by-state adoption of criteria for civil commitment based on demonstration of actual or likely imminent danger to self or others.[19] Transitioning large numbers of persons with serious mental illness from settings where their symptoms were managed around the clock to the community where they were delegated responsibility for their own care put them at risk of symptom recurrence. This often resulted in police intervention. The community-based care that was supposed to sustain living outside state hospitals was either unable to meet their needs or insufficiently available.

Persons with serious mental illness who could not understand the police, who were aggressive or in "the wrong place at the wrong time," became offenders. Once caught up in the criminal justice system, such vulnerable persons were exposed to the "get-tough" public attitude toward crime that arose in the 1990s. Those who had repeated arrests faced the consequences of mandatory sentencing and "third-strike" laws.

The criminal justice system was used to reinstitutionalize at-risk persons when their behavior crossed a very low community tolerance threshold.[20] Responsibility for these vulnerable citizens effectively had been relocated from the mental health system to the criminal justice system, and, more specifically to the law enforcement and correctional subsystems.

TRANSINSTITUTIONALIZATION

Persons with serious mental illness repeatedly moving alternatively between the community and correctional facilities constitutes the meaning of transinstitutionalization.[21] The rise of the prison population and the number of inmates with mental illness coincident to the drastic decline in the state hospital population would seem to demonstrate the face validity of the transinstitutionalization proposition. However, does it hold up under empirical scrutiny?

One study provides some perspective: incarceration of individuals who otherwise would have been treated in a state hospital accounted for 7 percent of prison population growth between 1980 and 2000, but less than 30 percent of the individuals comprising the reportedly high proportion of inmates with mental illness in prisons in 2000 would have been in a state hospital if that level of care were an option for their disposition.[22]

It is not a question of how many persons with serious mental illness are incarcerated because the absence of care appropriate to their needs led to their inappropriate imprisonment: it is that such outcomes occur at all with any regularity. Persons with serious psychiatric disorders do not do well in prison. Their behavior often conflicts with prison policies, which subjects them to punitive treatment such as solitary confinement.[23]

Calls have come for reopening state psychiatric hospitals to reduce the incidence of transinstitutionalization. It is argued that state hospitals are indispensable to meet the needs of patients effectively and to minimize transinstitutionalization.[24] The need is for a twenty-first century model of long-term psychiatric care using evidenced-based, recovery-oriented therapies that actively treat patients whose illness cannot be addressed adequately in outpatient care. This would break the ongoing cycle of crisis intervention, psychiatric hospitalization, homelessness, and incarceration endured by too many persons with serious mental illness.[25]

Police officers are frustrated with the emergency department/community revolving door. Sometimes this dilemma is resolved by arrest and jail, which at least slow rapid release back to the community from emergency departments.[26] Arrest is still a likely option to an officer dispatched several times during the same week, perhaps the same day, to the same situation with the same result. Taking the person into custody satisfies the immediate interests of all parties except the patient—who may be safe, but possibly on a fast track to the county correctional facility.

GROUPS AT RISK OF CRIMINAL JUSTICE CONTACT

Members of the populations discussed in this section are vulnerable to possible incarceration after drawing police attention, largely because the criminal justice system focuses more on offenses than on offenders. Groups with special needs also are disadvantaged in dealing with the criminal justice system because of the symptoms or side effects of their disorders or disabilities.

Persons with Serious Mental Illness

Serious mental illnesses (SMI) are especially debilitating and comprise a large segment of psychiatric disorders. They have been defined as follows:

> Serious mental illness (SMI) refers to individuals 18 or older, who currently or at any time during the past year have had a diagnosable mental, behavioral, or emotional disorder of sufficient duration to meet diagnostic criteria specified in the diagnostic manual of the American Psychiatric Association and that has resulted in functional impairment, that substantially interferes with or limits one or more major life activities.[27]

Schizophrenia, bipolar disorder, and major depression are the disorders most commonly associated with SMI. Characteristics of SMI include:

- ritualistic preoccupation with certain activities
- being suspicious

- unpredictable outbursts
- seeking quiet or isolation
- changes in mood
- demonstrating bizarre behavior

Persons with SMI are at greatest risk of inappropriate incarceration because of behavior or offenses related to their illness or its symptoms.[28] Persons with SMI, particularly schizophrenia, have been most affected by past and present deinstitutionalization efforts.[29] However, persons with other psychiatric disorders nevertheless may find themselves in detention, jail, or prison if they manifest SMI-like symptoms. This is especially likely to take place if the individual has a co-occurring alcohol or drug abuse addiction disorder.

The loss of contact with reality and experiencing things that are not happening are the SMI symptoms likely to bring the individual into contact with police officers at some point.[30] They may involve extreme agitation, grandiose or disorganized thinking, or frenzied speaking. This is psychosis and involves delusion and often paranoia, and those subject to such symptoms typically are treated with psychotropic medications and other therapies.[31] However, this treatment may be terminated because the individual does not believe it is necessary, a prescription is not refilled, or sometimes because of a short stay in jail.

Substance abuse, homelessness, panhandling, pilfering food from stores, and not bathing are baseline features that make persons with SMI stand out to law enforcement. The odds of police involvement rise precipitously when delusional behavior enters the picture. Examples are someone who received a message from the CIA or FBI assigning them a secret mission, a person who randomly assaults people on the street because they intend to kill him, damaging a satellite dish or antenna because it is transmitting signals into the person with SMI's brain, or trashing a restaurant because it is intentionally poisoning customers. Very infrequently, the delusions can result in serious injury or even in death, such as if "the voices" command violent acts for whatever reason.[32]

Persons with SMI can be grouped according to their criminal histories.[33] The first group has arrest histories largely for public order violations. These individuals best fit the profile of "the criminalized mentally ill." They are arrested for simply displaying the signs and symptoms of SMI in public. The second group commits "survival" crimes, such as prostitution, shoplifting, and minor drug sales, or crimes to supplement the limited financial aid from Social Security or other programs. The third group has backgrounds of street crimes, including robbery, burglary, assault, and battery. The first group is most amenable to jail diversion by police officers.

Persons with Mild Intellectual Disability

Intellectual disability (ID) is a common developmental disorder. However, individuals with ID in mild to moderate ranges may not always be recognized as disabled. Individuals with ID have been found to be at an increased risk for manifesting mental illness rates higher than the general population.[34] *The Diagnostic and Statistical Manual of Mental Disorders* (DSM-V) defines intellectual disability to be present when an individual has an intelligence quotient (IQ) score of 70 or below.[35] Current diagnostic criteria focus on adaptive functioning and the ability to carry out routine living skills. The American Association of Intellectual and Developmental Disabilities notes an IQ score of 70 indicates a limitation in intellectual functioning.[36] This group is categorized as mild ID and constitutes the majority of individuals with ID. Mild ID is marked by slow cognitive development and intellectual functioning not at the same levels as individuals without ID.[37] Despite this, their conceptual, social, and daily living skills enable them to fulfill basic requirements of community living with little or no support.

Persons with mild ID may have police contact for minor offenses, carrying out criminal acts beyond their comprehension, and taking responsibility for an offense without understanding the consequences.[38] They may draw police attention because of an inability to grasp the meaning of behavioral cues or be inappropriate with peers or the opposite sex. They may have a high degree of impulsiveness and a low frustration tolerance.

Various characteristics of mild ID may complicate encounters with police officers.[39] The individual may not grasp the seriousness of the situation. He may not understand a question but may give an answer to please the questioner and hide his disability. He may smile inappropriately and be unable to be still even when told to do so. If others are present, he may mimic their responses. He may be overwhelmed by "officer presence" and act suspiciously or furtively in response.[40] He may be unable recall facts or details regarding the incident. These aspects of this type of disability are compounded if the individual is "dual disordered" (i.e., has mental illness as well as ID) or is abusing substances.

Advocates for persons with ID offer some advice for police officers. Physical appearance, speech, and ability to sign their name (e.g., to a statement) do not mean disability is not present.[41] Research has shown that police officers correctly identify the presence of ID less than one-third of the time.[42] Persons with ID may overreact emotionally but not deliberately. When faced with such "bad" behavior, officers should try de-escalation techniques and minimize the use of force.[43] If a suspect appears to have ID, the officers should avoid framing questions in a way that may lead or direct responses.[44] A useful guideline for officers who find themselves interacting with a person who may have ID is to keep in mind that how the person relates to the officer will be different from that of a person with SMI.[45]

Autism Spectrum Disorders

Autism Spectrum Disorder (ASD) affects nearly four million Americans. It is described as a spectrum disorder because of the wide variation in the type and severity of symptoms that may be seen among individuals with the disorder.[46] ASD is 4.5 times more prevalent in males than females.[47] The disorder is characterized by impaired social interaction and communication, repetitive behavior, and restricted interests. Some adults with ASD need significant support to manage routines of daily living, whereas others function independently. All may confront abuse, stigma, comorbid mental illness, financial hardship, and other stressors, such as abuse, bullying, and exploitation. They may be more prone to extreme negative emotions in high-stress situations because of their inhibited cognitive and emotional control and limited ability to use proper coping skills, comprehend their need for help, and find support and services.[48]

Adults with ASD can exhibit severe limitations in social skills, verbal communication, and the ability to reciprocate emotional cues.[49] These limitations prevent them from maintaining supportive interpersonal relationships. This lack of social connectiveness restricts their sense of value and belonging. This may increase the tendency to engage in self-harming and self-destructive behavior. Adults with ASD often have insight into the nature of their disorder and how it makes them different.[50] This may lead to difficulties with persons in authority. Police officers may encounter individuals with ASD who confess to offenses they had nothing to do with because of a desire to please.[51]

Identifying adults with ASD can be problematic because signs may be masked by impaired communication, strained social interactions, cognitive deficits, and inappropriate behavior.[52] They may experience extreme stress when presented with screening questions by those who conduct an interview without insufficient sensitivity to their needs.

Adults with ASD may not comprehend instructions unless they are clear and concise.[53] They may have a limited vocabulary to describe their own emotions. Assessments may be tedious because of processing delays and the need for extra time to comprehend and respond. If the questioning proceeds too quickly for the individual to process, he may stop participating, possibly become hostile, and react very inappropriately such as suddenly approaching or moving away.[54]

The inability to make eye contact, and discomfort maintaining it, may make him seem deceptive. He may appear less convincing, which may lead the officer to believe that the individual is hiding, evading, or minimizing responses. These unusual behaviors may lead to misjudging the emotional state. He may appear calmer than he is due to a limited range of emotional expression. He may suddenly make an unexpected, exaggerated response if touched because he does not understand how his actions may be misperceived.[55] Police officers should speak calmly and softly, use short phrases (e.g., "Get in the car now"), avoid slang, and be ready to repeat and rephrase questions or directions.[56] They should approach adults with ASD in a nonthreatening manner and maintain a safe distance in the event that the individual suddenly moves in their direction.[57]

Adults with ASD who interact with officers unfamiliar with their condition are likely to be arrested. Interpersonal threats and being a public nuisance may bring adults with ASD to the attention of police. Other offenses may make diversion of persons with ASD difficult at the patrol level. These include telephone or internet stalking, inappropriate sexual contacts, downloading child pornography, and being a gullible accomplice in shoplifting or drug dealing.

Fetal Alcohol Syndrome Disorder

Fetal Alcohol Spectrum Disorder (FASD) affects up to 5 percent of the U.S. population but often goes unrecognized. Those with FASD typically experience a number of adaptive, cognitive, and executive functioning deficits and face many social, educational, and vocational challenges. Adults with FASD may often "hide in plain sight" while diverting attention from their disability. This may lead a criminal justice professional to miss or minimize the degree and nature of disability in someone they see as uncooperative.

Research suggests that the deficits caused by prenatal alcohol exposure may contribute to an increased risk of criminal justice system involvement later in life.[58] Some factors, such as learning disability, may play a role. But mental illness, substance abuse, poor supports, social isolation, poor executive functioning, and impulsivity also increase their risk of incarceration. Many individuals with FASD experience comorbid psychiatric disorders; and a sizable number, abuse substances.[59]

One area that places adults with FASD at a disadvantage in their dealings with the criminal justice system is executive functioning.[60] This is the ability to plan, to comprehend cause and effect, to infer or deduce consequences from potential actions, to think logically, and simply to pay attention. It may be difficult for individuals with FASD to see optional solutions to the problem at hand. In addition, they can have difficulty controlling their emotional response.[61]

Police officers may encounter suggestibility and inclination to give a "right answer" when faced with uncertainty and an interrogator perceived as authoritative.[62] Individuals with FASD can react emotionally beyond that typical of those without this disorder. Once such an outburst has occurred, it is difficult for them to calm down. For some with an inability to plan, a simple cry for help can turn quickly into an apparently threatening or even dangerous situation for anyone in their vicinity.

Persons with FASD are highly susceptible to victimization. They may have contact with police officers because they are the victim of an offense rather than the perpetrator. Abuse, bullying, other forms of victimization and self-injury are common in persons with FASD.[63] These experiences inure them to emotional pain and may lower their resistance to potential self-harming behaviors. Often, abusers repeat the physical, sexual, or verbal abuse or neglect because those with FASD often have a diminished ability to read social cues, avert abuse, or sense the danger around of them.

Traumatic Brain Injury

Traumatic Brain Injury (TBI) is not a developmental disability, but those who experience it have special needs that may put them at risk of police contact. TBI results from a head injury by impact or penetration that affects brain function. It is a major public health problem in the United States. About 1.5 million TBIs occur annually in this country.[64] Most TBIs are treated in emergency departments. An estimated 250,000 yearly involve hospitalization. An unknown number of TBI sufferers receive no medical care. In these cases, the symptoms and consequences of the TBI may never be connected to the head injury.[65] TBI severity is based on how long the individual lost consciousness when originally injured. Mild TBIs are the most prevalent and include concussions. Falls, motor vehicle accidents, assaults, and suicide attempts account for most TBIs.[66]

TBI affects cognition, mood, and behavior as well as deficits in attention, communication, learning, and information processing. TBI may have lasting negative effects on judgment, decision making, problem solving, and insight. TBI is linked to depression, apathy, anxiety, and emotional lability. Post-injury aggression and hostility are common in TBI patients.[67] Depressed patients with TBI are significantly more aggressive and hostile than depressed patients without TBI. This tendency to violence may bring those with this condition to the attention of police. TBI fosters criminal justice exposure in many ways.

Impulsivity, disinhibition, and intemperate outbursts are factors in TBI because of damage to areas of the brain that control these functions. These may lead to police contact with consequences compounded by problems taking cues, maintaining attention, keeping eye contact, violating personal space norms, and taking direction.[68] Behavioral nonconformity may result in criminal charges. TBI is also comorbid with substance abuse, which increases possible criminal liability.

Given their proclivity to engage in behaviors that may constitute criminal offenses and their likelihood of negative encounters with police officers, persons with TBI have high risk of incarceration. From 25 percent to more than 80 percent of adult inmates in county jails and state prisons have sustained a TBI at some point in their lives.[69] TBI may affect the ability to navigate the judicial system, take advantage of safeguards protecting rights, and use legal counsel effectively.

Persons with TBI generally do not do well in correctional environments. They have more rule infractions than inmates without TBI.[70] This may lead to longer sentences, harsher treatment, and less access to services. Parole presents a new set of challenges involving keeping appointments, complying with treatment, maintaining employment, and not repeating the behaviors that put them in jail.[71] Reoffending, coupled with an inability to meet the requirements of community supervision, finds many offenders with TBI rearrested and reincarcerated within a year or less.[72]

Persons with TBI, except veterans to some degree, have not received much attention as targets for diversion from the criminal justice system. A greater focus is given to those in the correctional system with this disability.[73] The uneven availability of training on TBI is equaled by the unavailability of community-based resources in most areas for police to refer those with TBI whom they encounter. This may change as more attention is given to the role of trauma in fostering criminal justice contact.

THE CRISIS INTERVENTION SPECIALIST PROGRAM: AN EDUCATION-BASED JAIL DIVERSION STRATEGY

Montgomery County Emergency Service, Inc. (MCES), a nonprofit psychiatric emergency service in Norristown, Pennsylvania, has provided behavioral health crisis intervention training to the law enforcement community since 1976. The training is part of a broader mental health provider-based jail diversion effort that regards the police as partners.[74] It was initiated after two former state hospital patients released as a result of deinstitutionalization took their lives at the county prison after being incarcerated for minor infractions.

Crisis Intervention Specialist (CIS) training is continuously offered to municipal police departments and other county, state, and federal agencies including correctional officers, probation officers, State Parole, FBI, Homeland

Security, the Pennsylvania State Police, and court personnel. Trainees come from the tristate greater Philadelphia region and beyond. Trainees also are drawn from many special police forces such as National Park Rangers, the regional transit authority, AMTRAK, and colleges and universities. In addition to sworn officers, CIS training is provided to police academy cadets.

CIS instruction covers crisis intervention skills, familiarity with signs of mental illness, and relating safely to individuals with mental illnesses. It increases empathy of police officers for individuals showing signs of possible mental illness or developmental disability, lessens the probability of injury associated with police contact, and decreases the probability of criminal justice system involvement and incarceration. The program trains hundreds of law enforcement professionals annually. Its founding philosophy was that the first responder to a mental health emergency should have the skills and knowledge to intervene safely.[75] CIS training is approved as a continuing education elective for police officers in Pennsylvania by the Municipal Police Officers' Education & Training Commission (MPOETC).

CIS training involves a three-day "police school." Completion qualifies trainees as a Crisis Intervention Specialist able to resolve mental health crises encountered in the course of their duties. The topics covered are:

- introduction to forensic mental health and jail diversion
- overview of the mental health system
- mental health law and the Pennsylvania Mental Health Procedures Act
- crisis intervention techniques
- treatment options—"talk" and drug therapies
- psychiatric medications
- "psych 101"—mental illness/intellectual disability and other disorders
- substance abuse
- suicide awareness

CIS-trained officers can provide basic crisis stabilization, assessment, conflict resolution, and referral to appropriate community services. The CIS program equips police officers with what they need to know to effect diversion where a person with SMI or special needs may first have contact with law enforcement. If trained officers recognize mental illness at this point, they can take the person to help, not to the station.

The objectives of the CIS program are:

1. To provide crisis intervention and stabilization to those with serious mental illness and other at-risk individuals
2. To interview and assess individuals experiencing a behavioral health crisis

3. To pro-actively resolve conflicts and de-escalate potentially violent situations without the use of force
4. To use local community-based mental health crisis services to divert mentally ill individuals from the criminal justice system when appropriate
5. To make referrals to applicable local community-based services
6. To use state mental health laws and procedures to arrange involuntary psychiatric evaluations and hospitalization, when indicated

CIS training provides police officers with a knowledge base and skill set to increase their effectiveness as part of the community crisis intervention system. It contributes to reducing criminalization and stigmatization of those with mental illness. It enables police officers to interface with crisis centers, hot lines, mobile crisis teams, and other gatekeepers to the local community mental health system in their jurisdictions.

The CIS syllabus is as follows:

Day One

- Introduction to Forensic Mental Health and Jail Diversion
- Overview of the Mental Health System, Policy, and Funding
- Mental Health Law
- Crisis Intervention

Day Two

- Treatment Options
- Psychiatric Medications
- "Psych 101"/Mental Illness
- Substance Abuse

Day Three

- Suicide Awareness
- Inpatient Unit Rounds

CIS training begins with an introduction to forensic mental health and the concept of jail diversion of the mentally ill. This includes a review of treatment options and their advantages over arrest, booking, and incarceration. This is followed by an overview of the community mental health system, how the system is structured, and how it is accessed. They learn the contact points and how to make referrals to providers that can help individuals with the types of problems likely to be encountered in the course of their duties.

Trainees are oriented to the roles of the county and state in mental health policy and regulation, as well as the basics of funding streams and reimbursement. They are grounded in the mental health law and the criteria for voluntary and involuntary psychiatric evaluations and hospitalizations.

Trainees are familiarized with techniques for communicating and interacting with someone in crisis. They learn verbal and nonverbal de-escalation techniques. They are taught active listening skills, how to set limits on a situation, and negotiation strategies. The principles of trauma-informed care also are addressed.

Trainees are given a basic understanding of the signs and symptoms of serious mental illness and psychiatric disorders such as schizophrenia, major depression, and bipolar disorder. Recovery, mental health wellness, and trauma awareness concepts are incorporated in CIS training. MCES involves volunteers from the National Alliance for Mental Illness's (NAMI) "In Their Own Voices" program, who share their first-person experiences as part of the training whenever possible and practical.

Pharmacological and non-pharmacological treatment modalities are looked at next. Trainees are acquainted with the most commonly prescribed psychiatric medications, and with their indications and side effects.

Trainees are oriented to the co-occurrence of mental illness and substance abuse and the consequences for relapse, crisis, and hospitalization. An overview of substance abuse is provided with a focus on the abuse of alcohol and other substances.

All trainees completing the CIS program receive a certificate of attendance, a CIS patch, and CIS pin.

CONCLUDING COMMENTS

What Police Mental Health Crisis Training *Cannot* Do

Police mental health training is seen as part of "the answer" to high rates of mental illness in county and state prisons. We must not overpromise what this training can do. Here are some caveats:

Mental health training for police officers cannot fix or compensate for community behavioral health system shortcomings/deficits.
A mental health system must be operating for police training to work. Where inpatient and outpatient resources exist, they must be ready to change policies and practices (e.g., hours of operation) to facilitate interface with police.

Mental health training will not reduce police involvement with persons with serious mental illness in their community.

Police training can only increase the safety and effectiveness of officer encounters. It is up to the mental health system to help those it serves function in the community without engaging in behaviors that draw police attention.

Mental health training will not eliminate the inappropriate incarceration of persons with serious mental illness.

Street-level police contact is not the only portal to criminal justice contact for persons with SMI. The criminal justice system can be entered at many points. Mental health training and screening must be applied at those points. Jail diversion requires buy in by criminal justice components beyond the police.

Mental health training alone will not create collaboration and trust between police and mental health providers.

Some approaches to police crisis intervention training are inherently police-based. Depending on how they are implemented in a community will determine how fast the mental health providers move out of their silo and toward a partnership with the police and criminal justice system in their community.

Mental health police training will not reduce the need for and use of inpatient psychiatric care in a given area.

Hospital, emergency department, and crisis center diversion is not a duty taken on by police officers when they complete training. Some mental health calls may be resolved on-scene with a referral or brochure. However, training promotes case finding as suspected signs of serious mental illness compel assessment rather than arraignment. As the number of trained officers grows, and as they come to trust the emergency mental health services they work with, police referrals will rise. A good example is the psychiatric emergency service where the author is employed. More than 60 percent of referrals are from the fifty-plus police departments in one county.

Police mental health training is part of the solution to diverting persons with SMI and special needs from the criminal justice system. As part of this strategy, the mental health system must gain more understanding of the methods, culture, and constraints of the criminal justice system in relation to persons with serious mental illness.

Part II

ORGANIZATION

Chapter Four

Alignment within Organizations

Frank Mielke and William Mossman

INTRODUCTION

As part of a team, athletics or otherwise, you recognize the importance of team members pulling together for a common cause. Building on that theme, law enforcement success in diverting the mentally ill out of the criminal justice system and into treatment requires that members of the organization be aligned around this common cause. In other words, members of a law enforcement agency must pull together for the common cause of diversion.

PERSPECTIVE ON ALIGNMENT

Before examining the subject of alignment, a simple concept at face value, it's important to understand the subtleties in the nuances of this concept.

For the purposes of this discussion, view alignment existing at three levels in the organization and think about the forces that drive alignment at each level.

The levels and forces are identified in table 4.1.

It is important to reconcile the concepts of alignment and leadership, recognized with some prominence in table 4.1.

1. We assume that the reader of this book aspires to leadership and we wish to present the integral part that leadership plays in organizations.
2. Total vertical alignment cannot exist without leadership influencing the tactical component in the execution of diversionary strategies.
3. We significantly limit the application of leadership to the concept of alignment only. To go beyond those boundaries clearly exceeds the capacity of this book.

Table 4.1.

Level	Characteristics	Forces	Threats to Alignment
Strategic	The police chief is the prime mover shaping the attitudes, culture, and behaviors toward a common goal (i.e., diversion). The attitudes, culture, and behaviors are reflected in the agency's mission statement and filter down to policies and procedures.	An inherent belief in the financial, regulatory, public safety, and moral imperatives of diversion.	Failure to embrace the imperatives and the inability to balance the everyday challenges that confront a law enforcement agency. Such threats may include budgetary constraints, compliance, or the inherent rejection of the four imperatives.
Tactical	Policies and procedures are consistent (aligned) with the mission and strategies regarding diversion.	The mission statement, in words and actions, drives the development of policies and procedures.	The mission statement, or the behaviors at the strategic level, suggests that efforts to divert are receiving lip service. When the mission and strategies are not understood, nonalignment is the result.
Execution	Frontline personnel understand what is to be done and why it is to be done.	Frontline officers behave in a manner consistent with the mission and with compliance to policies and procedures.	Frontline officers reject the notion of diversion. They are dissuaded by their own philosophies and competing demands: "I don't want to babysit someone in crisis; I joined the police force to catch the bad guys." Nonalignment occurs because frontline supervisors don't have the time, patience, or skills to address these objections effectively.

WHY ALIGNMENT?

The necessity of alignment is both intuitive and well recognized as an organizational quality. The lack of alignment results in organizational dysfunction that Kofman and Senge characterize as "fragmentation."[1]

When organizations are aligned, behaviors are predictable. Consider why you opt to frequent a particular restaurant:

- The quality of the meal is consistently good
- The behavior of the waitstaff consistently meets your expectations
- No surprises come with the bill
- The ambience of the restaurant is always clean and inviting
- Any combination of the above

This example demonstrates positive alignment because the restaurant demonstrates positive, consistent, and predictable qualities.

For law enforcement encountering an individual in crisis, alignment can be positive, such as a police officer steering that individual to treatment instead of incarceration, and such behaviors are consistent with a department diversion strategy. Further, given the description of the incident, the behaviors of the responding officers are predictable. In other situations, alignment can be negative. In these situations, it's predictable that a response to an individual in crisis involves "cuff and carry," either to a hospital, crisis center, or jail with the foregone conclusion that the end result is an arrest. Such behaviors may be viewed as negative, but if they are consistent with the culture and policies of the organization, the organization can be viewed as aligned. In other words, alignment can be around both positive and negative strategies and culture.

An example of the latter is terrorists groups seeking death and destruction. Their devotion to their cause and dedication to their ultimate goals render them an aligned organization.

With a negative response to an individual in crisis, the responder opts for a short-term solution and the transfer of the problem to someone else, be it the medical, mental health, or judicial system. Some justify such a transfer as being in the best interest of their organization, citing that it's not their job to act as crisis interventionist. Unfortunately, such thinking fails to recognize the larger issue when those with mental illness are incarcerated. In fact, they may be contributing to the cycle of recidivism and faced with the associated recurring and increasingly problematic challenges surrounding the issue of treatment and incarceration. It's unfair to characterize all "cuff-and-carry" options as negative; some of these options are warranted.

An example is the very combative crisis patient who demonstrates an immediate threat to herself or others.

Most situations fit into the gray area of uncertainty. When these situations occur, the predictability of the highly aligned organizations is high, and the patient most certainly will wind up either in jail or in a facility receiving treatment. In most organizations, leaders can predict with some level of certainty how particular members may respond, either negatively or positively, but with the remainder there is that level of uncertainty.

Alignment is rarely absolute. Rather, alignment exists at some point in a continuum from the negative to the positive, as demonstrated in table 4.2.

Table 4.2.

Certainty	Uncertainty	Certainty
Negative Response		**Positive Response**
Options are aligned with incarceration over treatment.	Response may be positive or negative depending on the attitudes and values of the individual responding and the severity of the episode.	Options are aligned with treatment over incarceration.

Table 4.3.

Influences	Individual in Crisis	Outcomes
The Details (Who, When, Where, What, and How)		Diversion/Incarceration

The challenge for leaders is to move their department in the direction of a positive response with high levels of certainty. Such movement starts with leaders believing in a strategy of diversion in the best interests of the constituents they serve. They provide training, encourage behaviors, and monitor compliance. They "walk the talk" and make balanced decisions in the interest of the community, the men and women they lead, and for the individual in crisis. They talk openly and candidly about a particular response identifying things that could have been done better along with things that went well to reinforce positive behavior and to recognize those who made a positive contribution to the incident. Everyone is on the same page, contributing to the predictability of behaviors.

Here's what happens in an aligned organization that embraces a strategy of diversion: A police officer encounters someone in crisis. The officer pulls the cuffs or exercises a violent takedown *only* in the face of imminent danger. With less serious cases, the officer starts with a preliminary diagnosis until help arrives from the behavioral health professionals. By training or experience, the officer knows that a depressed individual may need a hug. The officer also knows never to try to hug an autistic individual. It's recognized that a hug is an appropriate intervention and does not compromise his sense of identity as being strong and stoic. The officer recognizes that the hug, particularly for males with a sense of machismo, does not detract from his manhood. The end game for the police officer is not incarceration but treatment while not jeopardizing his or her own safety or the safety of the public or the individual in crisis.

In "fragmented" organizations, leaders who embrace a strategy of diversion are frustrated because members in their organization behave inconsistently. Some react too quickly and set a course of incarceration. As previously noted, by going into the criminal justice system the condition of the patient may become exacerbated, lead to recidivism, and the police again may be confronted with that same patient. A variety of reasons contribute to the disconnect or lack of alignment between leaders and followers, which will be discussed later in this chapter.

What happens with an ineffective diversion strategy? Baton Rouge District Attorney Hillar Moore commented on an annual report analyzing officer-involved shootings that resulted in death either of an offender or lawmen. According to Moore's statement, "50 percent of the officer-involved shootings was with a suspect who suffered from mental illness."[2] The findings in Baton Rouge are consistent with research by the Ruderman Family Foundation. They report that almost half of the people who die at the hands of police have some kind of disability.[3] Although the term "disability" is not defined, we assume that the majority of these deaths occur among those with some form of mental illness.

The absence of an effective diversion strategy can have tragic results. Consider the case of Jason Harrison from Dallas, Texas.

The mother of Jason Harrison, a man with bipolar and schizophrenia, wanted help to get him to the hospital because he was off his medications. She had made this request before without incident and requested someone trained to handle the mentally ill. The police arrived at the house and observed that Harrison was fumbling with a screwdriver. Shouts to drop the screwdriver quickly were followed by shots fired by the police officer.

As with many incidents of this nature, conflicting accounts come from the public, family, and the police with respect to the body cam and Harrison's behaviors that allegedly incited the police.

It is not our intent to indict the police but to raise the question of alignment. Could the police have behaved differently acting to:

- Ensure their own safety?
- Protect the mother?
- Support a strategy of diversion if one had existed?
- Alter the outcome in Harrison's interest?

It is worth discussing one facet of alignment: the barriers to it.

BARRIERS TO ALIGNMENT

A variety of barriers exist, but perhaps the three most significant are:

1. poor leadership
2. lack of a viable mission or vision
3. culture

The importance of leadership is obvious. However, three facets of leadership are worthy of consideration, especially in the context of diversion:

1. defining the leader
2. situational leadership
3. task/results orientation

DEFINING THE LEADER

In their research, Barge and Carlson[4] recognize the importance of frontline leadership and its applicability to law enforcement.

Individuals hearing the term leader immediately assume this to be the police chief or superintendent. However, the importance of frontline supervisors as leaders cannot be overstated. Patrol officers, who respond to an individual in crisis, establish the initial pathway to incarceration or into treatment and exercise incident leadership. The frontline supervisor influences the patrol officer on almost a daily basis. The supervisor provides direct communication and supervision. The supervisor's attitudes and belief in the organization's mission, vision, and strategy shape the attitude and behaviors of frontline supervisors and, in turn, patrol officers, clearly providing leadership in the organization.

Peer influence is a complicating factor. Strong bonds among patrol officers are demonstrated by the extraordinary response to the call of "officer needs assistance." Peer-to-peer bonds are strengthened in off hours. Frequently, police officers socialize with the family of their peers, strengthening the bond with their significant others. This is an opportunity for a spouse or partner to commiserate with others about the challenges of shiftwork and the fear generated by the constant threat of danger. No one else understands what cops and their family go through.

Leaders publish and promote practices and strategies; vetting occurs in conversations among peers. The results of these conversations can materially influence the level of compliance to diversion efforts.

It falls to the frontline supervisor not to attempt to break up these peer-to-peer relationships, but rather, recognize them and enlist the support of those individuals among the ranks who don't have title but are a clear influence.

SITUATIONAL LEADERSHIP

Law enforcement operates in both a "red zone" and a "green zone."

In the red zone, police officers are chasing bad guys, guns are drawn, and the danger level is high. We've seen countless examples of gunfire erupting and officers rushing to the scene as others run away. At other times, a police officer encounters someone in crisis unsure of the outcome. There is an element of uncertainty when facing behaviors that may require an arrest with a noncompliant and potentially combative individual. In these types of incidents, training and instinct kick in and the adrenaline flows. The red zone is the reason why many individuals join law enforcement.

The alternative environment is the green zone, characterized by administrative tasks ranging from budget preparations and writing reports to reporting incidents and completing the required paper work necessary to place someone with mental illness into treatment. The green zone does not occupy a lot of top-of-the-mind awareness for a newly sworn officer, nor do these activities enjoy favor with the experienced officer.

A diversion strategy encompasses elements of both red and green zone environments. Previously mentioned training prepares an officer to confront a dangerous, combative individual where the red zone climate requires that force be met with force. Transitioning to the green zone requires training, instinct, and patience—lots of patience.

A successful diversion strategy requires leaders to immerse themselves in the green zone to develop training, goals, strategies, and programs. It also requires constant reinforcement of the drivers of a diversion strategy. At times, force is necessary, and we are confident that officers will protect life and property. At other times, leaders will help officers to control their natural instincts for the greater good: keep the person in crisis out of jail and diverted into treatment.

TASK/RESULTS ORIENTATION

Like many professions, law enforcement behaviors are governed by procedures. Training prepares officers to do those things necessary to de-escalate a crisis situation. When failure occurs, the response of "I did what I was supposed to do" is unacceptable. A successful outcome starts with a positive mind-set and employs training and learned skills. Instincts guided by mind-set increase the probability of success. It involves the recognition that circumstances vary widely.

It falls to the leader by word and deed to establish the appropriate environment that blends a task (follow procedure and training) and results (strive to do the right thing). The effective leader is relentless in the pursuit of the goals of the organization, including diversion; just doing the required tasks and activities is not enough. The appropriate mind-set is an attitude of success guided by training and skills.

The appropriate mind-set is guided by living the "spirit" of the strategy versus a "letter of the law" strategy. Police officers performing in accordance with the letter of the law focus on completing a task without necessarily regarding the ultimate outcome. Those living the spirit of the law recognize the ultimate goal and act accordingly in compliance with policies and regulations.

LACK OF MISSION OR VISION

It's difficult to imagine a successful organization or endeavor without a clear understanding of self (mission) or aspirations (vision). The mission and vision unite individuals and guide their behaviors in a common cause. These two elements strengthen alignment, improving the likelihood of a successful diversion strategy.

It's not enough just to write a statement, either mission or vision, that has literary appeal. The statements must be easily understood, realistic, relevant, and compelling. The old adage "do as I say, not as I do" doesn't work. The behaviors, including what leaders say and do, must be consistent with the mission and vision statements.

CULTURE

The traditional profile of a policer officer is characterized by stoicism, strength, and someone who takes control in a crisis situation. Diversion requires compassion over stoicism, accommodation over strength, and understanding over control. The response to the criminal might be significantly different for an individual experiencing a mental crisis. The combative patient requires restraints while the placement process is conducted. Frequently, bed demand exceeds supply, and patients wait in some not so comforting environments. The use of force is consistent with law enforcement culture and traditions. For many, compassion, accommodation, and understanding are countercultural.

Culture can be a powerful influence on behavior. The leader who recognizes the power of "old-time" thinking will find it very difficult to implement a successful diversion strategy. Changing culture is a daunting task.

Aligned organizations just don't happen, which begs the obvious question: How do organizations achieve alignment? The path to alignment starts with understanding the theories of alignment.

THEORIES OF ALIGNMENT

A working description of alignment is everyone working in concert toward a common goal. This description is simplistic in its presentation but challenging in implementation, requiring a review of various theories and research.

A more comprehensive definition and discussion of alignment is: "A collection of ideas which set forth general rules on how to manage a business or organization. Management theory addresses how managers and supervisors relate to their organizations in the knowledge of its goals, the implementation of effective means to get the goals accomplished and how to motivate employees to perform to the highest standard."[5]

In this section of the chapter, we offer four theories or models that impact alignment within organizations:

1. Balance
2. Navy Seals
3. 7S Framework for Organizational Effectiveness (7S Model)
4. People-Centered Organizational (PCO) Theory

Balance

Conflict is inherent within individuals and in organizations. A police officer may serve in any of the following roles:

- police officer
- significant other

- parent
- member of a social, community, faith-based, athletic groups, or myriad like organizations

Consider obvious causes of conflict and stress for a police officer serving in myriad roles. Job scheduling may require absence from significant family events. Shift assignments inconsistent with circadian rhythms may create tension with loved ones. Witnessing, or being part of, a traumatic experience may alter one's mood. Coming home with a happy face is highly challenging in these situations. The police officer is required to align the responsibilities of the job with other roles. In other words, the police officer is required to maintain a sense of balance among all of these conflicting demands.

Similarly, organizations are subject to various, sometimes conflicting demands. Leaders in law enforcement must answer to politicians who are not always sympathetic. Community leaders often view police officer behaviors through a very narrow lens. In the face of these demands, law enforcement leaders strive to maintain loyalty to the people they command.

We know that for human beings, the inability to cope or maintain a sense of balance has consequences. Individuals in extreme emotional stress will develop ulcers. At this level of imbalance or inadequate coping mechanisms, where stress gets the upper hand, balance is lost and ulcers develop.

Consider the issue of balance and a patient requiring medication. The physician will review the patient's medical history before prescribing medication. The pharmacist, filling the prescription, will ask similar questions and instruct the patient on the proper way to take the medicine. The unwanted reaction—side effects—to the medication can range from discomfort to death. In other words, the ingredients in the prescription are not aligned with the body's needs, causing an unwanted reaction or imbalance.

Other more subtle implications appear when it comes to balance and the human body.

In response to the question "How do I prevent cancer?" an oncologist replied, "Be happy!"

This apparently glib response has a medical foundation. He went on to explain that we all have cancer within us, but the immune system is important because it fights off the cancerous viruses. So, can a smile, a real smile as a manifestation of happiness, improve the immune system, and, by extension, prevent cancer? Because this is not a medical journal, we respond with a definite "maybe." But this example demonstrates the complexity and interconnectivity of systems in individuals, and by extension, organizations as they function by systems. For the human being, a balanced disposition may deter serious illness. For organizations, a balanced culture supporting alignment deters unnecessary detention of individuals in crisis by the criminal justice system.

Balance for individuals is not a new concept; it can be traced back multiple centuries to the Chinese. Traditional Chinese medicine is based on a holistic approach that addresses the whole including the body, mind, and spirit. Chinese medicine views the body as a system in balance. When the body has an imbalance, illness occurs.

By comparison, we can view a functioning organization as a system in balance. When an organization is not in balance, negative outcomes can occur; in the case of Jason Harrison, that outcome was death.

The Harrison case identifies four parties to his incident whose interests must be kept in balance. The four parties are:

1. the public,
2. the organization,
3. the responder, and
4. the patient (Harrison).

The Public

We define the public as those outside the organization, which includes the citizens and visitors to the community protected by law enforcement.

In the Harrison case, his mother falls into the area of the external environment, a topic covered in the next chapter.

The Organization

The organization must be aligned externally to a series of interested parties as well as internally. However, the organization cannot be viewed as a simple and homogeneous entity. In a large law enforcement agency, members are male and female, of varied races, ethnicities, religions, and sexual orientations. They have different life experiences shaping diversity and potential barriers to alignment.

In our research, respondents were asked to identify a series of demographic factors including:

- age
- length of service
- position (from patrol officer through police chief or superintendent)
- military and combat experience
- attendance at various training sessions

These demographic factors were cross-tabulated with the response to a series of questions. The results are shared later in this chapter.

In the midst of all of this diversity, the organization's goals and strategies are a unifying element to improve the organizational alignment. It is intuitively obvious that individuals in the organization must be aware that such goals and strategies exist, must understand them, and that those goals and strategies be aligned with individual beliefs. Finally, the goals and strategies must influence behavior.

Goals and strategies should drive the behavior of the police officer. In addition to complying with organizational strategy, the police officer must keep herself/himself safe along with the public, and where appropriate, divert the patient into treatment.

The Responder

At times, the police officer is the first responder to a crisis incident. The officer makes an initial assessment and in no certain order confronts a series of questions:

- What am I required to do as defined by procedures?
- How do I protect the public, those who might be in danger?
- What does my training tell me to do?
- What is in the best interest of the individual in crisis?
- How do I protect myself?
- What are the consequences if I fail to react in a timely and appropriate fashion?

A police officer, potentially conflicted by these demands, reacts. The level of organizational alignment and the severity of the incident will influence the response. In a highly aligned department with the unlikely potential of harm, the officer predictably will lean toward a decision to incarcerate or a decision of diversion based on the department's mental illness strategies. When the forces of alignment are weak, either in support of or a rejection of a diversion strategy, the outcome is difficult to predict.

The Patient

Goals and strategies provide a framework for decision making. When diversion goals and strategies are known, agreed to, and consistent with the police officer's values, an appropriate decision will be made whose benefits accrue to the patient.

At the point of contact with a person in crisis, police officers make decisions, often without the luxury of time, and faced with someone potentially deemed to be a danger to himself or others. As we learned in chapter 3, not all patients are alike and not all causes of a crisis are the same. Essentially, the needs of the patient must be aligned with what the organization, through the responder, can provide.

In other words, the benefits of a balanced decision aligned with the financial, regulatory, public safety, and moral imperatives serve the interests of all involved.

Navy Seals

Jeff Boss is a former Navy Seal who writes about organizational alignment. He opines that a high-performing team doesn't operate at an elite level based on the performance of just one or more high-performing individuals. We can apply Boss's thinking to crisis intervention. In an aligned organization, positively disposed to treatment over incarceration, individuals perform at a high level when intervening with an individual in crisis. The positive disposition occurs with each encounter. No headlines scream of a wrongful shooting. A successful alignment strategy is not dependent on the performance of a few. Everyone must be on the same page. If not, fragmentation occurs, and fragmentation has consequences. The police, acting inconsistently, may put themselves at risk of injury or sanctions because their behaviors are recorded by an iPhone-equipped audience. The police may incarcerate a patient who otherwise might be directed to treatment.

In many respects, what a Seal has to face has the variability and potential volatility that a police officer confronts when dealing with an individual in crisis. Does the individual in crisis have a weapon? Is he a veteran, combat trained and potentially suffering from PTSD? Are others in the immediate area in danger?

In the midst of variable and potentially volatile situations, consider Boss's five factors contributing to organizational alignment:

1. a clear and meaningful purpose
2. clear goals
3. a practical strategy for achieving those goals
4. daily (even hourly) plans and priorities that kept us on track toward executing our strategy
5. metrics that define success[6]

These factors all are linked in law enforcement's quest for diversion.

Point 1—Purpose, diversion, is both clear (divert those in crisis into treatment) and meaningful. Meaningfulness is framed by the four imperatives mentioned in chapter 1: financial, regulatory, public safety, and morality. Purpose applies equally to Seals and law enforcement. In addition, organizations must ensure that the purpose is clear to everyone who is a part.

Point 2—Clear Goals and *Point 3—Strategy* are situational, reflecting on what a Navy Seal might encounter. These same points can apply to a police officer coming on scene with an individual in crisis. Goals may vary from restraint and shipment to a jail to a strategy of de-escalation, leading to treatment. In an aligned organization, both goals and strategies influence the behavior of the police officer. Further, goals and strategies are reinforced with training, which is highly influential in shaping individual behavior.

Point 4—Daily Planning and Setting of Priorities is closely connected with training where goals and strategies are reinforced, thereby shaping individual behavior. In addition, police are deployed to the geographical areas that represent the highest level of risk requiring police intervention. Daily briefing sessions provide the opportunity to share critical information and to develop coordinated responses when necessary. At times, critical information reshapes priorities.

Point 5—Data, Supporting the Metrics, indicating diversion successes or failures, are limited and vague for law enforcement.

Consider that reports on the number of inmates in jails and prisons largely are based on estimates. For example, it is estimated that approximately 20 percent of inmates in jails and 15 percent of inmates in state prisons have a serious mental illness.[7] We offer several observations that influence reporting:

- We assume that the methodologies developing estimates are reliable and the resulting data is statistically valid;
- Although the data is reliable, it's still not a precise portrayal of reality—it's an estimate;
- On a global basis, we can rely on current estimates to frame an understanding of conditions. However, data are less reliable at the regional or local level;
- Capturing data at the agency level is largely ignored; and
- The definition of mental illness, specifically as it applies to those in crisis, is inconsistent.

The last bullet refers to the inconsistent definition and understanding of mental illness. As can be seen in chapter 3, a range of illnesses and disorders must be considered. In the midst of all of this, one of the most consistent definitions used in the behavioral health field is "serious mental illness" or SMI.

The National Institute of Mental Health defines SMI as a "mental, behavioral, or emotional disorder resulting in serious functional impairment, which substantially interferes with or limits one or more major life activities."[8]

The definition is open to wide-ranging interpretations and points to the challenge of data collection. Can we truly measure something when there are inconsistencies in the definition of what we are trying to measure? The impediment to measurements resulting from a lack of consistent data does not limit the application of the Navy Seal model; rather, it underscores the compelling reason to improve data-capturing mechanisms.

Our understanding of the diversion landscape, associated with moral, financial, public safety, and regulatory imperatives, is based on educated guesses. Although chapter 2 addresses the understanding of mental illness, our ability to codify illnesses in the criminal justice system is woefully inadequate.

The overarching strategy regarding a data collection process requires a balance between gathering as much relevant data as possible and not being a burden to the police officer who must provide the data. After all, who likes paperwork?

We propose the following guidelines for a data-gathering process:

- Use agreed-upon codes that facilitate tabulation of the data
- Identify location of incident (home, public street, retail establishment, etc.)
- List patient profile (age, gender, marital status, military status, etc.)
- Identify disposition (released to family, hospital, mental health professional, or others in the criminal justice system with the intent of pursuing criminal action)

This is not an exhaustive list but an attempt to stimulate conversation. Developing a robust information system requires discussions with vendors who provide such systems along with input from the ranks who must use the system.

Without data, we don't know whether diversion strategies are working and, perhaps more important, why. We must know when and why a response to any incident is either successful or unsuccessful. A robust information system contributes to alignment. Such a system will:

- promote the communication of results to celebrate successes or rectify failures;
- serve as the foundation for meaningful discussions with everyone in the organization; and
- evaluate results that may adjust strategies, goals, and objectives.

Data must:

- emanate from a carefully constructed system;
- be easily understood;
- be widely disseminated; and,
- serve as a unifying force within organizations, a clear contributor to alignment.

Data drives a basic model:

7S Framework for Organizational Effectiveness (7S Model)

If you have a basic understanding of systems theory as introduced in chapter 1, the 7S Model will make a lot of sense to you. The origins of the model can be traced back to 1980 to the collaborative efforts of Tom Peters with Robert Waterman, Tony Athos, and Richard Pascal, academicians and consultants at McKinsey Consulting Group.

At the core of the model is shared values, which has an obvious connection to the subject of internal alignment. The remaining six components of the model are structure, systems, style, staff, skills, and strategy.

Each of the 7Ss does not operate alone but, at maximum effectiveness, in a synergistic fashion contributing to alignment or shared values.

The model has a number of uses. The most appropriate application is the development of strategy, in this case strategy of diversion. Other applications include changing organizations, identifying the potential for future change, and merging organizations.

The 7S Model was developed with private sector, for-profit organizations in mind. However, we believe that the components of the model have wide-ranging applicability, including to diversion, as follows.

Strategy

An effective strategy is one that is widely understood and is supportive of the organization's mission and vision, which, in turn, is a reflection of organizational values and culture. Law enforcement is a value-driven sector obviously not motivated by profit or market share. It serves to protect the public, and we frequently are reassured when police officers act in accordance with values they share with the communities they serve. Newspaper accounts of acts of heroism and kindness reinforce our trust in law enforcement. Further, we are saddened to see line-of-duty loss of life, a manifestation of an ultimate sacrifice. On the other hand, wrongful deaths at the hands of the police officer raise consternation and concern. Regardless, the pledge to protect persists, and responsible law enforcement agencies seek to establish and maintain community trust.

Diversion is also a value, driven by the moral imperative to steer individuals in crisis toward treatment over incarceration.

Structure

The organization chart is a visual representation of an organization's structure. The chart defines the chain of command and accountabilities in terms of who reports to whom and who is responsible for what. The chart may show geographical accountabilities where, for example, Platoon A is responsible for the northern portion of the community and Platoon B is responsible for the southern portion of the community. The chart also may show specialty areas, such as homicide, burglary, traffic investigation, or other specialized units.

For law enforcement agencies in suburban and rural areas, developing a specialized behavioral health unit would be largely impractical but may work in larger departments in urban areas and where the incidence of encounters with the mentally ill may occur more frequently. In chapter 8, we talk about pairing select police officers and crisis workers in the interest of promoting diversion.

Systems

This portion of the 7S Model covers the processes and procedures that guide day-to-day activities. Often, law enforcement agencies address diversion through procedures that identify what has to be done and who to contact when encountering an individual in crisis.

As previously noted, the lack of clear and consistent definitions and cumbersome regulations regarding involuntary commitments complicate the development of procedures. The ambiguity contributes to inconsistent behaviors and the lack of alignment governing diversion activities. It's incumbent on leadership to develop effective procedures and to do so in concert with members of their organization. Involving widespread participation in the development of procedures can be cumbersome. Leaders must strike a balance between the practical (developing effective procedures with frontline involvement) and the ideal (involving everyone).

This portion of the model is closely linked to the next item, skills.

Skills

Much has been done to improve the skills of law enforcement encountering an individual in crisis. Examples include the CIT model, or the Memphis model as it is sometimes known; the CIS model that has proven to be very effective in southeast Pennsylvania and with organizations that are national in scope such as AMTRAK, among other training offerings (see chapter 3 for additional details). These trainings tend to be intense, and some cases cover a number of days. Mental Health First Aid (MHFA) is another very popular training method, shorter in duration, which has been adapted for educators, law enforcement, and the general public. MHFA is an effective primer, enabling people to perform in an appropriate manner before either a law enforcement officer or a skilled crisis worker arrives.

Staff

We often see pushback on diversion efforts where law enforcement leaders cite staffing shortages as a deterring factor. Leaders feel that it is an inappropriate expenditure of resources to have a law enforcement officer "babysit" someone in crisis. In their opinion, these types of situations take precious time that could be devoted to catching the "bad guys."

Staffing decisions reflect a number of influencing factors including population size, crime rates, and the financial conditions of the community and its ability to adequately support law enforcement. These factors are appropriate considerations, but leaders also must include the financial, moral, public safety, and regulatory imperatives associated with mental illness in the decision-making mix.

Style

Clearly, law enforcement includes an element of machismo. Many prefer the rough-and-tumble behavior required to take down the bad guy as opposed to a soft and fuzzy approach necessary with someone in crisis. Fortunately, this attitude is changing. The vast majority of new hires for police positions have undergraduate degrees including courses in psychology. Their education prepares them to apply the skills necessary to handle someone in crisis. Although we've seen improvement, a lingering attitude of toughness, embraced by many law-enforcement officers, is difficult to reconcile with the requirements of dealing with someone in crisis.

7S Model and the Survey

To further demonstrate the applicability of the model, we draw on the previously mentioned survey.

The following table identifies each of the 7S factors linked to the survey components. The scores were developed from a seven-point Likert scale, levels of agreement and disagreement where 1 is the most least desirable score and 7 is the most desirable score. Note that the survey is not a complete assessment of the 7S components, but it does provide some insights. When reviewing the table consider the following:

- Regarding strategy: for the purposes of this comparison, the strategy is diversion, and the remaining elements help shape its effectiveness.

- Regarding staffing: the 7S Model lists recruiting, training, motivation, and reward. For the purposes of this review, trauma is included as a factor that has clear implications for motivation.

7s Factor	Survey Component (refers to survey statement)	Scores
Shared values	**Internal Alignment Indicators:**	
	(14) Awareness of policies	5.23
	(15) Agreement with policies	5.20
	(16) Policies influence behaviors	4.73
	External Alignment Indicators:	
	(7) Partnership with mental health providers	4.98
	(8) Confidence in mental health system	4.31
	(7) Satisfaction of timeliness by mental health system	4.97

The responses provide insights for both internal and external alignment within the context of shared values. The #14, awareness, score is the highest at 5.23 and the #15, agreement, score at 5.20 is lowest. Note that the #16, policies influence behaviors score, at 4.73, is the lowest of the internal alignment indicators.

It's important that police officers be aware and agree with policies. But the critical question is: Are policies influencing behaviors?

The influence on behavior score may be influenced by the style score, specifically the score addressing comfort disagreeing with the supervisor. In other words, if the supervisor is to be effective in implementing policies and the associated influence on behavior, the supervisor must listen to his or her subordinates, answer questions, and keep an open mind to disagreements.

7s Factor	Survey Component	Scores
Strategy	(14) Awareness of policies	5.23
	(15) Agreement with policies	5.20
	(16) Policies influence behaviors	4.73
	(17) Consistency of philosophy	4.97

Note that some survey questions are applicable to one or more 7s Factors. This factor introduces a new survey component for consideration, namely, #17, consistency of philosophy. There is a difference between strategy, used in the 7sFactor model, and philosophy used in the survey. What we can extrapolate from the survey results is that consistency, in this example, is marginal at best. We opine that philosophy is universal in nature and prevails throughout the organization, influencing behaviors. Further, we believe that strategy is more specific, guiding behaviors and task performance. Therefore, reflections on philosophy should have a corresponding influence on strategy.

We offer these comments based on observation, as opposed to a rigorous approach of empirical evidence, therefore requiring additional research. The ensuing discussion may shed additional light on the issue or suggest the need for further research. At a minimum, the data should spark a greater appreciation of the interaction between philosophy and strategy, and methods to improve both.

7s Factor	Survey Component	Scores
Structure	(9) Supervisor has information	5.46
	(10) Supervisor shares information	5.14
	(11) Information secured from peers	5.15

Normally, the organizational chart provides a graphic representation of the hierarchy defining who reports to whom and, therefore, the structure of the organization. The survey adds an additional dimension to understanding alignment by extending the discussion of structure to communication flow that may be vertical from supervisor, statement #10, to subordinate or horizontal, statement #11, from peer to peer.

In a paramilitary organization, such as law enforcement, we traditionally expect a command-and-control structure and vertical flow of information. However, we recognize strong peer-to-peer influences in law enforcement where officers may ride with other officers on a regular basis. We also see extensive off-hour socializing involving families. Here, significant others commiserate about the impact on family and relationships from rotating shifts or the safety concerns they have for their law enforcement love ones.

Finally, consider a cop's response to the call "officer needs assistance." Nothing will stand in their way to respond.

7s Factor	Survey Component	Scores
Systems	(3) Differentiate mental versus nonmental episode	5.26
	(4) Adjust response appropriately, mental health	5.61
	versus nonmental health	5.36
	(5) Influence appropriate intervention	

Systems provide step-by-step instructions for task completion. Police officers follow individual tasks within the system to effect an arrest that may start with an observation and lead to taking a suspect into custody. At each step along the way, the officer must be aware of the law, interrogation techniques, takedown methods, among others, all leading to a potential arrest. Likewise, tasks within the system to deal with the mentally ill start with #3, differentiating, continue with #4, adjusting, and culminate with #5, influencing the appropriate intervention.

On the surface, the results appear to be positive. However, on further analysis, we identify the obvious: the greater the experience, the better the result for differentiating, adjusting, and influencing.

Accelerating the capabilities for a new officer in these three areas is problematic given that, in the early stages of a police officer's career, he is faced with a plethora of training requirements that deal with knowledge of the law, local regulations, and methods of how to deal safely with the public while protecting themselves. Unfortunately, we know that the failure to exercise these three system components effectively can have highly negative outcomes. It falls to the leaders in both law enforcement and their strategic partners to balance a multitude of competing demands.

7s Factor	Survey Component	Scores
Skills	(1) Adequacy of training	5.11
	(2) Comfort with crisis situation	5.56
	(3) Differentiate mental versus nonmental episode	5.26
	(4) Adjust response	5.61
	(5) Influence appropriate intervention	5.36
	(6) Know whom to contact	5.19

Some of the statements in this factor are repetitive, showing that the relationship between survey results and 7s factors is not one to one.

For this factor, we introduce two new statements. The first, #1, adequacy of training, although satisfactory, falls below other measures that are skill dependent, namely, statements #2 through #5. We deem this a positive result, showing the receptivity of the audience to additional training.

It's also reassuring to know that #6, the identification of the contact, is also positive. Unfortunately, the "confidence" score, #8, is poor at 4.31.

7s Factor	Survey Component	Scores
Staff	(20) Trauma profile	4.19
	(21) Management support with trauma	5.03
	(22) Employee attitudes toward trauma	4.73

We linked a specific aspect to the staff factor, namely, trauma due to the prevalence of trauma among law enforcement agencies. The treatment of trauma is presented in detail in addendum A. The data, consistent with a general understanding of trauma, suggest a less than desirable trauma profile, #20.

The survey then delves into various aspects of trauma, including the level of management support, statement #21, which shows positive results.

Unfortunately, employee attitudes toward trauma, #22, is problematic. Practitioners dealing with mental illness, intense stress, and trauma strongly advise that those who feel intense stress or who have been traumatized seek help. This flies in the face of the machismo attitude of police officers: "I can handle it myself."

7s Factor	Survey Component	Scores
Style	(12) Consistency of leadership team	5.09
	(13) Comfortable disagreement supervisor	4.25
	(18) Management support of decision	5.15

Style is similar to culture. This section addresses survey components #12, consistency, #13, two-way communication, and #18, management support.

The score for #12, consistency, is generally positive. In other words, respondents report that leadership does *not* follow a practice of "do as I say, not as I do." Inconsistency on the part of the leadership team leads to a great deal of skepticism, fracturing internal alignment.

The essence of #13 is "two-way communication," the lowest scoring statement among the style factors. The reasons vary but fall mostly into the category of not enough time, arrogance ("I know better than to listen to someone else"), and skill (where individuals have not been trained properly).

When considering the 7S Model, critically examine each element and determine whether it promotes or detracts from the strategy. In other words, what is the level of alignment? For most departments, the scarcity of resources may be a deterrent to conducting a vigorous analysis. However, we see value in examining each of the seven components and rating your organization's performance.

People-Centered Organizational (PCO) Theory

Dr. Miles Overholt is a practicing psychotherapist, widely recognized for his treatment of individuals and families whose lives are adversely impacted by an array of psychotic influences. He is also a practicing management consultant and president of Strategia Analytics (SA) whose work, in part, is reflected in his book *Building Flexible Organizations: A People-Centered Approach.*[9] The theory identified in this book is recognized as being ahead of its time and describes how employees and organizations fit together to create high performance. Overholt's use of the word fit is consistent with the term alignment and how leaders in law enforcement can improve diversion. In addition, he is the team leader and codeveloper of Measuring the Alignment of People and Processes© (MAPP), which continues his research on organizational alignment and identifies an organization's DNA.

At the core of his work is people-centered organizational theory (PCO Theory), which, in part, recognizes that people behave in both predictable and unpredictable ways and offers a framework to facilitate change. Change is at the core of Overholt's work, so we include PCO Theory, recognizing that a successful diversion effort requires organizational change.

Overholt recognized that in the 1980s, executives, consultants, academics, and organizational researchers began to realize that existing organization and management theories inadequately explained how to channel human behavior in the face of change.

An explosion of theories followed—built on proven, past theory, attempting to explain and predict how organizations react to sustained and intense change. Some theories explain an organization's ability to change by its leadership, those who by sheer power of persuasion might pursue a strategy of officer safety or community policing. The theory also helps explain a reluctant response to municipal or legal commands. Unpopular changes often fail to embrace the true values of the organization, are not sustainable, and are seen as disingenuous by members in the organization, thus exhibiting Kofman and Senge's characterization as fragmented.

For law enforcement, the winds of change are powerful, creating a "duality of police work on several dimensions," according to the Pew Research

Center.[10] Consider some of the results from their research, not as a nice or an interesting piece of information, but as a backdrop for making change in the face of conflicting pressures within their organizations.

Table 4.4.

Statement	Percent Agree
Work as a law enforcement officer nearly always or often makes them feel proud.	58
Work often makes them feel frustrated.	51

Frustration for those who feel proud of their work may cause significant internal strife leading to stress. The subject of stress and trauma is covered in chapter 6. The forces of frustration may also detract from internal alignment. Frustration is a natural segue to questioning leadership effectiveness, and by extension, the goals and objectives of the organization.

Table 4.5.

Statement	Percent Agree
They have been thanked by someone for their police service in the past month.	79
They have been verbally abused by a member of their community in the past month.	67

Fortunately, the Pew study shows that a high percentage of participants were thanked for their service. Unfortunately, however, two-thirds of the respondents have been abused verbally by some member of their community in just the past month. The polarization of the community is another source of stress. Further, it significantly tests the resolve of law enforcement to pursue its mission and vision in the face of a community with highly varied opinions.

Overholt blends theories into a systems perspective to explain and predict how an organization responds to change in all situations. In the late 1980s, he developed the people-centered organization theory.

PCO Theory is based on a simple premise: Organizations are living, dynamic entities, composed of people. People are complex creatures who respond and adapt to external and internal environmental pressures in both predictable and unpredictable ways. Organizations are full of these environmental pressures—new regulation, new oversight, and leadership reflecting a political climate in flux, diversity, community expectations, and changing strategies regarding those with mental illness. The best way to lead people in a common direction is to have as many organizational pressures possible guide members in the same direction, reducing unpredictable responses and adaptations. To accomplish this, leaders need to create an organizational design, along with procedures consistent with the organization's strategy. This consistency or alignment guides members to achieve the organization's goals.

Like looking through a diamond to see the many facets of light, using PCO Theory allows the viewer to understand, explain, and predict organizational change from multiple perspectives. Whatever the situation dictates, PCO Theory facilitates an in-depth view of the organization to predict how an organization, its departments, and its people will change. It enables the leader to determine the most opportune point to introduce change in an organization to produce a specific outcome.

Overholt and his colleagues used the theory as a thinking tool to develop strategy, create organizational design, assess organizational strengths, and develop operating strategies and tactics. Leaders find the theory an excellent tool to structure and guide their strategic thinking. Leaders and followers have found it to be a common, nonjudgmental language to discuss how to make radical organization change.

Two factors serve as a prerequisite for change: alignment and congruency. Note that Overholt's definition of alignment differs from the definition in this book. He states that alignment occurs when an organization meets the requirements of outside influences such as citizens, politicians, regulators, and societal demands and needs. In the case of the mentally ill, the motivation for alignment may be:

- fear—resulting from regulatory pressure;
- economic—recognizing the cost of litigation or recidivism;
- image—recognizing the adverse publicity that results from an incident with negative outcomes; or
- compassion—a legitimate concern for those in crisis.

In reality, organizations respond to a combination of these factors, some more important than others.

Overholt describes congruency, which we refer to as alignment, as "all their (the organization) components aligned with each other. The components fit together, reinforcing and supporting each other. Congruency (alignment) is a dynamic process, a shifting interchange among organizational components as each respond to changes in the whole and to changes within itself."[11]

Consider some of the following changes requiring the organization to adapt to maintain congruency/alignment:

- A new process, introduced by the district attorney, requires additional areas of investigation in domestic abuse cases before the officer can initiate an arrest. The detectives complain that this adds extra and unnecessary paperwork, but leadership doesn't buy the complaints, opting instead to be compliant with the DA's requirements.

- In the interest of improving community relations, all members of the department are required to meet residents in local coffee shops. Most feel that chitchatting or listening to complaints is not a productive use of time.
- In response to community activists and an unfortunate incident involved the shooting of a deranged individual, members of the department are required to attend some form of training. They respond but grudgingly, feeling that all are being punished because of the misdeeds of a few.

These types of situations test leadership effectiveness. They require leadership to balance the legitimate complaints and reluctance of their members with the need for compliance. Further, the leader must comply without sacrificing personal values. Where such mandates violate personal values, the values of their members, or those embodied in the department's mission/vision, the leader must exhibit the courage to stand up for what is right.

According to Overholt, seven drivers of behavior influence the organization's ability to achieve and maintain organizational alignment, factors that determine leadership's ability to navigate the organization through change. This navigation requires a level of balance between external and internal values.

Table 4.6 identifies, describes, and positions the drivers in a law-enforcement context. We pose the questions to help shape our research and to measure organizations.

Overholt recognized that leaders wanted to use a systems-based analysis to match systems-based thinking. He also wanted to gather baseline data to measure and track how their organizations changed over time as they made specific interventions—changing department heads, improving training and readiness, or implementing new technology to fight crime. Consequently, using PCO Theory, Overholt and his team began to develop an instrument powerful enough to capture the dynamics of an organization from multiple points of view and from multiple levels: employees, teams, functions, and organization.

Over five years, Overholt developed, revised, and modified the instrument to create the Organizational Flexibility Profile® (OFP). Clients such as Atlantic Electric, Graphic Controls, GTE, Johnson & Johnson, Sandoz, and the Wilmington Police Department found it to be an excellent measurement tool. Statisticians, psychologists, systems modelers and researchers, most at the PhD level, were added to Overholt's team to ensure the Organizational Flexibility Profile's validity and reliability.

RMCG consultants and researchers, encouraged by the strong validity testing results, began to reach out to other disciplines. Along with Dr. Rick Jones, author of *Risk-Based Management: A Reliability-Centered Approach*,

Table 4.6.

Driver	Description (per Overholt)	Key Questions
Leadership	Locus of power, decision maker	What are the decision-making skills? What is the nature and frequency of contact?
Philosophy	Publicly stated and articulated values and beliefs	Are members aware of a diversion philosophy? Is this philosophy consistent with strategy?
Formal Organization	Set of hierarchical structures (chain of command), reporting relationships; reward and control systems	Is the organization chart consistent with reality? Who makes or influences decisions?
Informal Organization	Network of friendships and acquaintances that links people together	How strong are the peer-to-peer relationships? Is the informal organization an asset or detriment to strategy implementation?
Work Environment (Culture)	Normative set of beliefs of how the organization operates	What are the feelings of the members about their agency? Is trauma a detriment to individual performance?
Work Processes	Work steps that determine daily operations and links that provide information for decision making	How flexible are the processes that drive the organization? Is there a mechanism to secure patrol officer input?

A prime example of poor work processes can be found in chapter 1, in the confusion about who should follow through with the involuntary commitment. We learned that the confusion contributed to the murder of an innocent individual.

Behavior	Set of interactions between individuals and groups within the organization	Do behaviors support such critical management systems as decision making and conflict resolution?

the research team linked the OFP to the taxonomy of the American Institute of Chemical Engineers to create the Organizational Risk Profile (ORP). The ORP provides data revealing root causes of failure and accidents. In addition, it identifies the degree of risk inherent in an organization and the actions needed to correct the exposures. The components of the taxonomy include those listed in table 4.7.

Table 4.7.

Root Causes	Management Failures
1. Lack of strategic communication system	1. No effective two-way communication system
	2. Confused reporting lines
	3. Poor information exchange
	4. Insufficient employee involvement
2. Lack of technical understanding	1. Expert knowledge not present
	2. Poor organization and planning
	3. Management failed to resolve technical problems
	4. Inappropriate written procedures
3. Management structure	1. Inadequate definition of roles and responsibilities
	2. Inadequate safety organization
	3. Complicated decision-making process

The theory and instrument provided the foundation for a root cause analysis process, a systematic way to identify the underlying contributors to negative outcomes.

Using the root cause analysis process in law enforcement has significant potential. A number of unfortunate incidents lend themselves to this analysis process, such as wrongful deaths and the treatment of the mentally ill. In order for this process to be effective, leaders in law enforcement must be sufficiently mature and self-confident and recognize that the organization itself, or its leader, may be the root cause of the problem.

Combining the theory (PCO), instrumentation (OFP, ORP), and application (root cause analysis) provided the foundation for research in both the public and private sector.

RESEARCH AND PROFILES ON ALIGNMENT

Following through with Overholt's work, Audubon Management Consultants (AMC), with an array of strategic partners, completed a series of assessments, both funded and unfunded, revealing critical insights about organizational behavior and alignment. There were 829 participants from thirty-six police departments. A successful effort to divert those in crisis is contingent, in large part, on the behaviors of the first responder, in this case, the police.

Specifically, the research sought to measure alignment through awareness, understanding, and agreement with the strategies of the organization. Further, the research sought to measure the influence on strategy.

Table 4.8 shows results by statement. Scores were based on a seven-point Likert scale, where the higher the score, the better the results.

Table 4.8.

Statement	Average
12. The behavior of the leadership team is consistent with my department's philosophy as I understand it.	5.07
14. I'm *aware* of our department's mental health policies.	5.23
15. I *agree* with our department's mental health policies.	5.20
16. Mental health policies in our department *influence my behavior.*	4.73
17. The philosophy reflected in mental health emergencies is consistent with my personal philosophy.	4.97
18. I feel comfortable that my department supports my decisions regarding mental health issues.	5.15
Total	**5.06**

PROFILE BY STATEMENT

Table 4.9.

Statement	Low	High	Average	Standard Deviation
12.	3.75	6.33	5.21	0.53
14.	4.13	5.77	5.32	0.38
15.	4.33	5.88	5.28	0.33
16.	3.71	5.75	4.79	0.41
17.	4.10	5.82	5.06	0.43
18.	4.00	6.00	5.27	0.45

Overall alignment scores fall into the acceptable range except for Statement 16, which reflects policy influence on behavior. The gap between the high and low averages is material, suggesting a fairly wide response to this statement by department.

As with other research AMC conducted, the response pattern is consistent. Scores deteriorate moving from awareness to consistency, then fall off precipitously with regard to the influence on behavior.

Perhaps the most important statement is 16, which reflects policy influence on behavior. The insights from this statement can be gleaned from a variety of influences; perhaps most important is leadership.

Management researchers and practitioners concur that the key to organizational effectiveness lies with its leaders. Clearly, it's incumbent upon leadership to establish the mission and vision, and the supporting strategies, as well as to provide the necessary resources. But the key to the execution of strategy lies with those who interface directly with patrol officers, such as sergeants, supported by those of higher rank such as lieutenants and other command staff members.

This narrow focus on leadership factors is limited to two important components:

1. "supervisor has the information"
2. respondents "get the information"

The responses are included in table 4.10.

Table 4.10.

Statement	Average
9. My immediate supervisor has the information and knowledge I need to do my job.	5.46
10. I get the information I need to do my job from my supervisor.	5.14
Total	**5.30**

It is our experience that scores for Statement 9, "supervisor has the information," are consistently higher than those contained in Statement 10 where the respondents "get the information" from the supervisor (table 4.11).

Table 4.11.

Statement	Low	High	Average	Standard Deviation
9.	4.11	6.25	5.23	0.46
10.	3.00	6.00	4.98	0.70

Statement number 10 has a significant gap between low and high, and a corresponding high standard deviation.

A logical link between leadership and communication is addressed in the next two statements (tables 4.12 and 4.13).

Table 4.12.

Statement	Average
11. I get the information I need to do my job from my peers and others within the department.	5.15
13. Members feel comfortable disagreeing with supervisor in circumstances other than a crisis.	4.25
Total	**4.71**

Table 4.13.

Statement	Low	High	Average	Standard Deviation
11.	4.25	6.33	5.19	0.41
13.	3.71	5.33	4.50	0.36

The results with Statement 13 are consistent with virtually every organization we assess—namely, the inability for individuals to disagree with supervisors.

For organizations going through cultural change, such as those associated with attitudes and behaviors regarding the mentally ill, it's important that members of the organization be given the opportunity to disagree. Often, the level of disagreement is based on lack of understanding of the strategy. Therefore, leaders should look to these types of discussions as an opportunity to clarify, reinforce, and promote, rather than as a personal affront.

This ability to disagree, reflected in Statement 13, often characterized as two-way communication, was cited by the American Institute of Chemical Engineers in its research on high-profile catastrophes such as Bhopal, Chernobyl, and the Space Shuttle Challenger, among others.[12]

In the case of the Challenger disaster, an engineer voiced his concern about launching under certain atmospheric conditions. His comments were ignored, and what followed was a disaster of catastrophic proportions.

CONCLUDING COMMENTS

The effectiveness of any effort involving two or more individuals requires consistency of behaviors. For diversion, front-line employees, backed by like-minded leaders, strive to avoid incarceration for an individual in crisis without a risk to themselves or others. We refer to this level of consistency as alignment. It is simplistic in presentation, but implementation is far more challenging.

Leaders must present and demonstrate through their own actions a widely understood and accepted mission and vision. Those encountering someone in crisis do not compromise the traditional law enforcement persona but must exercise a new set of de-escalating behaviors. At no time should the officer put herself or others in unnecessary danger. Leaders must overcome the inertia of culture and promote counterintuitive behaviors.

The task is daunting, but organizational theories, PCO Theory, 7S Model, organizational practices by Navy Seals, and the concept of balance help leaders navigate through these turbulent times. The financial, regulatory, public safety, and moral imperatives demand superior performance, a level of performance shaped by organizational alignment.

Chapter Five

Alignment among Organizations

William Mossman and Frank Mielke

INTRODUCTION

In the previous chapter, you learned about alignment and how important it is within an organization to achieve a goal. You also learned reasons why alignment isn't always easy to achieve, even in a single organization with clearly defined goals, policies, and mission; it takes more than just a defined set of rules or policies. To truly achieve the goal, it requires all players to be of the same mind-set and to act in a predictable, consistent manner. If that is difficult to achieve in a single organization, imagine how much more difficult it is when multiple organizations are involved. Now imagine what happens when those various organizations have policies, procedures, and cultures that differ from one another. Imagine, too, that the challenge increases exponentially when cultures are at cross-purposes.

A succesful diversion program requires cooperation between law enforcement and a variety of external organizations. We will identify some of the organizations that are key players in diversion of the mentally ill from the criminal justice system and into treatment. We also identify some common ground opportunities and present research findings from our "external alignment survey."

LAW ENFORCEMENT PERSPECTIVES

If the criminal justice system is truly about justice, then penalties should fit the crime. Locking up someone who has not committed a crime, or locking up someone who committed a crime who wouldn't have if she had received the proper mental health treatment, is an injustice. It perpetuates the individual's suffering, it diverts resources from jails and prisons, and it stagnates society's efforts humanely to address the long-standing issues of those suffering from mental illness and other behavioral issues.

At their core, police officers want to do the right thing. They express frustration when situations go beyond their control and an individual in crisis suffers. They seek to comply with the safety imperative to protect people and property when such threats present themselves. They also seek to comply with the moral imperative, to do the right thing. They get frustrated when situations require them to go beyond traditional police activities. The more cynical officers respond that they do not want to "babysit" someone in crisis. They want to get back on the beat. They want to catch the bad guys.

KEY PLAYERS

Most municipalities and states in the United States have some form of mental health department. These departments administer services through various program offices. For example, in Pennsylvania, the Chester County Mental Health/Intellectual & Developmental Disabilities Department contracts with an independent company called Valley Creek Crisis Center to provide phone counseling, outreach visits, or a hospital stay. The Crisis Center fields the calls for persons in actual crisis. These calls usually come from family members, counselors/therapists, and the police. The mission of these departments is to intercept the person in crisis as quickly as possible and get him to a treatment facility.

These organizations provide myriad services for the patient and their families, but for the purposes of this chapter, we will focus on the goal of treatment over incarceration. When a call is received, it involves a person in crisis who is or may become a danger to herself or others. The crisis worker will evaluate the person's behavior and, if severe enough, may petition the court to issue an order for an involuntary commitment.

This is where law enforcement comes in. When all other alternatives for a peaceful and voluntary submission of the person in crisis have been exhausted, force may be necessary to end the dangerous or violent behavior. Police are well trained and well equipped to handle uncooperative and/or violent people. The purpose of the police is to maintain or restore order and to protect life and property. That goes for their own safety as well. An incapacitated police officer is incapable of helping or protecting anyone. To make matters worse, the police officer has a weapon that becomes undefended if he becomes incapacitated during a struggle.

A primary responsibility of a police officer is to investigate crime and arrest the offender. Liability is attached every time a police officer takes someone into custody. That person's welfare becomes the police department's responsibility. Police exercise great care when taking someone into custody because if they hurt the person unnecessarily, they most likely will be sued. Even if they use justifiable force and the person is injured, they still may be sued.

It has been well established in court that police may use whatever force is necessary and reasonable to overcome the force being applied against them. In a perfect world, when someone is acting up and a police officer gives him a lawful order to stop, he would stop and all would be fine. But we don't live in a perfect world, and some people won't stop voluntarily. When it becomes necessary for a police officer to force someone to stop, the police officer can't use the same level of force the offender is using to counter the efforts of the officer. This would lead to a stalemate, and the offender would continue with the behavior. Because this interaction can't end in a tie, the officer must escalate the level of force to overcome the offender's resistance. If the officer and the offender are evenly matched, the officer won't be able to overpower the offender. When this occurs, the officer has to escalate the force to incorporate some type of pain compliance technique to make the person submit.

This is the time that all officers dread: the camera phones come out and the officer's actions are live-streamed on social media. Force never looks good, even when it is applied with restraint. The offender will fight until it hurts too much to continue fighting. Depending upon the pain threshold of the person resisting (or his level of intoxication), this could lead to physical injury that might require medical attention. The citizenry viewing the encounter on social media might side with the officer once they see how out-of-control the offender was, but few will stand by the officer when the person injured was mentally ill. A violent criminal might have "had it coming" once he decided to square off with the police. But the police should have "figured out a better way" once they realized that the person they were dealing with was mentally ill.

The National Alliance on Mental Illness (NAMI) was formed as a nationwide grassroots advocacy group that represents people in the United States who are affected by mental illness. NAMI acts to shape public policy through advocacy efforts and education for those suffering the effects of mental illness. NAMI is one of many groups who advocate for the mentally ill as well as their families and therefore serves as an interested party that influences external alignment.

So much focus is on the well-being and behavior of the person in crisis that family members often are overlooked. Family members serve as additional interested parties in the external alignment landscape. All too often, family members are not aware of services available to assist them in helping their loved one through their moments of crisis and what treatment opportunities are available. Family members also are concerned about the quality of life their loved ones might expect upon returning from some form of involuntary confinement. A treatment facility is a much more appealing option than incarceration in a prison.

Mentally ill people who are incarcerated are disproportionately victimized while in prison. Although they receive some form of treatment while incarcerated, mentally ill inmates are more likely to reoffend and find themselves back in prison, where they become targets once again. Concerned family members want their loved ones in a treatment facility, but a lack of insurance, or a lack of cooperation from a family member, or an overzealous police officer, or an uninformed judge could derail the family's effort for treatment over incarceration.

The interest of the community is well served when police officers are able to inform individuals of available services. In this regard, they are not acting as social workers, just aiding individuals in crisis and their loved ones to obtain needed help.

A few minutes of reflection will identify other interested parties, such as the local emergency room, where individuals in crisis may present themselves for help. The school system is a critical component in the overall mental health landscape. Children at the early stages of a crippling mental health or disability issue may act out, requiring police intervention. Clearly, it's advisable that protocols be established to define how and when police intervention should be brought to the school. Factories, office buildings, and retail establishments also should be included in the network. Too often, we see the catastrophic effects of workplace violence that could have been mitigated with a closer working relationship of these entities with the police.

Unquestionably, the network of players in the mental health arena is large and diverse, requiring a comprehensive approach to identify the players and establish plans and procedures for when an intervention is required.

CULTURE: CLASHES AND OPPORTUNITY

Key players and their roles as they apply to interacting with persons suffering from mental illness have been identified. The next step is to present ways in which these disparate groups can combine their efforts toward the ultimate goal of diversion.

This chapter discusses the external alignment of several different groups that share a common goal in the interest of those in crisis. Among them are mobile crisis units that respond to calls for help from family members, friends, or even the individual in crisis. Responding police officers seek to ensure that those in need receive appropriate treatment while keeping the peace and protecting life and property. Advocacy groups are concerned about the services provided to the family members as well as those suffering from mental illness. Each group has a specific mission that doesn't always mesh well with others because of differing policies and procedures.

It falls to leaders to link these groups in a cohesive manner. Leaders, regardless of the organization they represent, must be willing to work collaboratively. Egos must be set aside and common ground must be established. They need not see eye-to-eye on every topic, but they must be willing to communicate and collaborate. No one entity should be singled out as more important than another. All must view their individual contribution as one essential piece of a puzzle and find out how they best fit to maximize their contribution to the cause.

Mental health departments and advocacy groups are very helpful in organizing, educating, sponsoring, and promoting programs designed to divert persons with mental illness from the criminal justice system and into treatment. But the police departments have the most influence in this area because they are part of the criminal justice system.

For the purposes of this chapter, remember that when we are discussing persons with a mental illness, we specifically are addressing those who commit a crime that they might not have committed if they had been treated properly for their mental illness. The goal is to divert those people out of the criminal justice system and into treatment.

The typical first point of contact for someone with a mental illness who commits a crime is with a police officer. When a police officer is called to the scene of a criminal act and he encounters someone with a mental illness, he has a decision to make. Does this person need to go to jail? Or does this person need treatment for mental illness? Many factors go into this decision, but here's the point: this is the first opportunity for diversion.

If the police officer's mind-set is not aligned with those from the advocacy groups and the mental health specialists, her first reaction might be to charge the offender with the crime he committed and send him off to jail. After all, if a mental health issue is affecting the offender, he'll get help in prison. That may be the easy or expedient way to dispose of the service call, but it might not be the best way—especially if our true goal is justice. Remember, the penalty should fit the crime. Even though a jail sentence may fit the crime committed, is justice being served by locking up a person who may not even remember committing the crime, or who would not reoffend if his illness is treated appropriately?

Police agencies must commit to spending the extra time required to divert someone with a mental illness from the criminal justice system and into treatment. It must start with the police, because they are the most likely entity to make first contact with the individual who committed the offense. The police officer must try to work with the victim to gain cooperation. It is more difficult to divert someone out of the criminal justice system if the victim insists that the offender go to jail. Remember, the police officer works for the victim, not the offender. Police agencies risk losing credibility with the public if they appear to care more about offenders than they do about victims. However, all law enforcement entities should be guided by the concept of "doing the right thing." Advocating for victims is the right thing. Locking up criminals is the right thing. The line between black and white becomes pretty gray when we begin to talk about locking up people who really need treatment.

Let's get back to the victim. Let's say that the fictional "Johnny" has stopped taking his medication because he feels better and doesn't believe that he needs it. Johnny's behavior becomes more and more erratic. His family and friends notice the signs and question Johnny. Johnny tells them that he stopped taking his medication because the government is trying to poison him. Johnny's family recognizes that he is becoming delusional, and they know that when this happens, it isn't long before Johnny starts acting out violently.

One morning the family is awakened by the sounds of Johnny breaking things around the house. When his father intervenes and tries to stop Johnny physically, the father is punched and falls to the ground, injuring his arm. The family calls the police. When they arrive, they take Johnny into custody for assaulting his father and for criminal mischief for breaking items around the house.

In a case like that one, Johnny's family loves him, and they don't want to see him go to jail. Johnny was doing fine while he was taking his medication and being supervised by his family. But they are afraid that Johnny will be neglected and victimized if he goes to prison. What Johnny really needs is to go to a facility to get him back on track with his medications and counseling. However, Johnny did commit a crime and could be called to account for that.

Mental health specialists and advocacy groups would petition for Johnny to go to treatment instead of incarceration. The police officer could derail the wishes of these groups and the family if she wasn't in alignment with the goal of diversion. If the police officer is thinking in the same way as the family, she will petition the court to divert Johnny out of the justice system and into a treatment facility. If the judge is in alignment as well, he will make the decision to order Johnny into treatment.

It took a long time for the criminal justice system to come around to that way of thinking. But now "mental health courts" exist to carefully review the facts of certain cases and the offenders who commit those crimes. If criteria are met, the offender will get the treatment he needs and be spared incarceration.

Police departments are recognizing that they spend a lot of time repeatedly returning to the same houses, dealing with family disturbances involving a member with a mental illness. Sometimes these disturbances end in a violent encounter that lands the offender in jail for a period of time. When the offender gets out and returns to the family home, the cycle begins again. The old way of doing things doesn't seem to be working. When police departments take time to analyze the root cause of the problem, they discover that the family member with the mental illness is not getting the services or treatments he needs to address the behavior that keeps landing him in jail and using so much of the police department's time.

Prisons were among the first to recognize that they had become the dumping grounds for mentally ill people who, left to their own devices, could not survive in our society. Prisons became the de facto mental health facility for those without insurance who couldn't afford medication. Without medication, a person can't control the behavior brought on by mental illness. The mission of prisons, first and foremost, is to house those convicted of committing crimes who are paying for their crimes with their time. While people are in prison, they are wards of the state, and the state is responsible for their health and well-being. Gone are the days when one could simply "lock up all the crazies in the looney bin," where they were watched but basically left to themselves or warehoused until their release date or their death.

Prisons are now responsible to medicate, counsel, and protect inmates with mental illness from the general population who will take advantage of or victimize those who aren't able to defend themselves physically or who don't have the cognitive abilities to spot when they are being taken advantage of. Prisons recognize that many of their inmates are being dealt a disservice by being placed in a prison setting instead of a proper treatment facility.

Each of the entities mentioned above is a piece of a puzzle. Each piece has a unique specialization. Each has its own policies and procedures and missions. Each could manage to do its job independent of the others. And they have done so for a very long time. However, in order to accomplish a shared goal, they must be aligned externally. As mentioned earlier, that can only come from the direction of the leaders of the various organizations.

The previous chapter taught us about internal alignment. This chapter explains external alignment and why that is more difficult to achieve. As discussed in chapter 4, internal alignment is what single entities try to achieve. It requires a leader with vision who is able to persuade those under his command or those he supervises to share in that vision.

It always is better to gain voluntary compliance by educating everyone in the organization on the importance of a particular goal. Success rates are higher when everyone is on the same page and everyone approaches the goal with the same level of enthusiasm. Sometimes not everyone "buys into" the idea or goal. When this occurs, it is still possible to achieve a level of alignment. It just has to be mandated or required through policy or regulation.

One may understand the goal but not necessarily agree with it. In this case, the skeptic will have to be brought "in line" through regulation. If an action becomes mandatory, then the person will comply or no longer be part of the organization. So, it is possible to create a level of alignment (internally) with the right leader and the right policies and objectives.

That isn't always the case when one is trying to create a level of alignment externally. The internal policies of a police department have no binding authority over an outside entity such as a county health department. An advocacy group can't force a police department to comply with the group's internal goals and objectives. For instance, advocacy groups might petition police departments to transport persons with mental illness or behavioral issues in the front seat of a cruiser, with their hands restrained or cuffed in front of their bodies to reduce stigma and maintain the person's dignity.

Police departments have strict guidelines in regard to transporting persons in their vehicles. Even a cooperative detainee will be required to sit in the backseat and will most likely have her hands cuffed behind her back. This is a safety measure both for the officer and the detainee. Sometimes these are commonsense measures, sometimes policies mandated by the department's insurance carrier. This is why communication and being open to discussion and debate are qualities that leaders need if they will ever find middle ground and work toward alignment.

The following is an experience that I (Mossman) had during a training symposium I was invited to attend. The topic of the exercise was how best to interact with someone in crisis. It was held in a large room with twenty-five or thirty people sitting in chairs placed in a large circle. Nothing was in the middle of the room, so everyone basically was facing each other, and a free-flowing discussion was taking place.

Most of the participants worked in the mental health field or worked for some type of mental health support group. I was the only police officer in the room. During the discussion, observers made several references to how some police officers handled some "person-in-crisis" calls. The observers were very critical of how the police responded and how they handled the situation. They questioned the application of force and criticized the number of police responders as "overkill."

The person telling the story was a family advocate who was called to a house to help calm a fifteen-year-old boy with a mental illness. The boy's behavior had become more and more erratic, and the parents were losing the ability to keep him calm. They had spoken over the phone to the boy's case worker and to the advocate. They also called the Crisis Center to begin the involuntary commitment process because it was apparent that the boy was going to become dangerous.

While they were waiting for the process to run its course, the boy erupted and began to get violent and destructive. Having lost all control of the situation, the parents called the police. They explained the situation and pleaded with them to come quickly before something really bad happened. When the police arrived, they entered the house and immediately engaged the boy in conversation in an attempt to see what had upset him so much and what they could do to calm him down. They explained who they were and why they were there. They tried to talk with the boy to calm him down, but their presence only seemed to increase his agitation.

At one point, about five officers were in the house. As the boy's agitation increased, he lashed out, and the five officers immediately pounced on him. The advocate detailed how the boy screamed and struggled while the five officers were all over him. This had a very traumatic effect on the boy's parents, who began screaming at the officers to get off their son and to stop hurting him.

One can imagine how chaotic the scene must have been and how frightened the boy and his parents were. Why does it take five police officers to control one fifteen-year-old boy? Why did they have to throw him to the ground and pounce on him? Why didn't they stop when the boy cried out in pain and panic? Why didn't they listen to the parents when they ordered the cops to get off their son? The consensus of the room was that the police were totally out of control, that their use of force on a boy in crisis was excessive and probably led to further trauma.

It was apparent to me that from their point of view and with those limited details, they believed that the police acted in an irresponsible manner at best, and in a brutal manner at worst. They didn't understand police tactics. I could have sat there quietly and let the discussion continue, which ultimately would have perpetuated their uninformed view. Or I could have taken offense at their critical and uninformed comments and snapped back that the police acted in accordance with their training and their policies and that they should not make critical remarks without knowing all of the facts. Instead, I treated that moment as an opportunity to educate some uninformed but very well-meaning people.

I stood up from my chair and walked to the center of the big circle. I announced that I would try to explain why the officers acted as they did and then asked for someone to enter the circle with me and force my hands behind my back. I didn't get any takers the first time, so I asked again. Again, no takers. I then invited multiple people to join. I told them that I would resist as hard as I could, but that I wouldn't hurt anyone. All they had to do was get my hands behind my back, and I would consider myself "in control" and stop resisting immediately. The only restriction I placed on them was that they couldn't hurt me.

I stood there alone in the center for a minute or so looking at each person in the circle. Because no one took me up on my offer, I asked the group why. One person said that I was too big to take on one-on-one. I replied that I had invited multiple people to come up at the same time. Someone else said that I was trained and might hurt them if they tried. I replied that I told them that all I would do was resist forcefully, but I wouldn't hurt anyone. The unpredictability of the challenge's outcome unnerved the group, and they basically just sat there looking at each other and at me.

Now that I had their attention, I asked the group if anyone knew why the boy's parents had called the police instead of simply calming their son. After all, they knew him and his triggers better than anyone. The case worker was very acquainted with the son, as was the family advocate. Why did all of these people, who knew the son extremely well, call the police, who had never met the boy? The answer was obvious. Because he was out of control. He was too strong for them to restrain and he could not be reasoned with—not even by the people he loved and who knew him best.

The police were called because the boy had to be "forced" back into control. There's that word again. Force. As I mentioned earlier, the application of force is never pretty. Police are trained in the application of force. Police are ready at all times to restore order. People call the police when a situation has degraded beyond their control. Another way to say it is that they call the police when their ability to persuade someone peacefully to stop doing something harmful, dangerous, or illegal proves useless. If someone could be persuaded peacefully to cease his actions, then force wouldn't be necessary and the police would not have been called.

People want to call the police when force is necessary, then dictate to the responding officers how they are to apply it. That is not how police conduct business. Police are trained to assess a situation quickly and then act. If the boy had just been ranting, or being uncooperative, the officers would have continued to try to "talk him down" to get him to the point of cooperation. But that wasn't case here. The boy would not be reasoned with, and then he lashed out in an aggressive, threatening manner. Until that moment, the police had options. When the boy's actions removed all options, the police acted with what they had left: force.

In the first place, the police were called to apply force. The question is whether they used restraint in its application. Was the force reasonable? While most people in the symposium agreed that the application of force was warranted to prevent injury and property damage as the boy's behavior escalated, they felt that five officers tackling the boy to the ground was excessive and unnecessary.

At that point, I reminded the group about when I first stood up and challenged them to force my hands behind my back but not to hurt me. I told the group that police are not trained to fight to a tie. Police must win every time. As mentioned earlier, if the officer is an equal match to the offender, then the officer won't win, and the offender will continue. That can't be allowed to happen. That is why officers carry several weapon options on their duty belts. They can choose a chemical agent, which creates a burning sensation when applied to the skin or eyes (commonly known as mace or OC spray). They have an impact weapon such a baton with which to strike a person. Many have an electrical shock device (you might have heard of the brand name Taser). And, of course, they carry a sidearm or pistol. All of these options except the pistol are designed to impart some level of pain to gain compliance.

In the scenario depicted above, it would have been very easy for an officer to beat the boy with a baton until it hurt so much that he submitted. The officer would have walked away unscathed (which is good for him), but the boy would have been injured and suffered for several days.

Or the officers could have sprayed the boy with the chemical agent. While he was distracted by choking and feeling an intense burning sensation for the next forty minutes, they could have tackled and subdued him. This wouldn't have been as good for the officers: it places them at risk while wrestling the boy. But it would have been slightly better for the boy, because he would only suffer for about forty minutes instead of several days.

Finally, the officers could have shocked the boy with fifty thousand volts of electricity delivered through two barbed probes shot into the boy's skin from the Taser. Again, this would have been good for the officers because they wouldn't have risked injury while wrestling the boy. But the pain from an electrical shock is intense and forces the recipient to fall to the ground without being able to break his fall. The body seizes up, and the person loses control of his muscles. He simply falls over from a standing position and lands on whatever is around. This isn't good if the surface is hard, or tables are around.

So, from among all of these options for forcing the boy to comply while limiting their own exposure to injury, the police chose the one option not listed. It placed them in harm's way but ensured that the boy was not injured. The police chose to overpower the boy. By bringing in four or five officers, they were able to overpower the boy without hurting him.

The officers usually are yelling at the boy to stop resisting so he doesn't get hurt. One officer grabs the right arm, one grabs the left. One officer grabs the right leg, one grabs the left. They bring him to the ground where their weight makes it more difficult for him to struggle and their overwhelming combined strength makes it easier to restrain him securely for transport to a medical or behavioral facility. It may look terrible to the parents who are witnessing this mayhem, watching their son scream and fight to escape. The point is: The boy can struggle and scream all he wants. He's not getting away, he's not hurting anyone, and he isn't being hurt.

Remember, the police are ready to go one level higher on the force continuum scale than the level of force being presented to them. The harder a person fights, the more force will be required to subdue him. This is the point where parents and loved ones start demanding that the officers let their loved one go and stop hurting him. This is when things can go bad; the people who called the police may turn against them. A family member is sure to be recording the scene, and as I mentioned earlier, the application of force is never pretty.

Imagine you are a police officer who is called to a house where someone you've never met is out of control. You step into the house and notice a shirtless man bleeding all over from self-inflicted cuts. He is throwing furniture at people but immediately freezes and stares at you when he first notices you. He doesn't respond in any way when you start to talk to him. Then, out of nowhere, he starts screaming that you'd better shoot him right now or else. Someone in the house is recording you with a cell phone while two others are yelling at you to stop the man but not hurt him. "He's usually a nice guy, but he's off his meds right now and doesn't know what he's doing" someone shouts.

After I explained that what looked like a "pile on" of excessive force was the police officers' best option to gain control of the boy without hurting him (while also placing themselves in the most vulnerable position for injury), the group began to see the incident in a different light. They needed to be educated in police tactics: to know about all of the weapons and tools at our disposal to regain order, and to know that the police officers were working in the boy's best interest. The family advocate admitted that although the scene looked horrific at the time, the boy did emerge unharmed.

These scenes are traumatic but can't always be avoided. The group needed to realize that in instances like the one described, police are reactionary. The officers described did not know what was going on inside the house prior to the call. They reacted to the call for service from the parents. When they got to the house, they asked what was going on and instructed the boy to cease his actions. They then reacted to the boy's next actions. When the boy lashed out in an aggressive manner, they reacted by taking control of him. When he escalated his force to escape, they escalated their force to maintain control. When the boy de-escalated, they de-escalated, and so on.

Police have a duty to act when criminal activity is taking place or when lives or property are threatened. Police react to what is being presented to them. Police realize that they are a "necessary evil." They can't get there fast enough when someone needs help. But nobody wants to see them in their rearview mirror. Police often are viewed as uncaring or callous when they have to use force, because they can talk about having to hurt someone like they were talking about ordering lunch. Civilized society doesn't act that way and is repulsed when overhearing conversations of the application of pain in such a cavalier manner. But that is the world police live in. The police have to be prepared to fight and win when they have no one else to turn to and when all other peaceful options have been exhausted.

That was an eye-opening experience to a group of educated, intelligent, and well-meaning people. Until that point, many of them hadn't ever put themselves in the shoes of a police officer trying to do his best with an unpredictable person who isn't processing reality like those around them. That experience sparked an interest in finding out more about why police do what they do. They recognized that sometimes application of force is the only option. And that application looks different to different people. Subsequently, they weren't so quick to judge. They approached police tactics with an open mind. This marked the beginning of an alignment between different and unrelated organizations that happened to share common goals.

RESEARCH AND EXTERNAL ALIGNMENT

Intuitively, we recognize that law enforcement *alone* cannot always effectively address an individual in crisis. Frequently, the situation requires support from a mental health specialist.

The following series of statements addresses how well law enforcement works with others who participate in an intervention with an individual in crisis. The level of cooperation at the point of contact significantly impacts the outcome—namely, does the individual go to jail or go to treatment?

The research of law enforcement agencies in Southeast Pennsylvania and southern New Jersey posed a series of statements regarding external alignment. These statements are profiled in table 5.1.

Table 5.1.

Statement	Average
6. I know whom I can contact to ensure that a detained individual will receive appropriate attention.	5.19
7. We work in partnership with mental health providers.	4.98
8. I have confidence in the mental health system as it relates to policing.	4.31
19. I'm satisfied with the timeliness of service provided by the mental health system.	4.19
Total	**4.67**

The averages represent the weighted average of each statement where results of 5.5 and above are positive and scores between 4.0 and 4.5 are marginal.

We believe that the timeliness of service average contributes to the lack of confidence in some scores. In other words, as timeliness improves, so does confidence in the mental health system.

Table 5.2 demonstrates the level of consistency or inconsistency by each participating department. The "average" score is unweighted as opposed to the average score above that is weighted. In other words, the average on this table represents the calculation for the average of each individual department not weighted by the number of participants from that department.

Standard deviations show a level of consistency for Statement 6, "knowing who to contact," but are volatile when it comes to the issue of partnership, demonstrated in Statement 7.

Table 5.2.

Statement	Low	High	Average	Standard Deviation
6.	4.11	6.25	5.23	0.46
7.	3.00	6.00	4.98	0.70
8.	3.08	5.50	4.23	0.62
19.	2.63	5.75	4.14	0.81

The data supports the anecdotal evidence of the silos that exist between the mental health system and law enforcement. The timeliness of service is a frequent complaint and is demonstrated in the data where the average for Statement 19, "addressing timeliness," is the lowest in this scale.

The differences between low and high scores are particularly pronounced and the standard deviations are somewhat higher than normal. Standard deviations, in particular, suggest a level of disparity that may be attributable to the differences that exist between the two largest participating counties in the survey.

In these counties, we know that the philosophy regarding crisis intervention and the manner in which involuntary commitments are handled is remarkably different.

CONCLUDING COMMENTS

External alignment between disparate entities requires the leadership of those entities to be open to discussion, compromise, respect, and recognition of the contribution of the outside entity toward a common goal, objective, or philosophical imperative.

Chapter Six

Building Emotional Muscle Memory

The New Frontier for Addressing Law Enforcement Trauma

Michelle Monzo and Patricia Griffin

INTRODUCTION

Sadly, we are recognizing the extent and impact of trauma. We live in a climate of political and financial instability that is a stressor in our everyday life. Add to that the exposure to and experiences of life's dramatic events.

We mourn the loss of a loved one. We agonize over failed marriages and relationships. We become depressed with failures in our careers and despair at not achieving our own goals.

Now, we realize that safety is not guaranteed in our schools, churches, temples, and mosques, at nightclubs or in shopping malls. Indeed, the gathering of a large group of individuals can be a target for both domestic and international terrorism.

These are the stressors and trauma that plague the general population. Police officers are members of that general population, experiencing the same political and financial stressors and the fear that family and friends, and in particular their children, are potential victims of horrific experiences. They carry these thoughts with them on "the beat," where they must address the victims of violence and accidents. They maintain hypervigilance in the face of potential danger. They fear that the simple issuance of a traffic citation may turn life threatening. As they perform their tasks, they wonder whether they are in the crosshairs of those who would destroy them.

Welcome to the world of law enforcement.

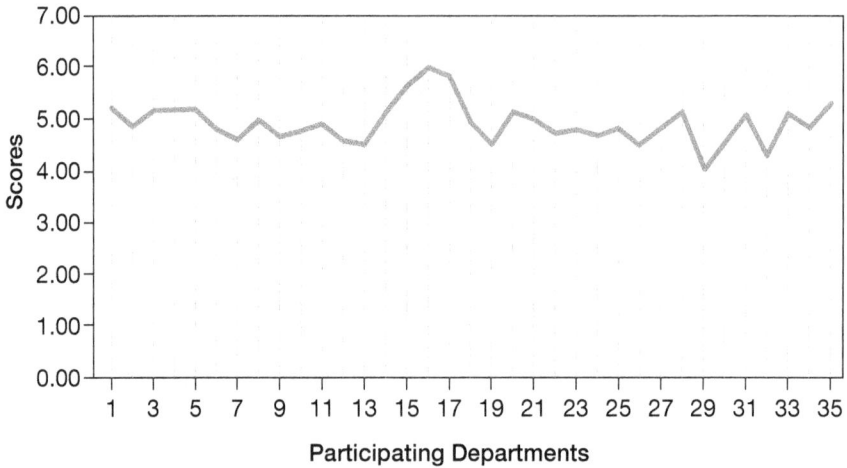

Participating Departments

Figure 6.1.

Note:
    Scores range from 1 to 7; the greater the score, the better the result.
    Excludes results for one department that had only one respondent.
    Scores for the thirty-five departments are presented in random order.

If we are going to address the subject of trauma, we must keep several items in perspective. First, police must contend with trauma and stress both on and off the job. This makes them particularly vulnerable to the consequences of trauma and stress.

Second, if we expect law enforcement to be mental health interventionists, we should require that they have the proper mind-set and the mental health soundness to address some very difficult situations.

Third, we must recognize that one of the four faces of the mental health system is to respond to police officers in need. It's not enough just to have a transfer facility for those in crisis, or an effective mobile crisis unit, or an effective mental health training curriculum. The mental health system must respond to all in need, including police officers.

Against this backdrop, we face police attitudes that run contrary to professional opinions that encourage those who face extreme stress or are exposed to trauma to seek help. The results of our survey suggest otherwise.

What follows are the responses by individual department addressing the question of how to handle trauma. Unfortunately, the results are consistently below desired levels. Handling trauma on your own is a prevailing—but not desired—strategy for law enforcement.

The President's Commission on 21st Century Policing recognized that the general health and welfare of police officers is critical for themselves, their colleagues, and the community. The Commission stated, "Officer wellness and safety supports public safety . . . An unhealthy officer cannot serve their community effectively, and can be a danger to himself, their colleagues and the community they serve."[1]

This chapter will examine behaviors that can ameliorate stress and trauma while also supporting police officers' mental, physical, and emotional well-being. They fall into three categories:

1. Mental—depending on the organization and local practice, this may be voluntary or mandatory referral.
2. Critical Incident Stress Management (CISM): Group Crisis Intervention—the small-group environment provides a space that may normalize behaviors to abnormal situations. These small-group debriefings allow each individual who experienced the event to share physical, cognitive, emotional, and/or behavioral reactions to it.
3. Peer Support

Dealing with an individual in crisis requires a sense of wellness by the interventionist. Table 6.1 contains the trauma profile as reported by participants of the 2019 survey detailed in addendum D of this book.

Note that this is not a clinical diagnosis of trauma. That type of representation goes far beyond the scope of the survey. However, it does take into account different responses from different individuals in the face of trauma. In other words, seeing a grizzly sight may be more traumatic to one individual than another. The approach the survey used takes into account individual variances and reflects their own categorization of trauma.

Table 6.1.   Reported Trauma Experiences

Trauma Experience	Number	Percent Total, All Responses
No experience	30	3.82
Few experiences, non-traumatic	88	11.21
Many experiences, mostly non-traumatic	154	19.62
Few experiences, some traumatic	179	22.80
Many experiences, many traumatic	180	22.93
At least one life-altering experience	70	8.92
Many life-altering experiences	84	10.70
Total	**785**	**100.00**

A growing body of evidence suggests that stress and trauma are contributors to officers' maladaptive behaviors, including a higher incidence of divorce, substance use disorder, suicide, and early death compared to the general U.S. population. These problems cannot be ignored. The sources of stress and trauma go beyond the workplace and include past experiences as well as dealing with everyday life. Individuals are not able to forget such influences when they arrive on the job.

To illustrate, we offer a case study from the the CIS Police School, a crisis-intervention school for law enforcement and criminal justice personnel operated by the Montgomery County Emergency Service, Inc., in Norristown, Pennsylvania. It illustrates how training officers in appropriate mental health identification and interaction has opened the door for them to reflect on their own mental well-being. We conclude the chapter by identifying other model practices.

PAINTING THE PICTURE

A rookie officer was the first to arrive on the scene at a multi-vehicle crash. The driver of a pickup truck struck a minivan, which then toppled over the median strip and was struck by an oncoming sedan. The drivers of the truck and sedan incurred minor injuries. The driver of the minivan, a woman, was critically injured. She spoke her final words, "My daughter, save my daughter. I love her," to the officer. The mother then lost consciousness and died on the way to the hospital. Her eleven-month-old infant, who was in the backseat, was pronounced dead at the scene.

The sergeant and three other officers arrived shortly thereafter. The sergeant asked, "Are you OK?" The rookie responded, "Yes, it's a bad one, but I'm OK." They processed the scene and returned to the station. The chief was concerned about his rookie because it is widely acknowledged in the law enforcement community that the death of a child can be especially traumatic to process. Moreover, this officer had a child of his own, close in age to the infant that died. The chief called the Critical Incident Stress Management (CISM)/peer support team to request that someone meet with the officer.

After speaking with the rookie officer, the CISM peer believed that he was adjusting well to the event. But, during the course of their conversation, he mentioned the three other officers who were on the call. The CISM peer decided to speak with them. Interestingly enough, those three were more affected by the event than the rookie, all for different reasons. One was having personal problems; this event was an added stress and took a toll on him. The second officer recounted that this event brought back two other child incidents he had never talked about before. The remaining officer was affected by this particular event itself.

This story is all too familiar. Many times, without supervisory leadership awareness, access to a CISM peer, a trusted employee assistance professional (EAP), or other social supports, officers in need of assistance are "hiding in plain sight." Unfortunately, many of our police officers still are functioning in a "suck-it-up" environment compounded by the stigma of weakness. This leads to the cumulative effect of trauma, where each event adds a layer.

The result of not dealing with trauma as it occurs, repeatedly stuffing it down, usually leads to depression, anxiety issues including post-traumatic stress disorder (PTSD), anger, and compulsive behaviors—that is, substance abuse, infidelity, gambling, eating addictions, internet addiction, and other behaviors that eventually get an officer into personal and/or professional trouble.

Sadly, not taking care of his or her own mental health can lead an officer to suicide. More active-duty officers die from suicide than from shootings and traffic accidents combined. According to the group Blue H.E.L.P., in the first six months of 2019 at least 104 cases of officer suicides were verified. This compares to 167 for the entire year 2018. Of these, 159 were male and the average length of service was sixteen years.[2]

MONTGOMERY COUNTY EMERGENCY SERVICES "THE CIS POLICE SCHOOL": TRAINING LAW ENFORCEMENT AND CRIMINAL JUSTICE PERSONNEL AS CRISIS INTERVENTION SPECIALISTS

Montgomery County Emergency Service, Inc. (MCES) is a nonprofit hospital founded in 1974. The U.S. Department of Justice and the Law Enforcement Assistance Administration (LEAA) nationally recognized MCES as a model program. MCES established the Crisis Intervention Specialist (CIS) Police School in 1975 to train law enforcement and criminal justice personnel in dealing with individuals in a behavioral health crisis.

The aim of the basic three-day training is to educate and train police and criminal justice professionals how to identify symptoms of mental health and mental ill-health and to respond to individuals in a behavioral health crisis.[3] Interestingly, by the midpoint of day two, officers begin to identify with how their behavior and the behavior of their peers mirrors the symptoms of depression, hypervigilance, and anxiety previously explained. Moreover, they begin to identify how these lead to unhealthy behaviors, including excessive alcoholic drinking, divorce, and suicidal ideation—in themselves and in their peers. A statement they make regularly is, "Oh, my God, you are talking about me!"

Perhaps a police officer in crisis or on the path to crisis can get help through peer support.

What we have learned is that the Critical Incident Stress Management (CISM) Police School educational environment provides a nonthreatening space to explain the symptoms of trauma and open the door for considering questions such as, "Can I tough it out?" and "Am I cut out to do this job? What is wrong with me?" In this space officers begin to develop "emotional muscle memory."

Because of what was learned during the basic course, an advanced CIS Police School training curriculum was modified to address stress management, anger management, post-traumatic stress disorder, and healthy coping mechanisms. In essence, the course seeks to assist the attendees "how to survive the job, not hate everyone, and not want to retire to Montana where they never have to deal with a human being again." The foundation for the advanced class curriculum is based on not only how to "survive their shift" but also their career.

Organizations learn that their officers are experiencing mental and behavioral health problems in several ways: incidence of police suicides; events associated with critical incident stress management; 911 dispatch liability issues; the acceptance of the police drinking culture. Almost every police department has some form of employee assistance professional (EAP) who may be called upon to assist with mental health services should they be struggling or having experienced a traumatic event or cumulative stress.

Unfortunately, officers have voiced a lack of trust in the EAP. If the EAP comes under the department (internal EAP), then officers believe that if they go to the EAP, word will get back to their supervisor (or fellow officers) that they are depressed, anxious, not sleeping, or not doing well. This threatens their machismo self-image and prompts them to believe that it may put their job at risk because they may be perceived as not being fit for duty.

In addition, officers experience the departmental acknowledgment of trauma and organizational response in a negative way. For example, if the officer is made to talk to his EAP, the majority of officers do not believe that their supervisor or the department truly cares about them. Rather, referral to the EAP is more about minimizing the department's liability. Too often police officers say that "it is about protecting their ass."

This perception has validity. For example, one officer came to a CISM peer with a release form to turn over to the department all of his behavioral health records. The way that the letter was written, the officer felt he had to submit these records or leave his job. Yet, the peer was able to explain that according to the Americans with Disabilities Act (ADA), though the department may ask for mental health records, the officer is not required to release them.

Overall, many officers do not trust their administration. An officer who admits to experiencing anxiety, stress, depression, trauma, or other medical health issues is considered damaged goods. Officers do not believe that their administration would back them up if they seek medical or behavioral health services. Sadly, officers feel stigmatized.

In contrast to the lack of trust that many EAPs experience, the Montgomery County, Pennsylvania, CISM team has gained a trusted reputation through consistent positive interactions and ongoing support of officers. The Montgomery County CISM team is made up of approximately eighty-three persons, representing first-responder peers, mental health providers, chaplains, and four therapy dogs, who volunteer their time and efforts selflessly to assist first responders in crisis. Participation in the CISM team is volunteer, which has enhanced the value, credibility, and trustworthiness of this group.

Crisis Intervention Specialist/CISM peer support members have been called upon to assist an officer who either has been identified by the department as someone in need of services or the officer has contacted directly. The conversation often follows a variation of the "what ifs, should haves, could haves." An officer expresses, "What if I did this, should have done that, could have done something else?" Often, the officer is blaming himself or others for the outcome of the event/incident. A critical part of these encounters is for the CISM volunteer to create a safe space for the officer to experience the emotions and thoughts about the incident/event.

The recovery process does not stop here. It's beneficial to help the officer recognize that he did everything he could to achieve a successful outcome, even though it didn't end that way. CISM team members attempt to help the officer come to terms with his response to the incident for his mental well-being. The conversation unfolds like this:

> We are not superheroes. You did the best you could do, with what you were given on that day. Regardless of what was done or not done, you are the one not doing well right now. You need to be responsible for your own health and stress management right now.

The CISM team member instructs the officer to pick up the phone, call, and the member will connect the officer to the needed services. The member may also refer him to a trusted psychologist or medical provider. If the officer is blaming other people or other circumstances, the member emphasizes that we only can control our own actions, not the actions of others. More education is needed for the officers, police administrators, family, and significant others to help identify possible symptoms that may occur after traumatic events/critical incident/cumulative stress.

Police administrators and leaders also should take an active role in supporting officers' well-being, even when an officer says, "I'm OK." Most officers rarely admit they are not doing well due to stigmatization, fear of job loss, being placed on restricted duty, or appearing weak in front of their peers. A policy of mandatory referral to a CISM/peer support or mental health professional can ameliorate resistance to accessing mental health services. Mandatory referral reduces the risk that the officer will just keep plugging along. However, it is critically important that the officer be able to select a provider he trusts—whether a professional mental health provider or peer support.

CRITICAL INCIDENT STRESS MANAGEMENT (CISM)

Introduced in 1999 by Everly and Mitchell, CISM is an internationally recognized best practice "designed to stabilize the symptoms of distress, reduction of symptoms of distress, and improvement in adaptive independent functioning, or facilitation of access to higher levels of support"[4] following a crisis event. At its core, a CISM team provides debriefing for those who have been involved with a critical incident or traumatic event. What happens during a CISM debriefing is that officers who are directly involved can speak about their experience. This is helpful, because officers in the group can say, "I was affected, too," "I am not alone," or "I am not the only one damaged by this experience." Other functions of the CISM team could include rest information transition services (RITS), crisis management briefing (CMB), family intervention, organizational and community intervention consultation, pastoral crisis intervention, and defusing.[5]

While acknowledging the benefit of group support, several drawbacks associated with group CISM debriefings have arisen. First and foremost, one of the challenges or problems associated with CISM is that what may be traumatic for some is not necessarily true for others. In everyday parlance, what I bring to the table is different from what you bring to the table on any given day, and these differences are multilayered.

For example, let's imagine a fatal car accident where the mother was driving and her infant child was in the backseat, in a rear-facing car seat. One officer extracts the infant from the vehicle and takes the child to safety. Another officer provides aid to the mother, who is not likely to live, and is the last person the mother speaks to. A third officer is directing traffic and has no direct contact with the occupants of the vehicle. Although we may believe that we know who will be impacted more deeply, we have no way of knowing which officer has been affected. And, usually, no officer wants to be the first to say how her personal experience is bothering her.

Another possible barrier to the group CISM model is officers' reluctance to share their feelings in a group setting. Officers have negatively perceived the CISM model as being, in essence, too folksy and soft. Officers do not like to lay out their problems in front of their peers, nor do they do not want to be the first to wave their hand to say, "I've been affected." More likely they state, "This is bullshit. I don't know why I am here." This may either encourage another to speak up similarly or silence another member of the group.

It's important to note that a generational shift appears to be underway in this area. Some observers point out that it is pretty common to hear one of the older generations of officers say, "Suck it up, cupcake," but younger officers seem to be more aware of and willing to speak about their mental health. This may be the result of shifts in police training and education, higher education degrees, life priorities, and social awareness. The generational differences represent another important area of which police leadership must be aware.

PEER SUPPORT

In all likelihood, an officer will experience a traumatic event during the course of his career.

When that happens, peer support is increasingly recognized as an important component of officer wellness initiatives.[6] First responders and police are more likely to open up on a one-on-one basis, especially if they trust that person. Research indicates that the assistance of a trusted peer helps to build officers' self-confidence and removes the stigma of asking for help.

In one-on-one peer meetings, the leader will explain that nothing is documented and the information exchanged is kept confidential. In Pennsylvania, peers are protected from liability under the Good Samaritan's Act. Peers receive specialized training, so they know the question to ask about risk: "Are you telling me that you will hurt someone else or yourself?" Further, every peer officer who meets one-on-one with another officer has a mental health consultant to run issues past who can provide additional direction, if needed. This also ensures that a backup is there—someone else who knows what has been going on with the officer who needs assistance.

If an officer is not doing well, a peer specialist will try to connect that officer with a peer, a mental health provider, or a clergy member. A member of the Montgomery County CISM team, who has been working in the field for several decades and is widely respected in the region, often is called directly by a police chief. Most times, the CISM representative agrees to meet with the officer but states that she will be bringing along a police officer (who is the peer). Throughout this process, the officer has complete control—it is up to the officer; it is his choice.

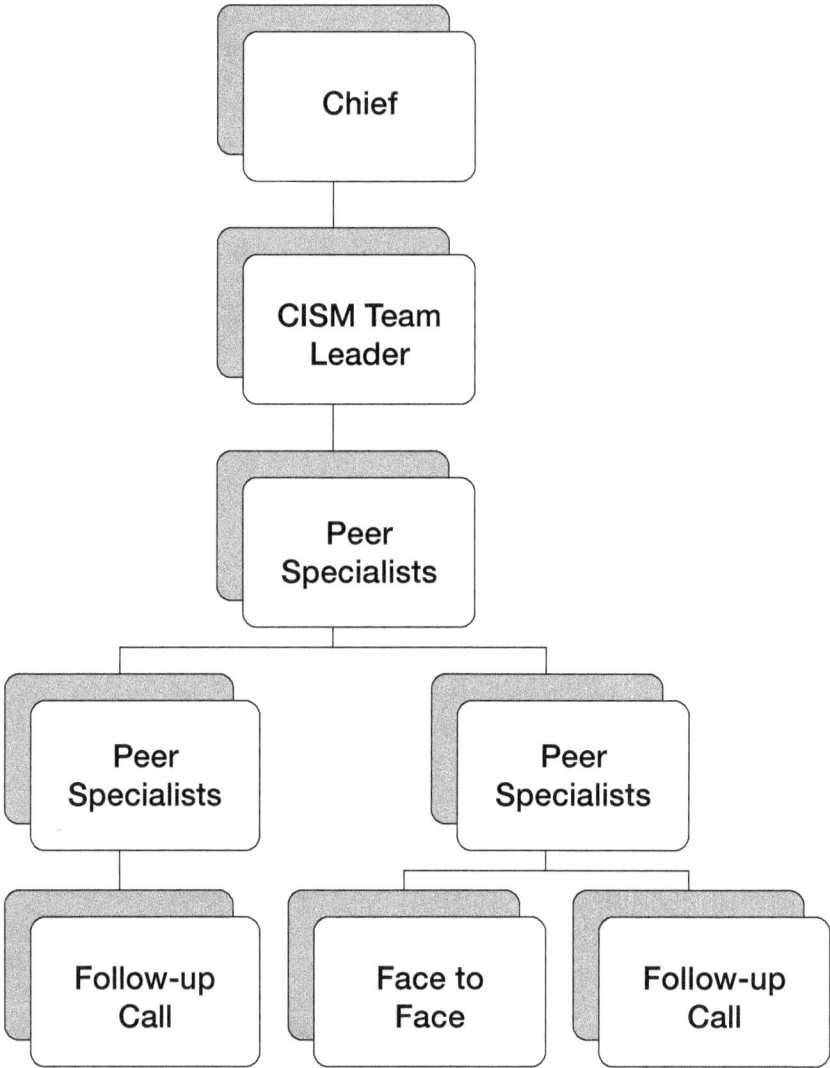

Figure 6.2. CISM Peer Referral Process

The process flows as shown in figure 6.2.

The Montgomery County CISM team has adapted the components of CISM that work through the expanded use of peer group support. The CISM team has a centralized call number. When a call comes through, the CISM team leaders, familiar with the strengths and job experience of the CISM volunteers, match on an individual basis by relatable background, taking into account the proximity of the volunteer to the officer, personality, job experiences, and the incident. For example, if an officer is involved in a shooting, that officer will be matched with an officer who has been involved in a prior shooting. Typically, departments do not debrief their own officers.

Police and first responders are more likely to seek professional help with the encouragement of a peer who has received help. When a group debrief follows a traumatic event, the group leader will have individual peers reach out to the first responders and check on them very often, setting up one-on-one interactions to offer support. This is in hopes of identifying a first responder who is not doing well but does not feel comfortable sharing that in a group. Moreover, the peer program has expanded in the Montgomery County region, now proactively reaching out to an officer rather than waiting for a supervisor or administrator's referral. However, this only happens when a member of the peer group knows the officer directly, recognizing that most officers will not talk to a peer unless that person is known and trusted.

In sum, the CISM team in Montgomery County evolved organically. Today it resembles a bit of integration of the CISM and the peer one-on-one model approach. A peer will reach out to an officer and ask, "Do you want to talk to someone?" If the officer says, "Yes," the next question is, "Who do you want to follow up with you?" A list of names is provided for other officers who have attended our training and their telephone number. We also have a list of professionals, psychiatrists, and medical providers we have identified as being culturally sensitive and trusted practitioners. The Montgomery County CISM team has discovered that after the initial debriefing, sometimes up to six months after the initial incident, it is necessary to revisit with the officer and sometimes the entire department, especially in cases of an officer-involved shooting or officer suicide.

CONSEQUENCES

The absence of a viable intervention for police officers experiencing extreme stress or trauma is tragic. Consider the case of David Colegrove, a thirty-year veteran of law enforcement who committed suicide in 2014, less than three months after retirement. This sad account is from his widow, Kim Colegrove:[7]

> David's problems can be traced back to when he was 21 and a first-year police officer. Following his involvement in a shooting, his badge and gun were taken away and was sent home for several days, not knowing what was going to happen. Finally, he got a call to return to duty the next day. There was no counseling, conversation or support.
>
> In the following years, he was subject to reoccurring stress symptoms that left him incapable of dealing with life's challenges such as change and uncertainty. Alcohol provided temporary relief.
>
> Two days after Thanksgiving, David took his life by his gun.

This doesn't have to happen. Early and effective intervention can influence outcomes. Kim Colegrove presents a series of symptoms with the admonition—get help. These symptoms include:

- chronic stress
- depression
- anxiety
- anger
- intense irritability
- aggression
- alcohol abuse/alcoholism
- drug use/addiction
- hopelessness
- isolation/withdrawal
- suicide ideation
- talk of suicide

SUMMARY OF RESPONSE STRATEGIES

In the previous section, the authors described three overarching strategies used to address mental and behavioral needs of police and first responders: Employee Assistance Professionals (EAPs), CISM, and Peer Support. Collectively, these strategies aim to meet the psychological needs of the individual officer—whether that officer has directly experienced a traumatic event, been impacted indirectly by a crisis, or is impacted by cumulative stress or trauma.

As noted, the impact of EAPs has been limited, due to lack of trust in confidentiality and credibility. Moreover, EAP referrals to psychological services have been hampered by lack of knowledge about the police culture and cultural sensitivity to this occupation. The CISM model, which offers group debriefing facilitated by a trained professional, is intended to provide a safe environment that may lead to mutual support and reduce social isolation. Yet, as noted, lack of confidentiality and the machismo culture may prevent an officer from disclosing in this group environment. The peer support model builds upon the strengths of CISM to offer social support and identification but offers the additional benefit of connecting one-on-one with an officer.

FUTURE CONSIDERATIONS: BUILDING ON EMOTIONAL MUSCLE MEMORY FOR EMOTIONAL SURVIVAL

As police and first responders increasingly have been relied upon to render support for community members with a mental or behavioral disorder, police training has widened beyond physical and tactical training to include coursework in how to interpret, understand, and respond to others' emotional states with confidence. Along the way, trainers have come to see the benefit of building an awareness of similar symptoms and behaviors associated with anxiety, stress, depression, and substance use by fellow officers. Police leaders and policing organizations have adapted preventive strategies, rather than intervention, to support officers' wellness.

For example, the Voorhees, New Jersey, police department will begin to offer annual mental health check-ups for officers. Another strategy, adopted by the Lower Providence Township Police Department in Montgomery County, Pennsylvania, requires that each officer meet with a CISM peer specialist annually. These movements align with the priorities set forth in the President's Commission on 21st Century Policing Report (2015) and seek to reduce the stigma associated with officers' health-seeking behavior.

SUMMARY

We believe that the women and men who make up our policing and first responder agencies are just like any other neighbor or community member—that is, until they took the "oath of office" and donned their uniform and badge. A symbolic, psychological, and physical transformation takes place, which makes these men and women willing to sacrifice everything for the protection and care of others. Although the job always has required officers to fulfill many roles (i.e., sometimes watchman, other times social worker, or enforcer), few argue that policing in the twenty-first century is different.

Throughout this book, the authors have described how police and law enforcement often are the first responders for aiding vulnerable populations in our community—those having a behavioral or mental disorder. Moreover, this subgroup ofttimes stresses limited policing resources and takes officers away from "real policing." Against this backdrop, we recognize that a legacy of flawed criminal justice policies, generational poverty, structural racial and ethnic inequalities, and insecurities from global threats and risks have contributed to a lack of community trust and support for police. The physical, mental, and behavioral toll of being a police officer in the twenty-first century finally is garnering attention.

In this chapter, we offer illustrations of how stress and trauma in policing contributes to officers' maladaptive behavior. The authors explain how training officers in mental health identification and how to identify and interact appropriately with those in a mental health crisis has opened the door for officers to reflect upon their own personal mental well-being, and as an avenue to build emotional muscle memory to use in their everyday encounters. The chapter concludes with a discussion of specific programs and practices.

Chapter Seven

Resiliency

Patricia Griffin and Darren Stocker

INTRODUCTION

Occupational socialization and stigma act as barriers to effective prevention and intervention programs for police and other first responders. Evidence is increasing that many police and first responders have been "hiding in plain sight." Their internal struggles and mental health are overlooked because, outwardly, they are high functioning—that is, until they are not.

The leading professional associations for police, the International Association of Chiefs of Police (IACP), along with their federal government counterparts—the Office of Community Oriented Policing Services (COPS), the Department of Homeland Security (DHS), and the Federal Emergency Management Agency (FEMA)[1]—have declared that their top priority is to break the silence born of shame and stigma associated with mental and behavioral health issues in the first-responder community. Moreover, the topic of officer wellness and safety is one of the six areas of emphasis, or "pillars," identified by the President's Task Force on 21st Century Policing (2015) for promoting effective policing.[2]

The present chapter explains the social ecological model of resilience and provides theory-informed research of wellness prevention and intervention strategies. It is a matter of importance to identify the individual choices, pathways, and/or interventions that serve as buffers against mental and behavioral illness.

We consider the following:

1. The capacity of officers to navigate their way to resources and maintain well-being;
2. The capacity of officers' physical and social environments to provide those resources; and
3. The capacity of officers, their families, and communities to negotiate in culturally meaningful ways for those resources to be shared.

RISK, STRESS, AND TRAUMA OF POLICE WORK

The President's Task Force also affirmed the long-standing belief that the same character strengths that impel officers to confront danger may be barriers to their resilience. Too frequently, the character traits that officers display in carrying out their duties—toughness, hardiness, and steadfastness—may under certain conditions prevent officers, their colleagues, and the police organization from seeking or providing needed services for mental and behavioral health.[3] Officers may be stigmatized and experience feelings of shame and weakness if they seek help.

Houser et al.[4] have reported that although the occupational fatality rate for law enforcement personnel is more than three to five times greater than the national average, the rate of suicide by law enforcement officers is even higher. Blue H.E.L.P., the not-for-profit organization run by active and retired police officers, reported 159 confirmed cases of law enforcement officer suicides in both 2017 and 2018, a 13.6 percent increase over 2016.[5] The concern has become so urgent that, since 2012, the IACP and the U.S. Department of Justice Office of Community Oriented Policing Services (COPS), in collaboration with representatives from the public health and research communities, have spoken out for the need to change the organizational culture of policing to support officers' mental health and wellness. Officers are being called upon to speak up for each other, talk to their peers, and address perceived or actual problem behaviors in their fellow officers as informal intervention efforts.

Whether responding to man-made or natural disasters, criminal or life-and-death events, or routine calls for service, first responders are regularly and repeatedly exposed to risk, trauma, and stressors beyond the range of normal human experience,[6] which may translate into maladaptive behaviors.

A review of the research reveals an abundance of literature that details disease, disorder, and dysfunction in the mental and behavioral health of first responders compared with the general population.[7] Misuse and abuse of alcohol and other drugs; overreliance on pain medication, benzodiazepines, and steroids; post-traumatic stress disorder (PTSD); and suicide are maladaptive behaviors associated with stress, workplace injuries, and trauma in public safety occupations.

Law Enforcement Work-Related Stress

Contemporary research points to the importance of understanding the impact of recurring and cumulative stress on an individual's physical and mental health; for example, owing to advances in medical technology and the field of neurobiology,[8] researchers have learned that "within the first three years of working as a first responder, the brain changes."[9]

In addition to generalized stressors related to interpersonal relationships, money, and work, researchers have identified more specific stressors related to "the job" of policing and public safety. These include work-related exposure to critical incidents and hostile communities and subcultures, as well as organizational stressors that limit officers' decision-making skills.[10] Research also points to a rigid hierarchy and bureaucracy; decreased sense of control;[11] and job-related problems such as poor equipment, unfair workload distribution, favoritism, and discrimination. The impact of these organizational stressors includes higher rates of heart disease, obesity, domestic troubles, early death, and suicide compared with the general population.[12] So harmful is the occupation of policing to officers' health and wellness that a recent text edited by John Violanti is titled *Dying for the Job*.[13]

When officers face high levels of stress and emotional strain, they must identify a way to deal with the impacts. Unfortunately, most officers turn to negative or ineffective coping mechanisms in response to stressors. Some ineffective mechanisms include alcohol consumption, repression of emotions, and violent reactions; more positive coping mechanisms may involve communication with a counselor, therapist, or loved one, or exercise to alleviate stress. Law enforcement requires assistance to identify healthy coping mechanisms and understand why the ineffective mechanisms are important to avoid. The stressors from traumatic events, along with the consequences of ineffective coping mechanisms, negatively impact law enforcement in relation to their physical and mental health, personal lives, and careers.

Officers' physical and mental health is the first area negatively impacted by work-related stress. Stress resulting from the experience of traumatic events can lead to anxiety, cardiovascular disease, depression, sleep disturbance, antisocial behaviors, and suicide ideation; and negative coping mechanisms, such as alcohol consumption or avoidance of emotion, lead to other unhealthy consequences. In extreme cases, officers may experience PTSD, and several studies report that close to 30 percent of law enforcement officers experience

PTSD symptoms or meet the criteria of a full PTSD diagnosis.[14] Unfortunately, many of the health consequences that result from stress will impact an officer for the rest of his life.

Officers' personal lives are the second area negatively impacted by work-related stress. The impacts of stress can result in changes in personality as well as strains on personal relationships. When officers avoid dealing with or discussing their emotions, everyone around them feels the effects. One study suggests that hiding their feelings from loved ones is the primary way officers handle occupational stress.[15] The lack of communication leads to isolation within relationships and other marital problems, such as separation or divorce. The added stress from dealing with marital discord only furthers the physical and mental issues previously discussed. The negative coping mechanisms of alcohol and hyperaggressiveness can tragically lead to violence against loved ones as well. This can result in further degradation of the relationship and even legal action against the law enforcement officer.

Officers' future careers and their departments are the final area negatively impacted by work-related stress. The continuous stress and subsequent health consequences can compromise the officer's ability to carry out her mission effectively. Police departments cannot responsibly employ or deploy officers who are unable to successfully protect the public, their colleagues, or themselves. Unfortunately, this could end an officer's career in law enforcement through either premature or disability retirement. Police agencies also feel the negative impacts of a force that is overly stressed and suffering from physical and mental issues, which may manifest as lack of productivity, an increase in turnover rates, excessive worker compensation costs, and health care use.

Therefore, agencies have a responsibility to provide the necessary support and treatment to their officers to ensure that they recover effectively from traumatic events. This also will help agencies understand and identify when an officer is ready and prepared to return to the field, and how that transition should progress. Programs to address mental health issues not only show a compassion for officers, but also result in a healthier, more productive workforce agency-wide.

PERSONALITY TRAITS, SOCIALIZATION, SUBCULTURAL NORMS, STIGMA, AND SHAME

Although the literature is mixed as to whether police and other first responders are predisposed to particular personality traits,[16] it is reasonable to presume that through the process of preemployment screening and testing, first responders have in common certain desired traits and abilities related to professional success.

More readily agreed upon is that police and other first responders share common values and norms imparted through occupational socialization, defined by Skolnick as the "working personality" of police. Most highly valued are the principles of integrity and honor in upholding the law, as embedded in the law enforcement Oath of Honor. The qualities of perseverance, reasoning, bravery, and toughness likewise contribute to the officer's social capital and trustworthiness among peers, as noted by Woody.[17] On the other hand, Reiner's characterization of the cop culture features a working personality that includes a sense of mistrust, cynicism, and pessimism,[18] whereas the expression of emotion or empathy is perceived as a weakness.

In a cry for help, Kristi Tausinga, a patrol officer in the Denver Department of Transportation, attempted suicide. Her blog post "I Am Tough, and I Don't Need Help" offered a personal account of how conflicted she felt about telling anyone of her opiate addiction and requesting assistance:

> I am a cop and cops "don't ask for help." We're tough, not allowed to be weak or show weakness. I don't know why I took all the pills. I guess I was hoping that my husband would find me passed out on the living room floor. I had been telling him I had an opiate addiction, but he did not believe me. I guess I did "too good" of a job hiding it. I figured if he found me passed out, he would call an ambulance or rush me to the hospital. THEY would tell me I needed help, which is okay. Then it would take the "weakness" off of my shoulders.[19]

Compounding the fear of being judged as weak by one's peers, officers fear reprisal by their supervisor for a perceived or actual lack of positive organizational support.[20] Speaking to his fellow chiefs of police at the Police Executive Research Forum, San Diego chief Bill Lansdowne confirmed what many supervisors know to be true: "Police officers are afraid to come to us when they are in trouble and they want help because they think it will negatively impact their career path and what we, as administrators are going to do with this personal information."[21]

Suspicion and secrecy may have their roots in the occupationally derived "code of silence," which has evolved to insulate and purportedly protect police from community complaints and uninformed external watchdogs. The code most frequently refers to the notion that if an officer crosses a legal line in carrying out duties, engages in corruption, or uses excessive force, "we" (police) can take care of "our own"; "we" can and will take care of "our" problems without the assistance of outsiders. Trautman suggests that the "us and them" code of silence may be an extension of the culture of machismo, also a feature of the communities of police and other first responders.[22]

Although the code may insulate officers from external criticism, it unwittingly isolates them from sources of assistance and intervention when needed. For example, organizational socialization and subcultural norms of toughness and self-sufficiency may hinder willingness to seek help for oneself or intervene on behalf of a fellow officer who is abusing prescription medications. Related, Callaghan states that avoidance of confronting a fellow officer is greater in the case of narcotics misuse or addiction than in the case of alcohol use because, whereas alcohol is legal, behaviors associated with the misuse of opioids, narcotics, and benzodiazepines are perceived to be illegal and in violation of the Oath of Honor.[23]

In most jurisdictions, the questions of whether an officer is taking a legal drug as prescribed, and whether that officer should be on active duty (e.g., able to carry a weapon and operate a motor vehicle), fall within the category of "fitness for duty." Though it is difficult to generalize, as policies vary by agency, common practices dictate that the officer reports the use of all medications to a medical officer or a supervisor, or that she may stay home and take a sick day.

In spite of routine stressors, cumulative stress, exposure to critical incidents, secondary traumatic stress, and internal organizational stress, the responsibility is overarching for law enforcement officers and other first responders to remain physically, psychologically, and socially healthy. In the *Nebraska Trooper Magazine*, Wineman has written that resiliency characterizes "a law enforcement officer's ability to: (a) quickly recover, both mentally and physically, from an overwhelming experience; and (b) translate that experience into positive practice. That is, the individual ultimately grows personally and professionally as a result."[24]

In common parlance, we understand resilience as the ability to cope and capacity for human development under conditions of stress. An individual's capacity to adapt is best understood in the context of the "local" social context, which includes access to resources, ability to navigate to these resources, and—important for law enforcement officers—normative expectations in their departments, in their homes, and in their peer groups.

A CONCEPTUAL AND THEORETICAL
MODEL OF RESILIENCE

The conceptual building blocks of positive psychology and learned optimism, along with the recognition that a holistic response to stressors (physical, social, and psychological) best contributes to wellness and health, are at the heart of resiliency theory. The social ecology of resilience theory aims to identify pathways for healthy growth and adaptability of individuals, organizations, and communities, in spite of external threats, by accounting for the protective factors resulting from embeddedness in a broader social ecological system. The components of resiliency research include prevention, intervention, education, and training.

Past research on resilience has been pursued along two paths: one placing emphasis on the centrality of resilience as a psychological trait and another perspective flowing from the community and social environmental supports.

A robust and influential ecological model of resilience in law enforcement and other high-risk occupations is the "Stress Shield Model of Resilience" developed by Paton et al.[25] The model seeks to explain how individuals adapt, rebound, and return to normalcy following exposure to risky environments or traumatic events. According to this research, resilience is an outcome of the individual's adaptive capacity and ability to make sense or give meaning to these events. In addition to this cognitive component, the Stress Shield Model attempts to measure the level of control the individual has over his environment and resources, including social supports. Paton et al. demonstrated that variation in officers' resilience is related to the interaction between individual, team, and organizational factors. The officers' past experiences, including previous training and education, along with a positive organizational climate, supervisory support, and trust, are important factors contributing to resilience.

Strategies for effective coping, adapting, and developing resilience in first responders have received increased attention, owing in part to greater understanding and more accurate diagnosis of PTSD following the Vietnam War and the Gulf Wars. Data from the U.S. Defense Medical Surveillance System (DMSS) showed a 544 percent increase in the reported incidence of PTSD from 2003 to 2013, but notably, a 50 percent decrease in the number of cases from 2013 to 2014.[26] Comparisons have been made between pathways to resiliency for military service members and for their domestic counterparts among police and other first responders. Their high-risk occupations carry many of the same stressors and mental and behavioral outcomes, such as PTSD, which is defined as:

> [A] reaction to a psychologically traumatic event outside the range of normal experience . . . [M]anifestations of PTSD included recurrent and intrusive dreams and recollections of the experience, emotional blunting, social withdrawal, exceptional difficulty or reluctance in initiating or maintaining intimate relationships, and sleep disturbances.[27]

The American Psychological Association's Task Force on Resilience in Response to Terrorism; the RAND Center for Military Health Policy Research;[28] the Resiliency Sciences Institute at the University of Maryland, Baltimore County; the Penn Resiliency Program at the University of Pennsylvania; and most recently the U.S. National Guard, FEMA, and the IACP, have been instrumental in advancing training for the military, police, and emergency responders. Such programs emphasize that resilient behaviors arise from taking care of oneself physically, mentally, and socially. When the focus is on resilient attitudes and behaviors, the emphasis shifts toward a positive orientation for understanding what must be done to enhance officer wellness and health during the course of the normal routine, as well as in preparation for and in the aftermath of a crisis event. A common theme is that resilient attitudes and behaviors stem from self-efficacy but are facilitated and contextually supported through the resources available in one's social environment.

Self-efficacy means having a positive belief in one's own ability to successfully complete a task.[29] Empirical research has emphasized the importance of preparation, prevention, and training for enhancing self-efficacy.[30] This includes a healthy lifestyle with physical training, exercise, nutritious food, and proper hydration, along with self-reflection, ongoing skill building, and a purposeful attitude toward one's work. In each of these areas, training and education can have a positive impact.

Understanding risk in a given context is a key component of assessing resilience. Studies of resilience have hinted at the role social capital and community-level support play in resilience. Pietrantoni and Prati noted that the availability of social support, seeking social support, and perceived social support positively impact police and other first responders' quality of life. The authors stated that variations in resilience are due to the combinations of individual characteristics, group dynamics, and organizational characteristics.[31] Meyer's study was one of the first to link social capital and collective efficacy with resilience research. Her research provides an elegant introduction for grounding the sociological understanding of these two concepts in resilience study. Meyer wrote:

> *Social capital* represents the resources available through individual social ties with others that can be activated to affect individual-like outcomes and outcomes for the entire network. *Collective efficacy* refers to the capacity of a group of people to work together for shared goals.[32]

In sum, Meyer's research points toward a multidimensional understanding of resiliency that accounts for how officers' social environment enables or limits their capacity to navigate risk, protective factors, protective processes, and social ecologies. The social-ecological model introduces the role that indirect relations, culture, and social structural elements play in developing and sustaining resilient behaviors. Further, the social-ecological model conceptualizes resilience as the adaptive capacity for growth—not solely a return to normalcy.

Case Study: Prescription Opioid and Benzodiazepine Use by Police Officers

Opiates are widely prescribed to those seeking relief from physical pain because they are effective. To simplify a complex neurobiological process, opiate pain relievers act to suppress pain and reduce pain transmission to the brain; they also may cause drowsiness and euphoria or a high. Narcotics such as fentanyl, hydrocodone, morphine, and oxycodone frequently are prescribed following surgical procedures ranging from dental extractions to hip/knee replacements and open-heart surgery.

Opioid pain medications are not intrinsically harmful; however, evidence is irrefutable that the risk of misuse and addiction is great. When police officers are impaired by substance use—including the use of prescription pain medications—their resilience, public safety, and the resilience of the organization may be threatened.

Griffin reports on opioid and benzodiazepine use by active and retired police officers in a large metropolitan police department.[33] Participants in this study identified pain control as the reason why they began to take prescription opioids. From that point in the discussions, two pathways were identified as contributing to opioid abuse: exposure to opioids during an acute pain episode and chronic pain management. Through this research, it was learned that officers' seeking help for, and recovery from, opioid abuse was best accounted for by the positive social supports and feedback mechanisms made available through the social network of the police subculture and policing organization.

The factors associated with officers' seeking help for opioid use disorder revealed three pathway themes—surrender, opportunity, and access—that connected prescription opioid-abusing officers to social supports and substance abuse professionals who aided in their recovery process. The process of giving up is referred to as "surrendering." Being confronted by a trusted peer, EAP, or supervisor may provide the opportunity to access social supports and resources. Despite individual feelings of vulnerability and shame, these supports, which are grounded in known and trusted components of the police subculture, act as protective systems for the officer.

In the literature about seeking help, surrender is associated with "hitting bottom."[34] Colier's description captured the concept quite richly, as she stated:

> Surrender arrives when we know that we cannot think or see our way through where we are . . . We don't give up to the situation, but rather, we give up to the notion that we *should* be able to or even *can* manage the situation, that we know anything that can help . . . As much as we are conditioned to never give up-in the case of surrender, giving up the mistaken belief that we are in charge offers a profound relief.[35]

A study by Satel, Becker, and Dan[36] of Vietnam veterans with PTSD illustrated the obstacles to surrender for soldiers, and similarly for law enforcement officers, whose training and experience have ingrained the importance of standing one's ground and fighting. Even so, their findings suggest, similarly to the present study, that resilient officers are able to develop a set of beliefs and attitudes that permit them to retain a positive self-identity, while successfully surrendering to their powerlessness. A finding that their research and the present study have in common is that specialized treatment programs and recovery support groups for police and first responders play an important role in supporting an officer, especially at the early stages of "surrender." Whereas psychological surrender at the individual level reflects officers' surrender to their powerlessness over opiate use, therapeutic surrender at the meso level references the process of surrendering that occurs in conjunction with treatment or clinical intervention.

ASSET-BASED APPROACH TO
HEALTH, WELLNESS, AND RESILIENCE

The recommendations of the President's Task Force on 21st Century Policing have suggested movement toward a holistic approach to officers' health and wellness. This approach is contrary to long-standing practices that give primary attention to remedying disease and health deficits. An asset-based approach is more likely to sustain individual, cultural, and organizational changes to support wellness and resilience over time.[37] Moreover, an asset-based strategy has the potential to empower officers and policing organizations to improve health outcomes for the individual officer and public safety. We conclude the chapter with a discussion of the social ecology of resilience and examples of asset-based strategies.

Griffin offers a conceptual model that considers individual strengths, along with those of the social and fraternal networks, the community, and assets and resources in the social environment.[38] Figure 7.1 depicts how an asset-based

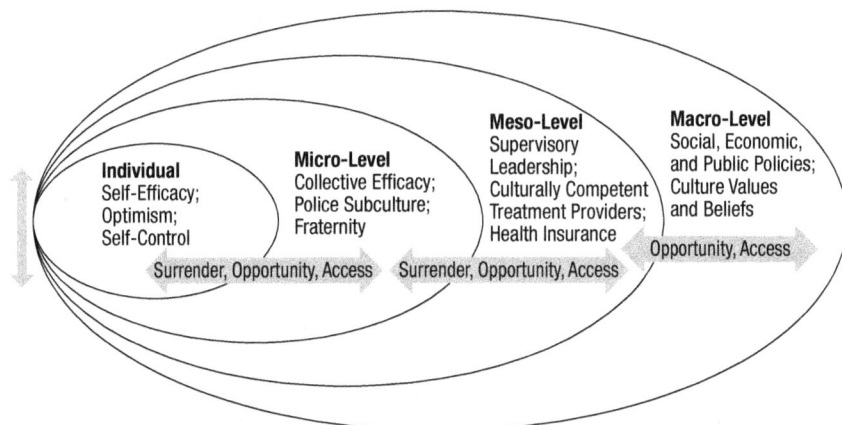

Figure 7.1. A Social Ecological Model of Resilience

approach relies on the interrelationship between individual and social supports to advance a culture of resilience and fitness for duty.

At the individual level, the focus is on identifying the personal history and trait factors that increase the likelihood of officers' engaging in healthy behaviors. In many departments, initial screening and hiring procedures evaluate applicants' social, behavioral, and physical characteristics. These procedures may be expanded or intentionally constructed to assess candidates' attitudes, beliefs, and behaviors that indicate willingness to learn, confidence in one's ability, and openness to vulnerability; they may be coupled with ongoing training and education throughout the officer's career. Together, these factors have been identified as ultimately enhancing fitness for duty.

The micro level examines close relationships that may increase the likelihood of engaging in healthy behaviors. A person's close social circle—consisting of peers, partners, and family members—influences behavior and contributes to the person's range of experience. Strategies at this level may include mentoring and peer programs designed to build or support healthy lifestyles and relationships.

Many examples showcase the success of peer support programs. First, research shows that the impacts of trauma can be minimized when using support provided by those closest to you.[39] A peer support program was found to mitigate the impacts of stress and resultant emotional fallout from a traumatic experience. In addition, peer support officers help "reduce sick days and job-related disability claims, keeps families intact, and lowers the rate of officers' suicides." For these programs to be effective, it is essential that the officers chosen to act as peer support officers are provided with appropriate training, adhere to strict standards, and are considered trustworthy by their peers.

The meso level includes the workplaces, neighborhoods, and other settings in which social relationships occur and seeks to identify the characteristics of these settings associated with wellness. Strategies at this level typically are designed to impact the social environment—for example, by reducing social isolation and by improving health opportunities, processes, and policies within workplace, family, and health-care settings. Officers must have the opportunity to engage with and have access to culturally competent treatment providers. Officers must not only know "where and to whom to go," these actions were possible because they had health-care coverage. As health-care costs continue to rise and cost containment through managed care is given priority, having specialized care may be an important consideration. Given the safety-sensitive nature of police work, policies at this level must also consider the need for public safety.

Finally, the macro level considers the broad societal factors that help create a climate in which officers' wellness and fitness for duty are encouraged or inhibited. These factors include social and cultural norms that support physical, mental, and behavioral health. Recent legislation that supports health insurance parity for physical, mental, and behavioral health is one such example.

Assets of the Police Culture as the Foundation for Wellness and Resilience

The distinct value of the culture of policing to officers' health is that the solutions are grounded in what has worked well for policing organizations and its members in the past. Whether the successful programs involve physical fitness, suicide prevention, deconfliction training, or the use of body armor—to give a few examples—the past and present practices aimed at advancing a culture of health and wellness for police and law enforcement officers and their organizations have a deeply rooted commitment to loyalty, fraternity, integrity, and honor. These same core values may be invoked to address workplace policies and officers' response to mental illness and substance use, rather than perpetuating a culture of silence, shame, and stigma.

An organizational change strategy may include wrap-around services that begin with education and training in the police academy and extend throughout officers' careers. The law enforcement officer's career begins with several months or longer, depending upon the jurisdiction, of academy training. Though most of the training academy curriculum includes mandated procedural, operational, and legal content, this substantive content should be infused with helping the officer to construct her personal habits of mind and practice to support lifelong wellness. This training also should include building relationships and identifying resources, procedures, and services that the officer or her family member may need throughout her career. When the officer is in the academy, that is the time when she is the most physically fit. This approach would seek to build on the ideal of physical fitness to effectuate desirable positive behavioral changes as well. In sum, by motivating police trainees at this critical point in their professional development, it is possible to imagine building behaviors that not only support physical fitness, but emotional or behavioral wellness.

Using the educational environment is an ideal venue for presenting the physiological and psychological components of substance use, but these may be insufficient without an anchor in the police subculture. The power and success for engaging officers in resilience have been linked to credibility and trustworthiness that emerged through either direct or indirect contact with others. Consequently, it would be beneficial to set aside formal and informal time for police cadets to engage with key stakeholders in the micro level, such as officers in recovery, peer counselors, EAPs, medical specialists, and family members of living or deceased officers who may have been touched by problems associated with substance abuse or mental illness. The academy is an opportune time for the health benefits provider to first engage with police cadets, who may be especially motivated to learn about employment benefits. Last, this is a critical time to explain the department's drug-free workplace policies with special attention directed toward fitness for duty and prescription medication use.

Continued annual training on substantive legal and procedural changes, along with continued firearm qualification, is required for most law enforcement officers. For many police departments, smaller departments in particular, having an officer at a training means one fewer officer on the street. A growing movement supported by the IACP and the State Chiefs of Police Association is to provide online asynchronous training that the officer may complete when he has down time on patrol. Departments may take advantage of e-learning opportunities for officers to acquire information and knowledge in substantive areas. Ideally, this would allow time for an onsite EAP or health specialist to provide ongoing face-to-face wellness coaching and training.

Many health providers, including the benefit organizations that contributed to the present study, have implemented multipronged wellness programs that support and monitor individuals with a chronic disease such as asthma, diabetes, or heart disease. In order for members to take advantage of these services, the benefit provider must have processes and procedures that ensure the confidentiality of members' health records. Whether real or perceived, officers may be reluctant to take advantage of health services if they believe this information will be shared with the department and used against them in the workplace—this may be particularly true as it concerns seeking help for mental or behavioral health. Yet, components such as outreach, education, ongoing support, and lifestyle coaching are important.

Outreach and progressive engagement with the officer must be balanced against the individual's right to privacy. A complementary strategy adopted by several drug and alcohol treatment facilities is to create an online portal where all subscribers and members enroll. This online community would provide targeted educational information related to substance use, particularly information germane to wellness initiatives that support the law enforcement community. It may be supported by an online chat forum to connect with a professional. The added strength of this approach is that a subscriber can gain information and support while remaining anonymous. It also brings together individuals who may be able to share their common experiences and solutions.

The family system is a key component for supporting officers' wellness and resilience. Often the family is aware of problem behaviors before they escalate and come to the attention of others in the workplace. Establishing an online health forum may be a valuable way for concerned family members to obtain needed information to bolster the officer's health and provide the family with resources they may need during difficult times.

Among the core values and strengths of the law enforcement occupation is a desire to be on the street and to "do police work." Most policing organizations require the officer voluntarily to notify her supervisor or the medical officer if she is using a narcotic or has an injury that could be limiting. In most cases, this would restrict the officer from being on active duty. When she is off the medication, she is expected to receive medical clearance to return to active duty. Having access to a medical specialist who not only understands a medical condition but also the police persona—that officer wants to be on the street—would be an asset for advancing officers' wellness and resilience. It is critical for officers to have access to culturally competent medical providers who can clear them for return to duty.

Last, police supervisors can play an instrumental role in advocating for organizational resources and supporting wellness initiatives. Specialized training on wellness and resilience should be incorporated into supervisors' professional development. Through their leadership, rank and file officers may benefit as well.

SUMMARY

This chapter elucidates and applies the social ecological model of resilience and provides theory-informed research of wellness prevention and intervention strategies. It is critical to recognize the individual choices, pathways, and/ or interventions that serve as buffers against mental and behavioral illness.

The research considered the capacity of officers to navigate their way to resources and maintain well-being; physical and social environments to provide those resources; and their families and communities to negotiate in culturally meaningful ways for those resources to be shared. Detailed are the risks and trauma uniquely associated with law enforcement as well as accompanying trauma that is widely experienced. Studies indicate that first-responders' experiences are outside the standard and frequently translate to maladaptive behaviors grossly above those found in the general population.

Therefore, it is important to understand the cumulative stress first-responders experience and the many unhealthy and destructive coping mechanisms they employ to try to alleviate the pressure and anxiety in their careers.

Part III

COMMUNITY

Chapter Eight

Innovation and the Community

Louis J. Beccaria and William Mossman

INTRODUCTION

The essence of this chapter is that the concept of community plays a major role in the development of a diversionary law enforcement mind-set and subsequent programs that may stem from it. For various moral, social, and economic reasons, diversion should be viewed as a necessary ingredient in making an efficient, effective, and well-functioning criminal justice system. When individuals who are not criminal at heart are diverted from the criminal justice system, everyone benefits.

This chapter highlights one such community, Phoenixville, Pennsylvania, and how it rallied around diversion as an alternative to dealing with certain kinds of situations presenting themselves to law enforcement. It will highlight two different case studies, the Hub Process (presented in further detail in chapter 10) and work around the situation known as adverse childhood experiences, or ACEs. These case studies will show how Phoenixville's enlightened school district leadership embraced the Hub Model as a diversionary approach and how health and human services individuals, led by the Phoenixville Community Health Foundation, are working to divert youth and future adults from having a life journey along the path of interaction with the criminal justice system.

Understanding Community

Community! Community! Community! We hear that word used in many different contexts. According to Webster's *New World College Dictionary*, the word "community" is broadly defined to imply having a similarity, or a likeness. It further is defined as a group of people living or working together having interests in common. It implies having ownership or partnership in something held in common.

When applied to the criminal justice field, application of the concept of community can offer a great deal toward diversion and innovation.

It becomes apparent that these two words—community and diversion—are linked. We say this because we do not believe it is possible to have reasonable, effective diversion without the input of the local community. Likewise, it is in the local community's best interest, for various law enforcement, economic, moral, and efficiency reasons, to have diversionary options at its disposal. In addition, one could make the case that community involvement is necessary to sustain diversion as well.

In the context of playing out this relationship between community and diversion, the reform or modernization of our criminal justice system is not just the purview of the criminal justice field as a professional discipline. Not hardly. The community-at-large has an important stake in this as a partner with a good measure of ownership of how criminal justice diversion is designed and plays out in its area. Remember: the criminal justice system needs diversion as a necessary element and requires the community as an important player to make it so.

In the past, when someone was acting out in public, the police would be called, and, upon their arrival, they would order the person to stop doing whatever was alarming the public. Persons with certain mental illnesses might not react to these commands in the "normal" fashion that an officer might expect. Police are trained to "force" compliance to restore order and public safety after they issue a legal command. When a police officer legally commands that someone stop doing something illegal, unsafe, disruptive, or alarming to the general public, that officer expects compliance. Most people recognize the officer's authority, and they understand the potential consequences of their actions if they don't comply. They might receive a citation; worse, they might be arrested. The thought of having to pay a fine or go to jail is deterrent enough for most people to comply with the lawful order.

When people continue to defy an officer's lawful order, the situation must escalate. A police officer doesn't have the luxury of walking away when someone tells him "No." The public's safety potentially is at risk if he walks away. So, if a police officer cannot gain compliance using a "hands-off" approach, speaking with the individual and giving clear verbal commands, he will have no choice but to escalate to a use of force. How much force the officer uses is dictated by the defiant individual's level of resistance. Oftentimes, the individual will continue to resist until it hurts too much to continue. Sometimes the resisting individual is injured during the struggle.

In the past, the general public didn't have much sympathy for the injured subject if he was the town jerk, or if he was drunk or high and looking for a fight. But a problem developed with police hurting persons who weren't complying due to mental illness. Openly defying a police officer because someone hates authority or because someone is drunk is one thing. Failing to comply with a lawful order because of an altered sense of reality, or an inability to process the situation quickly enough due to a mental illness, is something else.

The "community," on a national scale, no longer accepts that police are trained to restore order quickly and to escalate to force immediately if compliance is not readily achieved. The community now demands that police be trained to recognize someone in crisis, or someone suffering from a mental illness or a traumatic brain injury, who may need more time to process the officers' commands. The community demands that police officers be trained in de-escalation techniques so that force becomes less necessary and fewer people are injured fighting with police.

This training has a direct link to diverting individuals suffering from a mental illness away from the criminal justice system and into treatment. Here is the reason why: A trained officer will recognize that the individual in crisis (or suffering from a mental illness) will require more time to respond positively to the officer's commands. By taking the time that the individual needs, and using de-escalation techniques and other techniques learned through training, the officer is more likely eventually to gain compliance and be in a position to channel that individual into treatment.

However, if the officer is not trained, or does not have the patience to "negotiate and bargain" with the individual, that officer is more likely to resort to force to gain compliance. The ensuing struggle and potential threats that the individual makes toward the officer could be used to file charges. That individual may be incarcerated, and treatment may be delayed or may never come.

Training in de-escalation techniques and identifying persons in crisis, or with a mental illness, is an example of community playing an integral role in bringing about change to enhance the criminal justice diversion strategy.

Phoenixville, Pennsylvania, is an example of a community that has had the right ingredients for accepting the importance of diversion.

Phoenixville's history goes back more than 170 years when it was founded as an important location for the iron and steel needs of America's industrial age. The town is located on the banks of French Creek, its source of power to operate the plants. Likewise, Phoenixville (originally named "Manavon") had instant access to the Schuylkill River into which the French Creek flows. It was necessary for transportation of the iron and steel products produced at Phoenix Iron & Steel. The town was populated largely by European immigrants from Ireland, Poland, Hungary, Germany, and Italy, among many different countries, speaking different languages and possessing different cultural customs. They were bolstered by African Americans migrating from the South. All had one thing in common: to find a better economic life for themselves and their families.

Phoenixville grew rapidly during the latter half of the nineteenth century and well into the first half of the twentieth century. The borough thrived economically and culturally as a municipality. By the end of the 1960s, the town, at its zenith population-wise, was home to more than fifteen thousand people, a melting-pot community.

Most people were related to the iron and steel company in one way or another. For whatever reason—maybe their common reliance on the iron and steel company for their economic livelihood—they developed into a self-reliant community with a sense of brotherhood and sisterhood. They looked after one another and helped each other. Likewise, they developed a sense of pride in their humble steel town. Even today, pride and community are hallmarks of Phoenixville.

Around the beginning of the 1970s, the iron and steel industry was going through economic and international trade challenges of immense proportions. Phoenixville's iron and steel plant, after decreasing its workforce for several years, closed its doors forever. Enduring difficult times for about thirty years, its sense of community held Phoenixville together until a renaissance took place in the early- to mid-2000s. This revitalization turned this historic iron and steel town into an arts and cultural destination point for people from throughout the Delaware Valley region, essentially the area including southeast Pennsylvania, northern Delaware, and southern New Jersey.

Today, Phoenixville is vibrant, economically and culturally. It is a shining example of sticking together as a community, overcoming difficult odds for survival, and accepting new people and innovative ways of doing things for the community's survival and betterment. For example, it has become a very welcoming venue for Latinos seeking a better life away from economic hardships and the ravages of political dictatorships in their native countries.

One can see that Phoenixville's heritage is one of self-reliance, acceptance, innovation, and community. This heritage has set the stage for its ability to deal with current issues such as those apparent in today's criminal justice and mental health systems in northern Chester County in Pennsylvania, so it is not surprising that the concept of criminal justice system diversion has found a home in the greater Phoenixville area.

THE POTENTIAL OF FOUNDATIONS
IN RALLYING A COMMUNITY

An integral element of the Phoenixville community for over twenty years has been the involvement and work of the Phoenixville Community Health Foundation. The foundation has "community" in its name for a reason.

Since it came into existence in 1997 and became operational in September 1998, the foundation has practiced "community philanthropy." It has functioned with a keen sense of community that has far out-distanced its sole role: to give grants to area nonprofit, community-benefit organizations. Instead, it has totally immersed itself in the greater Phoenixville community by playing out various roles. Some that are relevant to this book's message about diversion are:

- Serving as an ambassador for Phoenixville, helping to develop and share a vision of what the Phoenixville community can be;
- Networking collaboratively with other community stakeholders to solve problems and institute change in needed areas;
- Taking on the role of a broker (not unlike that of a real estate agent) to bring parties together to address an issue;
- Serving as a catalyst to address a community issue that needs to be highlighted and acted upon;
- Functioning as a community builder to highlight the community;
- Serving as a trusted mediator for disparate parties in the community; and
- Being a capacity builder to help vital community organizations become stronger and more efficient, effective, and impactful.

Delving a bit into one of these roles, that of catalyst, can give the reader a sense of how the Phoenixville Community Health Foundation has helped, expending few or no funds, to bring about an acceptance of diversion as a concept to improve the criminal justice system as it applies to the greater Phoenixville area. What follows is a real-life example of how this intimate relationship between the foundation and the community has played out in the interest of diversion.

It started in 2005. Employing its catalyst role for community improvement, the Phoenixville Community Health Foundation, a private, health-conversion philanthropic entity serving nineteen municipalities (the greater Phoenixville community service area), set out to help address the thorny issue of access to mental health services for low-income individuals in serious mental health crisis. The immediate concern was their inability to be seen by a mental health professional therapist without waiting several weeks for an appointment at the new mental health agency. If these crises went unaddressed, these individuals likely could find themselves acting out in a way that ran afoul of the law and be captured into the criminal justice system.

MENTAL HEALTH, DIVERSION, AND ACTIVISM

The foundation formed the Greater Phoenixville Mental Health Advisory Council (GPMHAC) to help address this issue. This entailed calling together a broad cross-section of major players from more than fifteen different governmental and nonprofit, community-benefit organizations that potentially had a stake. Among them were the local police chief, officials from the Chester County Department of Mental Health & Intellectual Disabilities, several nonprofit mental health and social services groups, as well as a representative of the emergency department of the Phoenixville Hospital and the foundation itself.

It took several months to iron out the immediate situation for which the Advisory Council was formed, but progress was made and patients in mental health crisis began to be seen by the new mental health group in town in several days instead of many weeks. The Advisory Council could see its diversionary impact in this situation, but that was only the beginning. The group realized it could make a difference as long as the elements of "community" were in place.

Likewise, the group learned of the strong link between the mental health field and law enforcement. They were energized to tackle other issues at play in the greater Phoenixville area. All learned that the local police had much to offer in problem solving through their unique perspective and experience; the local police, in turn, learned many of the nuances of the Chester County mental health system of which they were not previously aware. One could call this "collaborative learning."

What elements of community were at play here? As we look back some fourteen years, when this first issue was addressed, the sense of community that developed, I believe, had the following elements at work:

Common Locale

The group was called together to address a mental health issue: that is, the lack of an urgent response for clinical appointments for those experiencing a mental health crisis, in a specific geographic area—northern Chester County and, specifically, the Phoenixville area.

Common Mission

The group defined its mission in addressing this immediate problem and others that came later: "To advocate for more efficient, effective, and impactful services for people in mental health recovery and to promote a better understanding of mental health issues in northern Chester County."

Rules of Engagement

As in any group activity, some rules were needed. Ours were:

- no private agendas were allowed;
- issues and frustrations were to be addressed with civility;
- participants must try to understand the viewpoint and pressures of others in the group; and,
- all needed to understand that compromise would be necessary if any solutions were to result from the discussions.

Representation and Roles

Players around the table represented different agencies with their own needs and their own rules, policies, and procedures influencing the issues at hand.

Learn from Each Other

It became evident not long after the GPMHAC began to meet that everyone involved had a big learning gap. Members confronted the fact that they often lived in silos in their everyday professional lives. It was apparent that the only way to resolve the issues was to replace the silos with a basket of collaborative learning about how things worked in the role that others played in the Chester County mental health and criminal justice systems.

Said another way, each player at each monthly meeting came to realize that all had a joint ownership stake in the solutions—and that they had the power to effect change in their community. Likewise, awareness of new, by-product concepts and programs arose, such as the Hub Model for dealing with at-risk students in the local Phoenixville Area School District and the ACEs (adverse childhood experiences) issue that has cried out for more public awareness.

Compromise

Flowing somewhat from those elements, the ability to compromise on previously held beliefs and positions was crucial to maintaining the sense of community and arriving at solutions. As a result of this process, other issues were brought up and discussed, and change was accomplished in a number of different areas, not the least of which were those related to diversion. A few diversionary successes are described below.

- Those in mental health recovery in northern Chester County came to know that they had an advocate.
- The idea for establishing the Gateway Housing Group, a nonprofit agency offering short-term crisis housing for those in mental health recovery, was born. Today, the successful Gateway Housing Group model has grown and has a countywide contract to offer housing for this population.
- Physical planning for the police lock-up section in the Phoenixville Borough's new borough hall/police station was highly influenced by discussions at the GPMHAC on the mental health needs of those arrested and jailed while awaiting arraignment.
- Spearheaded by the then Phoenixville police chief, Bill Mossman (a GPMHAC member), the Chester County Police Chiefs Association and the Chester County Department of Mental Health & Intellectual Disabilities began regularly scheduled meetings to initiate systematic changes in the processing procedures involving police and the mental health system.
- The GPMHAC's input influenced room design for safe isolation of mentally ill/acting out patients in the improved secure room in the emergency department of the Phoenixville Hospital.
- For the first time, a flow chart was developed as an outcome of GPMHAC discussions of how a person gets into the Chester County mental health system and what happens as they flow through the criminal justice system. The chart led to an increased understanding, triggering meaningful discussions.
- A crisis intervention services research study was implemented in 2015.
- Widespread support was generated for crisis intervention training (CIT) among mental health and criminal justice system stakeholders as a viable means for de-escalating crisis situations by police.
- Out of the GPMHAC deliberations, the Hub Model for dealing with difficult-to-solve case management situations with Phoenixville Area School District at-risk students was started in 2016.
- The GPMHAC gave birth to establishment of the Phoenixville ACES committee in 2016 to make the general public and the professional helping communities (i.e., faith-based groups, human services professionals, education professionals, and the medical community) of northern Chester County more informed about the long-term negative physical and mental health effects to children exposed to violence and other forms of trauma.

- Representatives of the GPMHAC were asked to participate in the Chester County "Stepping Up" program to provide better, timelier county mental health diversion services.
- Awareness of and support for the use of peer counseling in certain crisis interventions situations was promoted.

Thus, it can be seen, that when a pro-active sense of community participation is developed, good things can happen. Nothing solves problems and generates creativity like stakeholders exerting a sense of community through their collaborative participation. It is safe to say, that, at least in our general area, none of these diversion-related advances would have occurred if not for the catalytic efforts of the Phoenixville Community Health Foundation and the support of community stakeholders involved in the county's criminal justice and mental health systems.

LEADERSHIP

That is an overview of how the foundation was formed and one of the very important "spin-off" committees was initiated. One critically important element was left out: leadership! A number of very different organizations were asked to participate in a collaborative effort to achieve a goal. The problem, as happens so often when such disparate entities get together, is that each individual entity has its own priorities, policies, and specific mission.

Sometimes, two or more entities may not have gotten along well in the past, which may bring predisposed notions of how "this is not going to work if we have to work with them." Sometimes several similarly missioned organizations, which typically compete with one another for limited state and federal funding, are now on the same committee. The only thing preventing a well-meaning committee from dissolving into bickering, chaos, and further compartmentalization is leadership.

It cannot be overstated how important it is to choose the right leader from the very beginning. Two opposing groups will sit down together if they mutually respect the person who requested the meeting. Every organization has a leader, and leaders have similar traits. Leaders are comfortable being in charge; telling people what to do comes naturally to them. They don't typically approve of their authority being challenged and may feel insulted if they perceive that their opinions and comments aren't held in high enough regard. It takes a skilled leader to manage these strong, sometimes fragile personalities and mold them into a team with a common purpose. Each is a link in a chain that strengthens the committee and enhances the final outcome.

Our opinions on the selection of a leader and the associated characteristics are based on experience, observation, and intuition. Select someone who has a long-established reputation for personal excellence, without arrogance. The candidate should be widely respected by local governmental, cultural, educational, civic, and religious leaders. Make sure the individual does not rule through fear and intimidation, which do not foster open discussion or a sense of freedom to express creative or innovative ideas or methods. Look for the innate ability to foster collaboration and the keen sense to know when and how to redirect a conversation gently when it begins to go off course. A good leader allows leeway for free thinking and dialogue but knows when it is time to refocus the group on the task at hand. A sense of humor helps. People's time is important, especially when other pressing matters are vying for attention. If someone doesn't feel that his time was well spent, or that his input was validated during the meeting, he will not return. That loss will diminish the committee's effectiveness.

That is why it is paramount that the leader:

1. be universally respected by the other members of the group;
2. be someone who can skillfully navigate the disparate personalities and organizational missions, and gather them into a cohesive group working toward a common goal;
3. have the ability to add her two cents' worth without overly influencing the thoughts and opinions of the other members;
4. recognize when the group begins to deviate too far from the intended goal and refocus the group on the task at hand; and
5. have a clear vision of the group's purpose and keep it on track, methodically moving forward to accomplish the established goal or mission.

THE INFLUENCE OF COMMUNITY ON DIVERSION

In addition to the examples previously mentioned, we have seen how the influence of community has played a role in changing history. An abundance of examples could be cited; here are a few.

The advancement of civil rights for African Americans in the United States was accomplished out of a sense of community—that is, a community of civil rights activists in conjunction with the people they represent. The advances made in awareness of the harm of the primary and secondary effects of smoking to personal and community health is another, as is development of a greater awareness among most Americans of the need for a cleaner, healthier environment and the legislation that has followed to enforce measures to create it. This was the result of a sense of community on a national scale affecting change in the awareness of the need for healthier lifestyles.

In the criminal justice field, enlightenment about the importance and need for diversion reflects community influence. For the financial, regulatory, public safety, and moral imperatives, communities around the country have come to understand the importance of and need for diversionary practices.

Consider the moral imperative. Hopefully our society will become more educated and sensitive to matters of the human condition—specifically, to those suffering from mental illness. Out of a sense of moral decency, diverting people who, at their core, are not really criminals but individuals with a mental disease is the right thing to do. As we have shed the cloak of society's puritanical approach to life in general and have come to realize that mental illness is not a function of bad character, we have become more enlightened about affairs of the mind.

Just as we never have condemned a person to be of poor moral character because he contracted cancer, we have come to understand that mental illness is not a matter of poor character but a brain disease—a mental disease. This societal ah-hah moment has set the stage for criminal justice to be open to understanding this new way of thinking—essentially, through collaborative learning.

No less a reason for the criminal justice field to accept diversion as preferred for those suffering from mental illness is the economic calculus. In plain English, it makes good economic sense. In a world where financial resources are limited and becoming scarcer, using criminal justice funds as they were intended—to capture and imprison violators of the law—is the right path to pursue. Diversion of mentally ill people, no threat to our communities as serious lawbreakers, from the criminal justice system to the mental health system uses police resources more efficiently, unclog prisons, and, to employ the vernacular, puts square pegs in square holes and round pegs in round holes.

In addition, it is very difficult for those who need mental health treatment and who pose no serious lawbreaking threat to our communities, to receive it in nontherapeutic settings such as prisons and jails. Many mental illnesses can be controlled, and, with the proper treatment, can help people become normal, adjusted, and productive citizens in our communities. We would no more think of placing a person with cancer in a jail or prison as a means of dealing with their disease, so why would it make sense to do this with individuals who suffer from another form of disease, such as mental illness?

Case Study Models of Diversion

Diversion from the criminal justice system can mean providing new approaches to working with youth who otherwise may find themselves on the path to its front door. In the Phoenixville area, two program efforts at work right now can be legitimately regarded as diversionary. They are the Hub Process and the community effort to make more people, particularly educators, aware of the issue known as ACEs.

The Hub Process Model

The process began by recognizing that the traditional silo model of dealing with multiple-problem individuals and families, frequently seen by police by separate agencies, did not promote public safety and improve social outcomes. A better way was needed to redirect scarce public resources to meet the needs of individuals and families with elevated risk factors more effectively. In a sense, it was an attempt to implement and adapt the old adage, "It takes a village to raise a child" to "It takes a village to solve community social issues—one person, one family—at a time."

The Hub Process Model is a partnership approach to broker change through multiagency collaboration as a criminal justice system diversionary measure. Risk factors for those who are the target of help include:

- poverty
- homelessness
- unemployment
- physical and mental issues
- family trauma or instability
- substance abuse

For a Hub Process case to be legitimate, it must have a:

1. significant community interest at stake
2. clear probability of harm occurring
3. multidisciplinary nature to the elevated risk-factors
4. severe indication of harm predicted to the individual, family, or community

Adopting this model involves a mental criminal justice system shift from an "incident-driven" process to a "risk-driven" approach, triggered by immediate collaborative action based on identifying risk factors before incidents occur (see chapter 10 for exploration of the Hub in greater detail).

The ACEs Model

The second diversionary model is the ACEs Model. ACEs is an acronym for adverse childhood experiences. The ACEs Model was developed about fifteen years ago through the work of pediatric physicians in California such as Dr. Nadine Burke-Harris. They found in their research and clinical practices that childhood traumas can result in damage to brain development. This damage can cause changes in the functioning of the brain affecting a child's learning ability, social skills, emotional behavior, decision making, and long-term physical and mental health. When these traumas are prolonged, they can turn into toxic stress and create a multitude of health, social, and behavioral problems.

Adverse experiences that have been identified by pediatric research as stressful and traumatic in a child's life are:

- emotional abuse
- physical abuse
- sexual abuse
- emotional neglect
- physical neglect
- child's mother being treated violently
- substance abuse in the home
- mental illness in the home
- parental separation and divorce
- having an incarcerated parent

Although even one of these experiences can have a negative effect, having several of these experiences has the worst effect on a child and often results in physical and emotional health issues and social maladjustment. ACEs children, for example, often suffer such physical health maladies in later life as heart disease, strokes, and other preventable diseases because the body's ability to fight off infections is significantly reduced. As a consequence, children who have suffered traumatic stress and whose stress hormones are continually under attack often live shorter lives, sometimes by as much as twenty years. Lower tolerance for stress likewise can result in adverse social and emotional behaviors such as aggression, dropping out, and defiance of authority and the law. Exposure to trauma and prolonged toxic stress, because they affect brain development, can reduce a child's ability to learn and process information as well as create emotional problems in school.

Frequent or extended exposure to childhood ACEs experiences can increase a child's later life risk of such physical, mental, and social outcomes as:

- adolescent pregnancy
- alcoholism and drug abuse
- chronic obstructive pulmonary disease
- depression
- liver disease

- sexually transmitted diseases
- suicide attempts
- intimate partner violence
- social isolation
- criminal behavior

Resilience is the antidote in these situations. It can help reduce the effects of ACEs. Creating environments where affected children and adults feel safe and understood is important.

Helping affected children and adults identify and manage their emotions is critical. Establishing supports so that an ACEs child or adult has basic needs met, such as food, housing, clothing, and health care (both physical and emotional) is essential.

You may ask how ACEs relates to criminal justice diversion. If more people in a community were aware of ACEs and its causes, and if they knew better how to promote resilience, fewer adults who have suffered the mental health ravages of ACEs as children would find themselves afoul of the law. Many adults in today's prisons may have been saved from a journey of crime and had a chance at a productive life contributing in a positive way to society. Thus, diversion does not need to be a formal program, but it can be demonstrated in a community's better awareness of what contributes to crime and then trying to do something about it.

CONCLUDING COMMENTS

This chapter points out the role that the community can and should play in the development of diversionary practices in a criminal justice system to help make the practice of law enforcement more efficient, effective, and impactful for the community that it serves.

In the case of Phoenixville, the Phoenixville Community Health Foundation played a catalyst and leadership role in rallying its community around diversion via its work leading the Greater Phoenixville Mental Health Advisory Council to address mental health and issues that sometimes affected the Chester County criminal justice system. In addition, the foundation helped introduce the Hub Model to the Phoenixville Area School District to enable it to better deal in a preventive way with the health and human services problems facing some of its students.

What this chapter shows is that criminal justice diversion is doable if it is approached with a sense of open-mindedness, resolve, a willingness to learn new ways of solving problems, and leadership from the community.

Chapter Nine

Promising Practices and Programs

Identification and Analyses

Frank Mielke and Patricia Griffin

INTRODUCTION

In this book we established the foundation for change starting with the identification of needs framed within the financial, public safety, regulatory, and moral imperatives. We analyzed the landscape and presented a current state of mental health. Understanding the types of illnesses is important, so descriptions were provided for such disorders as autism spectrum disorders, bipolar disease, dementia, intellectual disabilities, schizophrenia, and traumatic brain injuries. We also recognized the importance of the wellness of the interventionist and addressed both trauma and resiliency.

As discussed in this book, if diversion efforts are to be effective, organizations must be aligned internally around common goals and externally with other systems such as the behavioral health system. We define diversion as diverting those with a mental illness out of the criminal justice system and into treatment where appropriate. With the help of special studies and theories of alignment, leaders can take the steps necessary to improve alignment. Because law enforcement doesn't exist in a vacuum, they must be aligned externally with myriad entities. Often, these entities have common goals but behave differently. Differences in values help shape culture that results in different policies, procedures, and behaviors that create conflict between law enforcement and the mental health system.

In the midst of all of these influences is the community that may serve as a focal point for positive change. The community is prominent in some examples of successful programs cited in this chapter; on a broader scale, it is at the forefront of social change.

Neither law enforcement, nor the mental health system, nor any other can be the sole driver for change. The interventionist, responding to individuals in crisis, may come from a family or the general public; from a 911 operator or police officer; or from a crisis specialist. In severe situations, a team of the aforementioned can best bring the situation to a successful resolution. In a quieter time, members of these disciplines, collaborating and embracing a spirit of innovation, provide meaningful solutions.

The cornerstone of diversion incorporates innovation and collaboration. Often, articulation of outcomes through reliable data spurs the collaboration. Stark and unambiguous numbers compel interested parties to do something. The failure to respond creates the potential for embarrassment, which leaders clearly seek to avoid. The need for data motivated the Audubon Management Consultants project team to undertake the survey profiled in this book.

The formula for change is clear: Information leads to collaboration, which then leads to innovation.

Innovation is required in the face of decades of challenges and continued frustration. Some progress has been made in diversion, but leaders must never rest on their laurels. Solutions may result from one individual's idea in one entity, but it requires nurturing from others with a different perspective, a function of systems thinking introduced in chapter 1. Implementation often requires a cross-functional effort from those with a different perspective coming from different organizational cultures.

Recognizing the importance of innovation and collaboration, the stage is set to analyze critically the personal and organizational characteristics associated with diversion programs. We offer several examples, along with critical analyses of what makes the endeavor successful and where pitfalls may render the effort a failure. These programs drive change supporting diversion and require the skills necessary for successful implementation.

When considering these or other interventions we propose several guidelines:

Remember, one size does not fit all.

Communities are unique in a variety of respects. Socioeconomic profiles vary widely and impact resources available for interventions. Recognize that collaboration is the key to success, but keep in mind the nuanced attitudes, behavior, and culture. Successful interventions can blend disparate factors. A successful intervention one community is no guarantee that it will be successful in others.

Do your homework.

Successful intervention requires an articulation of need. The research and data that articulate the need are necessary to align the intervention with the need. Researchers pursue meaningful discussions with all stakeholders identified in chapter 1 as interested parties to ensure full disclosure and understand the motivation for the intervention.

When considering an intervention, conduct an investigation with a risk/reward mind-set.

The risk is more than monetary, recognizing that people must put time and effort into a program. To delay the investigation or implementation of an intervention may continue to put patients in crisis at risk. A failed diversion program raises another critical question: Should the time and effort have been put into another program?

Ego is also a risk. Individuals do not want to associate themselves with a failure, so may resist involvement in particular programs. A fear of failure may override the potential rewards emanating from taking a risk.

Rewards may be both tangible and intangible. For a diversion program, tangible rewards may include higher rates of diversion, lower rates of recidivism, and an increase in public safety. Intangible rewards may include greater awareness of the financial, public safety, regulatory, and moral imperatives that may motivate other members of the community to pursue additional diversionary programs.

We draw on our collective experiences and diversionary efforts contained in the literature to examine promising practices and programs. We selected these examples because they embrace collaboration and respond to the financial, public safety, regulatory, and moral imperatives. Most important, these cases have a track record of success:

- Crisis Centers
- Partnering with Crisis Workers
- Hubs
- Youth Aid Panel
- Law Enforcement Resiliency: Programs of Promise

Building Evidence-Based Training for Law Enforcement: Crisis Intervention for Veterans

The purpose of this training module is to divert veterans in crisis away from the criminal justice system and into treatment. The program is endorsed by the Veterans Administration and is under review in several jurisdictions. It is characterized by:

- A focus on a well-defined segment of the population (veterans, in this case)
- A well-articulated needs assessment

- A multidisciplined project team, including a police officer, a crisis worker, a 911 call taker/dispatcher, and a veteran, all working collaboratively
- Monitoring and evaluation to promote continuous improvement

Perhaps, no greater imperative exists than to address veterans who suffer from post-traumatic stress disorder (PTSD) and traumatic brain injury (TBI). As current and former members of the military, they sacrifice on behalf of all. They leave family and friends and travel to remote and dangerous parts of the world. They are exposed to and witness horrific scenes, including the injury and death of fellow service members.

The primary audience for this training is law enforcement who, at times, interact with veterans in crisis. But the training can be adapted easily for other responders. For example, 911 call takers/dispatchers often are the first to receive an alert from a family member, friend, or civilian. The call taker/dispatcher must capture vital information to equip law enforcement to intervene effectively. Training provides an understanding of the veteran and the mindset of the caller, which shapes the necessary questions leading to potentially lifesaving information.

Emergency room personnel also treat veterans in crisis. We believe that beyond understanding the physical needs of the veteran, understanding the emotional needs leads to better bedside manner and a more holistic path to recovery.

Two factors provide a compelling reason to address veterans in crisis:

First, according to the National Center for PTSD, somewhere between 11 and 20 percent of veterans from the recent Gulf Wars have PTSD in a given year.[1] This compares to about 8 percent of the U.S. population who have PTSD at any given time.[2]

Second, the training and skills of veterans may render them more difficult and potentially dangerous to deal with. They may be more physically fit, trained in hand-to-hand combat, and proficient in the use of weapons. The interventionist, knowing that the individual is a veteran and may fit this profile, is inclined to approach the situation far differently than other crisis situations. Fearing for his safety, the police officer may opt for unnecessary force, thereby exacerbating the situation.

A series of interventionists or key players participate in the training as researchers for needs assessment, members in the training delivery team, or as recipients. They include: 911 call takers/ dispatch operators, law enforcement officers, crisis workers, or veterans.

Often, the call taker/dispatch operator is the first to receive a call for help. It is an opportunity to gather critical information if the call is from a family member or friend of the individual. Responses to critical questions will provide vital information for the responding police officers, such as:

- Is the individual in crisis a veteran?
- Are weapons at the location of the individual in crisis?
- Has the individual in crisis demonstrated unusual behaviors recently, and if so, what are they?

At times, the caller may be reluctant to share some information or not have the presence of mind to respond to these questions in a coherent manner. The dispatcher must handle the call with a level of sensitivity that will yield the appropriate vital information to law enforcement with the knowledge that time is of the essence. Handling such calls is appropriate and associated training for 911 call takers/dispatchers.

Law enforcement officers may have received crisis intervention or de-escalation training, but such training may not have sufficiently addressed interaction with a combat veteran. Even with such training, the intervention's effectiveness may be compromised, knowing that the veteran presents a greater danger than others in a crisis.

Frequently, the crisis worker is best equipped to address a variety of needs as demonstrated by the crisis patient, including veterans suffering from PTSD and TBI. However, circumstances may require the crisis worker and the police officer to work in concert to deliver an effective intervention.

In response, Montgomery County Emergency Service and Audubon Management Consultants, in conjunction with other specialists, developed a training module for intervening with a veteran in crisis. The training exists within a process to track attitudes, behaviors, and best practices to develop the evidence to support or indicate changes to the program. The curriculum and process draw on current training, theories, and practices to develop the next plateau for addressing veterans in crisis.

Development and delivery of such training is driven by a cross-functional project team whose members include experts in the areas of:

- crisis intervention
- law enforcement
- 911 call taking/dispatching
- veterans

The project team seeks to achieve the following goals:

Develop a comprehensive, community-sensitive training-needs assessment for police officers and for 911 dispatch operators and crisis workers who will encounter a veteran in crisis.

The needs must be sufficiently articulated for those who will provide, and those who will receive, the training. In other words, the training is not designed exclusively from one perspective (e.g., law enforcement), but rather presents a multifaceted response to need.

Develop and deliver interactive training sessions by an expert team in the areas of law enforcement, crisis intervention, dispatch operations, and veteran issues.

Notice that the delivery is conducted in an environment of interaction between those who deliver and those who receive the training. Often, attendees have had some experience with individuals in crisis, including veterans. As such, they developed a particular view and have specific questions regarding interventions. When one attendee comments or raises questions, all benefit from their experience. Further, the frequency of questions and the nature of comments may suggest the need to modify the training module.

Develop a data repository from participants, agencies, state judicial centers, the Veterans Administration, among others, to support evidence-based evaluation of the training.

This goal is influenced by a RAND Corporation study, which provided the following observation: "Agencies nationwide continue to search for effective strategies that reduce crime and build community trust. Yet, the policing profession lacks a robust capacity to conduct and broadly disseminate research that will help guide agencies in figuring out what works and what does not."[3]

Establish a framework for a rigorous, evidence-based process to evaluate the efficacy of the training.

The follow-up process of monitoring and evaluation (create a feedback loop) encourages sharing experiences, including what went right and what went wrong. This serves as input to the database cited above. Information is shared with all participants, promoting continuous learning and improvement of training. Outcome data also may be shared with the community at large and funding agencies.

Systematic and rigorous evaluation of the data creates the foundation for meaningful evidence-based practices. The intent is to standardize, systematize, and rigorously evaluate the data.

Contribute to the continued striving for best practice by all interested parties who can influence the development of effective interventions for veterans in crisis.

The process of capturing data cited above contributes to the identification, evaluation, and implementation of best practices. More important, perhaps, is the profile of experiences captured after the training and the responses and programs that emanated from such experiences. The overriding strategy is driven by the multidisciplined team developing and delivering a robust training program.

Project outcomes include:

- A well-articulated needs assessment that supports training for law enforcement, crisis workers, and call takers/dispatch operators;
- Materials for law enforcement, call takers/dispatch operators, and crisis workers when encountering a veteran in crisis;
- Published best practices that guide interactions with veterans in crisis and contribute to the development of best practices; and,
- Data that demonstrates the results of the training as a platform for continuous improvement.

The project team will measure the three key elements—attitudes, behaviors, and confidence—at three points:

1. *Registration*—Participants will complete a brief questionnaire at the point of registration. They will be asked for their name and e-mail with assurances that their information will not be shared except with the project team and only for the purposes of continuous improvement.
2. *Immediately after the training*—Participants will complete the same questionnaire they submitted at registration. Additional lines of inquiry will address such issues as trainer performance, adequacy of materials, and overall effectiveness. The process will capture best practices, either through feedback or discussions occurring during the presentation.
3. *Three months after the training*—The participants again will address the key elements of the training, provide updates on their experiences and any new best practices. The follow-up will request permission for a personal contact, if necessary.

Twelve months after the training, the three-month process will be repeated.

The results will reside in an electronic data repository and be updated each month after the training sessions. The data will:

- Guide any required modifications to the training
- Provide the foundation for articles and journals that may be published in the public domain
- Facilitate integration with other repositories for further research. Those repositories may include data from the Veterans Administration, state courts, Justice Policy Institute, and Bureau of Prisons, among others.

The ultimate goal is to improve knowledge, attitudes, behaviors, and confidence for police officers, 911 call takers/dispatchers, and crisis workers when encountering a veteran in crisis.

The training should show measurable improvements in:

- first responder appreciation of veteran issues;
- diversion as evidenced by reductions in incarceration and recidivism rates; and
- confidence by 911 call takers/dispatchers, police officers, and crisis workers when encountering a veteran in crisis.

As a result:

- Training for the interaction between veterans and law enforcement is improved due to veterans' input.
- Call takers and dispatchers will improve their skills at securing information vital to police officers.
- With support from various agencies, police officers and 911 call takers/dispatchers can be prepared, at the point of contact, to provide vital information to the veteran in crisis.
- The effort to reduce veteran suicides is enhanced because call takers, dispatchers, and police officers are aware of the signs.
- Project results will promote the integration of data among various agencies at the local, county, state, and federal level, leading to more effective practices and investments in the welfare of veterans.
- Best practices will be captured and made available in the public domain.
- Awareness of the nuances surrounding the interaction of a call taker, a dispatcher, or a police officer in the interest of diversion will be heightened.
- Rates of incarceration, recidivism, and suicide will be reduced.

Unique characteristics associated with this training module include the development by an interdisciplinary team acting in a collaborative manner, focusing on evidence, and, finally, a training module that is not "one and done." In other words, learning extends beyond the last day of training and provides continuous flow of learning experiences. Although on the surface the training may appear advantageous, challenges and pitfalls could lessen its impact.

A cost is associated with the training: it requires a leader to emerge from the various potential and participating organizations. This leader will drive the project and secure funds. Often, resources can be secured from grants or from municipalities convinced of the efficacy of the project. Without leadership, there is no project and no training.

Information is essential to an evidenced-based program and provides the foundation for continuous improvement. The previously mentioned RAND report cited the need to "disseminate information to all interested parties through interoperable systems in a manner to reduce information overload."

Characterizing the criminal justice system as being "data rich and information poor" has relevancy. Police officers complete detailed narratives that are partially codified. Various insights, nuances, and other valuable information are buried in narratives. Capturing this information in an easily accessible format is a daunting task.

The first hurdle in improving information flow is developing a consistent definition of terms. Different disciplines have different language, and translation often is a challenge in day-to-day communications. The problem is magnified when you link systems that use inconsistent terms.

Standardizing terms is a prelude to integrating systems. Differences in software, communication protocols, and operating platforms, among others, represents a daunting challenge and the potential for a sizable investment in technology.

Data collection efforts initially should be modest but gain momentum as the capture and dissemination of data expands. In other words, start small and build momentum.

Another challenge for the team is to overcome the illusion of invulnerability, a flaw in the decision-making process Irving Janis cited in his work on groupthink.[4] This illusion is associated with a project team that comes from value-driven organizations. Their quest is not to expand market share or increase profits: they protect individuals in need. Their work is noble and, in their minds, beyond reproach. These feelings may exist within individual team members or the team as a whole. Because of this illusion, a group insulates itself from outside input, constructive or otherwise. Enlightened members of the team, recognizing this potential character flaw, will help individuals and the team realize that "open-mindedness" leads to success.

Training in the interest of the welfare of veterans responds to a compelling moral imperative.

Crisis Centers

Ask police officers what kind of support they expect when encountering an individual in crisis, and invariably they will tell you foremost is a quick transfer of the patient to the mental health system for are three compelling reasons: First, because the right thing to do is to secure the right specialist to address the needs of the individual in crisis in a rapid manner. Second, they want to get back to the job for which they were hired, essentially, to get the "bad guys." Third, a timely and appropriate intervention decreases the likelihood that they will be required to respond to this person again.

It should be obvious that a patient in need wants a quick response. An individual suffering a heart attack needs a rapid response by a cardiologist. Have a severe laceration? The patient needs someone to relieve the pain and stitch the wound in a rapid manner. The need is no less great for someone experiencing a mental health crisis.

Law enforcement has made great strides in training and preparing police officers to deal with someone in crisis; frustration appears when the mental health system is slow to respond. Police bristle when, at times, they see themselves as "babysitters." The police officer wants an intervention in the shortest possible time both in the interest of the patient and of the people they were sworn to protect.

At the core of this discussion is collaboration between law enforcement and the mental health system that serves as the foundation for interventions, in this case, crisis centers.

Three elements influence collaboration between law enforcement and the mental health system as measured in table 9.1. The results, from the survey mentioned previously, center around the influences of partnership, confidence, and satisfaction with the timeliness of service. We gathered the responses from police agencies in two counties. In the interest of confidentiality, we protect their names.

Table 9.1.

Statement	Weighted Scores[1]		
	County A	*County B*	*Difference*
We work in partnership with mental health providers.	5.51	4.24	1.27
I have confidence in the mental health system as it relates to policing.	4.65	3.74	.91
I'm satisfied with the timeliness of service provided by the mental health system.	4.63	3.42	1.21

1. Based on a seven-point Likert scale; the higher the score, the more favorable result.

These two suburban counties are in close proximity to a large city and have similar socioeconomic profiles. They are contiguous, so they have some level of interaction between the police departments that border each other's county. One significant difference: County A has a crisis center and County B does not. Police officers in County B complain, continually and loudly, that they are at a disadvantage because they don't have a crisis center.

One might wonder why two counties, similar in many respects, have a different path to those in crisis.

Difference in philosophy is one factor. Mental health leaders in County B object to County A having a facility with both a crisis center and a mental health hospital at the same location. They contend that the transfer from the crisis center to the hospital is self-serving and may not be in the best interest of the patient. County A cites the oversight by its mental health department and the ethical practices they embrace. Further, County B cites the "asylum" type of ambiance of County's A facility. In response, County A points to several modifications and additions in furtherance of their efforts to create a warm, inviting environment.

It can be argued that County B has elected not to develop a crisis center for economic reasons. County A was able to take over an existing state facility with an annual rent of $1. County B made several attempts to establish a crisis facility in one of its hospitals, but they were short lived because the for-profit hospital failed to see the economic advantage.

The need for a crisis center is apparent: respond quickly and effectively to someone in crisis. The ingredients for success can be found in the following examples; foremost among them are innovation and collaboration.

McLean County, Illinois

Financial challenges did not deter McLean County in Bloomington, Illinois, from opening a taxpayer-funded mental health triage center. At a cost of $400,000 supported by sales tax proceeds, the center is intended to address deficiencies in community mental health services.[5] In other words, McLean County responded to two of the imperatives cited in this book, financial and moral.

Bexar County, Texas

When it comes to responding to mental illness, Bexar County is one of the most highly regarded counties in the United States. It demonstrates a sensitive and financially responsible approach to treating those in crisis. Bexar's journey began in 2002 with police training that steered the police officer with an individual in crisis to an emergency room or mental health facility. According to published accounts,

> Since its inception, Bexar County's program has diverted thousands of people with mental illness away from jail, saving money and winning national recognition. The problem is that, increasingly, there are no places to "divert" the person once dropped off at a local emergency department.[6]

Recognizing the dilemma of attempting to divert, but no place to divert to, Bexar County built a twenty-two-acre crisis center for psychiatric and substance abuse emergencies along with a place for the homeless. The process involves diversion from jails and emergency rooms into treatment. The estimated savings is almost $100 million over an eight-year period.[7]

Guilford County, North Carolina

The cost of a crisis center is no minor concern. With a population of 488,000, Guilford County, North Carolina, opened two facilities at a single location at a cost of between $15 and $20 million. The county sought financial support from a variety of entities, including the state of North Carolina.

The first facility is a sixteen-bed adult crisis center, a twenty-three-hour observation unit, and outpatient services for adults, adolescents, and children. The second facility contains sixteen beds and is a nonmedical facility that serves as an alternative to hospitalization for adolescents experiencing behavioral health crises.[8]

Jeff Phillips, vice chair of the Guilford County board of commissioners, cites the importance of collaboration: "This innovative project wouldn't be possible without the unprecedented cooperation of the organizations involved."[9]

Montgomery County, Pennsylvania

Too often, the fascination is with the new and unique, especially when innovation and collaboration serve as the foundation for such programs. The key question: "Are such programs sustainable"?

In response, consider Montgomery County Emergency Service (MCES) in Pennsylvania, a nationally recognized provider of behavioral health services for those in crisis and for those in drug/alcohol emergencies. The MCES offerings include experienced crisis workers, telephone support, comprehensive assessments, and referral information.

Law enforcement officers know that they can bring individuals in crisis to MCES and they will receive appropriate attention. Further, they are not burdened with the task of protecting the patient from danger to himself and to others until arrangements can be made to transport the patient to an intake facility.

A concurrent strategy for diversion is assisting law enforcement with mental health issues as a crisis responder and as a provider of training. The MCES school provides education and training on a range of subjects to help law enforcement deal more effectively with the mentally ill. Their law enforcement training, extending beyond the immediate geographic area, is national in scope.

The collaboration of MCES with law enforcement, which prepares police officers before a crisis situation through training and during a crisis, builds mutual trust and respect.

MCES was founded in 1974 and continues to be a model for other counties. In other words, the MCES model is sustainable.

Measures of Collaboration

The recurring theme in all of these examples is collaboration. We see collaboration among government, law enforcement, and providers in Texas, North Carolina, Illinois, Pennsylvania, and Texas.

In our survey, consistent with the material in chapter 5, we sought to identify the frequency and types of responses reflecting interfaces between law enforcement and various entities. Table 9.2 represents responses from seventy-four participants with the title of lieutenant and above. We believe that this is the group most likely to interact with the various entities.

Respondents were asked to characterize their interaction with various entities in terms of frequency and whether the interaction was positive or negative. The table focuses on frequent, positive interactions—hence opportunities to leverage the interactions in the interest of diversion. Results are presented in descending order.

Table 9.2.

Entity	Percent Frequent and Positive Interaction
Business Community	58.11
Educational System	50.00
Faith-Based Organizations	39.19
General Public	39.19
Judicial System	39.19
Health System	31.08
Funders	20.27
Labor Unions	20.27
Mental Health Hospitals/Agencies	18.92
Politicians	17.57
Advocacy Groups	16.90

All interactions are important. Those at the top of the list are intuitively obvious, whereas those at the bottom may be obscure and so deserving of comments.

Consider advocacy groups at the bottom of the list. Although advocacy groups and law enforcement may not need to interact on a day-to-day basis, they share a common and moral imperative: to do right by the patient. The advocacy group may have little opportunity to support a crisis center financial, for example, but law enforcement can capitalize on endorsements where a shared value and spirit of collaboration exist.

It's disappointing that the percentage of politicians, ranked tenth out of eleven, is as low as it is, given that local governmental leaders are instrumental in addressing diversionary needs. Politicians want to do right by their constituents, and they need to demonstrate their intent as well as their actions. A well-publicized program between law enforcement and local politicians sends a clear message. The financial, public safety, and moral imperatives will resonate with the community and increase the likelihood of support.

Interaction between law enforcement and mental health hospitals/agencies ranks ninth out of eleven. In many cases, the local emergency room is the intermediary between the police and the mental health hospital during an involuntary commitment. It's imperative that protocols be established between the emergency room and the police that center on protection. Appropriate questions include:

• What are the roles and responsibilities for emergency room personnel, hospital security personnel, and police?
• What arrangements must be made for equipment, restraints, and so forth?
• Should the emergency room be reconfigured for a secure room?

Ultimately, joint decisions must be made to protect emergency room personnel, other patients in the hospital, the police, and certainly the patient in crisis.

The emergency room is where the patient is given medical clearance before moving to an intake facility. However, the common interest is for de-escalation of an individual in crisis. A twenty-three-hour holding facility benefits law enforcement and the hospital emergency room. The patient is in the hands of competent personnel, specially trained to deal with patients in crisis, before moving to a mental health facility.

Although the emergency room response to someone in crisis is critical, remember that law enforcement can ameliorate or exacerbate the condition of the patient on delivery to a mental health facility. The two entities may be separate in the sequential flow of activities, the police must understand that how they handle a patient can influence outcomes.

Responses to the labor union entity, which ranks eighth out of eleven, are not surprising, given that the potential of labor unions is not widely recognized. A 2002 study by Columbia University cites the purpose of the report, in part, was "to describe the potential of unions as a connection to the workplace that is largely untapped and poorly understood by consumers and the mental health provider system."[10]

Law enforcement have opportunities for collaboration where the community has a concentration of unionized employees.

Partnering: Law Enforcement Officers and Crisis Workers

The concept extends from Boston, Massachusetts,[11] to Douglas County, Oregon,[12] where a police officer and a mental health professional together respond to those in crisis. The ride-along concept is making headway in Colorado with the help of the state. There, the Department of Human Services plans to distribute $16 million over the next three years to support ride-along and other diversionary practices. In January 2018 alone, the state planned to award $5.3 million, with as many as twelve police departments receiving the allocations.[13] The ride-along program presents the optimal collaboration at the front line.

A police officer and a mental health specialist work in concert to make diversion a reality, and the benefits extend beyond the obvious. At the point of contact with an individual in crisis, each one experiences what the other must do to de-escalate the patient. Each develops an appreciation of the contribution of the other. We recognize that the mental health and law enforcement communities have a strong informal network. The word spreads mouth-to-mouth by frontline individuals who, in this case, present a positive view of the other department. Police officers defend actions by the mental health system because they have observed the mental health specialist firsthand. Mental health professionals defend actions by the police because they have observed police firsthand.

The program has two limitations:

- *Geography*—Police or mental health departments covering a large geographical area usually are not ideal for a structured ride-along program. However, this does not preclude periodic ride-alongs, especially during periods of high-crisis activity. Such high-crisis periods may occur during the holidays, weekends, and so forth.
- *Population*—The population may serve either as a deterrent or incentive to ride-along programs. For example, in a large geographical area the population may be sparse and serve as a barrier to a ride-along program because the number of incidents is limited. On the other hand, a highly dense population may justify the use of resources for a ride-along program because the number of incidents is high.

The overriding criterion is the number of incidents the team encounters. The greater the number of encounters, the more likely a multidiscipline team approach is warranted.

Hubs

The hub concept originated in Scotland, was shaped in Canada, and is in operation in communities throughout southeast Pennsylvania. At its core, a hub group represents a collaboration of community leaders and organizations to address individuals at risk.

Various spinoffs of the basic hub concept work specifically with children at risk. A collaborative effort between the Norristown Area School District and the Norristown Police Department resulted in a children's hub modeled after the adult hub. According to Julie Knudsen, supervisor of pupil services for the Norristown Area School District, "The ultimate goal of the Children's HUB is keeping youth out of the juvenile justice system, so of course this created a natural partnership with the district and the police."[14]

Another example is a children's hub that serves the communities of Hartle-pool and Stockton, Ohio.[15] The children's hub is a partnership between:

- Hartlepool Borough Council
- Stockton-on-Tees Borough Council
- Cleveland Police
- North Tees and Hartlepool NHS Foundation Trust
- Tees, Esk, and Wear Valleys NHS Trust

Anyone can contact the children's hub with concerns about a child's welfare or safety.

It is our opinion that the hub concept capitalizes on the interests and resources of the community, is action-oriented, and is more likely to move children out of the criminal justice system and into an appropriate diversion, more so than any other diversionary program. In other words, it attacks the problem before children have any interaction with the criminal justice system (see chapter 10 for an in-depth review of a Hub model).

Youth Aid Panel

Dr. Beth Sanborn, the school resource officer for the Wissahickon School District in Pennsylvania, provided the details of the Youth Aid Panel (YAP) used in Montgomery County, Pennsylvania.

Growing in popularity, YAP offers an innovative approach to address juveniles at risk through the collaboration of the district attorney, the police, and the community.

In part, YAP serves as a diversion program because it steers juveniles out of jail and avoids exposure to factors that may contribute to mental illness during periods of incarceration. The goal of this program is to allow the juvenile to accept responsibility and be accountable for poor decisions. Through community service and guidance from invested community members, the juvenile can turn a negative choice into a positive outcome.

This program has been in existence since 2000. Prior to 2000, similar programs in jurisdictions within the county were overseen by the Montgomery County Mediation Center, but in 2000 the YAP fell under the responsibility of the Montgomery County district attorney's office.

The YAP measures outcomes through recidivism rate within a year of program completion. It tracks the number of referrals, the number of juveniles who successfully complete the requirements as well as the number who do not, therefore earning a referral back to the police department.

A juvenile must meet certain criteria to be eligible for a YAP referral. The crime committed must be a summary or low-level misdemeanor (and not traffic related), the juvenile must be under eighteen, must admit to their actions, and take responsibility for her involvement. Juveniles are ineligible if they have been arrested in the past. If the criteria are met, the police officer may use his discretion to refer the juvenile to the Youth Aid Panel. If restitution is due a victim, then paying restitution will be required for successful completion of the program. The juvenile also may be required to write the victim a letter of apology as part of the community service requirements.

An important factor in determining the appropriate community service is allowing panel members to learn about the juvenile's interest. Youth Aid Panel members want the juvenile to succeed. As an example, assigning a juvenile to work at a horse farm may set him up for failure if he has no interest in horses. Likewise, requiring a juvenile to volunteer at a hospital in an urban environment may be difficult without access to transportation. By learning the interests of the referred juvenile, local community service can involve an area of interest to him. For example, a juvenile who enjoys skateboarding/BMX cycling may pick up trash at the local skateboard park. A juvenile interested in hands-on labor may be paired up with a local mechanic or shop owner to see trade skills in action. Or a student may assist in an after-school homework club for younger children needing homework help or reading assistance.

At times, programs like these suffer from diminished attendance at meetings or a general sense of malaise. According to Dr. Sanborn, the experience with YAP is quite the opposite. Those truly invested in the success in their community remain involved. In Montgomery County, many panelists have been volunteering actively for ten to twelve years and show no signs of participation fatigue.

The interest in YAP extends beyond Montgomery County, and Sanborn cites numerous counties that have similar programs. They may be organized and run slightly differently, and housed under a different umbrella organization, but they have similar goals. Programs are in Philadelphia, Lehigh, Delaware, Chester, Berks, Lackawanna, Fayette, and Bucks County, Pennsylvania, and possibly more.

Law Enforcement Resiliency: Programs of Promise

Programs of promise have been started in at least three urban centers: New York City, Chicago, and the entire state of New Jersey. The foundation for resiliency among police and all emergency responders has been noted throughout the book. Positive attempts are taking place throughout the United States designed to reverse the tragic episodes of suicide and stress among all first responders, even as the majority of criminal justice leaders agree the trend continues to increase. For example, following the death of a third New York City police officer in June 2019, Police Commissioner James P. O'Neill said that, generally, police have a mental health crisis.

One programs has been implemented in New York City. Police Chief Monahan of the city police department hopes to increase services already in place for all officers of the department.[15]

Another program that works to assist the law enforcement community is the First Responders Wellness Center. According to Carrie Steiner, a clinical psychologist in Chicago and involved with the center, finds that police officers often state, "I'm the person that people go to when they're having issues, so how am I supposed to call somebody else for myself?"[16]

Generally, across the board, mental health advocates find that it is critical for police officers shed all sense of shame about mental illness within their profession. In one survey conducted by NBC New York, 78 percent of police officers across the country reported experiencing critical stress on the job, with 68 percent saying that stress triggered unresolved emotional issues. Another account generated by the U.S. Department of Justice in 2017 found that Chicago's officer suicide rate was 60 percent higher than the national law enforcement average.

The First Responders Wellness Center collected the numbers of police suicides during the past four years throughout the nation, showing a steady increase. The requirement to submit incidents to a central depository does not exist, and the numbers change periodically due to investigations that determine other crimes may have caused the untimely deaths. Still, these are the recent verified suicides to date: 2019—120; 2018—167; 2017—169; and 2016—142.

In New Jersey, following a series of suicides during the 1990s, a program was developed titled COP2COP. When the program was created, it was the first of its kind in the nation. The COP2COP program is a law whose purpose is suicide prevention, and it provides mental health support for law enforcement officers. Its impetus was the belief that all law enforcement professionals should have a confidential outlet where they could talk to peers who could understand and provide support without judgment and fear of losing their positions.

By 1998, the New Jersey Department of Personnel established a statewide law enforcement officer crisis intervention services hotline. Two years later, Rutgers University Behavioral Health Care (UBHC) was contracted to provide crisis intervention services to the law enforcement community. The result? The COP2COP program, which is supported by the Body Armor Replacement Fund.

This New Jersey law helped COP2COP become an essential program for law enforcement officers, averting more than 187 suicides in its ten-year existence. Though statistics have not been compiled nationally, most law enforcement experts believe the police suicide rate is higher than that of the general population, but because suicides among police officers often are reported as accidents or met with official silence, definitive numbers are hard to come by. The hotline is staffed by retired cops and cop clinicians who have a deep understanding of officers' concerns, problems, and family issues. COP2COP team members are trained in critical incident stress management (CISM) and respond to and conduct debriefings and defusing that result from a critical incident.

A new program, announced in July 2019 by the New Jersey attorney general, is designed to curb the rising number of police suicides by implementing a statewide program that teaches officers ways to better handle job stress.[17] Titled the New Jersey Resiliency Program for Law Enforcement, it requires that all New Jersey police officers complete a two-day training course on coping mechanisms by the end of 2022. The program calls for one member of every police department to implement the program and provide assistance to officers.

As others have indicated in New York City and Chicago, many officers fear that by telling others, their employment could be in jeopardy. By not talking to someone additional physical ailments, depression, and burnout multiply. According to the New Jersey attorney general, thirty-seven officers have died by suicide since 2016.[18]

CONCLUDING COMMENTS

Each example contains one or more characteristics. Some are new and show great promise; others have been around for a while and present processes and procedures outside the norm, but the effort itself shows remarkable sustainability. It falls to the leader to be the pioneer with efforts to improve diversion or reduce recidivism. The leader must be a responsible risk taker, recognizing that beyond the tangible commitments to the project is his own reputation. And although innovative programs may achieve increased diversion and reduced recidivism, the common denominator in all such efforts is collaboration. It does not fall to the criminal justice system alone to solve problems. Rather, it calls for collaboration among all interested parties, and, at times, it falls to local law enforcement to be the leader.

Chapter Ten

The Phoenixville EdHUB

A Community Approach for Children at Risk

Alan Fegley and Frank Mielke

INTRODUCTION

As a leader in the community, are you genuinely interested in diverting those with mental illness out of the criminal justice system and into treatment? If so, start with children at risk. Children who suffer from mental illness. Children, who because of environmental influences, may become incarcerated, and incarceration has consequences. For example, when juveniles are placed in isolation, it can severely exacerbate or even cause mental disorders that potentially affect them for the rest of their lives.[1]

In this chapter, we present the Phoenixville EdHUB that grew out of the confluence of three factors:

1. a proven model to intervene on behalf of those at risk
2. a proactive community
3. frustration

THE EDHUB: A RESPONSE TO A NEED

The data supporting the need to intervene in the interest of childhood mental wellness and divert youths into treatment are alarming:

- A study in the UK found that almost one in thirteen (8 percent) of young adults suffer from post-traumatic stress disorder (PTSD) following a childhood trauma.[2]

• According to the Centers for Disease Control and Prevention (CDC), "At least 1 in 7 children have experienced child abuse and/or neglect in the past year, and this is likely an underestimate."[3]

A CDC report published disturbing data indicating what is happening in our schools, with the potential of adversely impacting the mental wellness of a child. Results from a 2015 nationally representative sample of youths in grades nine through twelve show:

• 78 percent reported being in a physical fight on school property in the twelve months prior to the survey;
• 5.6 percent reported that they did not go to school on one or more days in the thirty days before the survey because they felt unsafe on their way to school;
• 4.1 percent reported carrying a weapon (gun, knife, or club) on school property on one or more days in the thirty days before the survey;
• 6 percent reported being threatened or injured with a weapon on school property one or more times in the twelve months prior to the survey; and
• 20.2 percent reported being bullied on school property, and 15.5 percent reported being bullied electronically during the twelve months before the survey.[4]

The CDC also identified four categories of risk factors:

• Individual Risk Factors (e.g., exposure to violence and conflict in the family)
• Family Risk Factors (e.g., parental substance abuse or criminality)
• Peer and Social Risk Factors (e.g., association with delinquent peers)
• Community Risk Factors (e.g., high concentration of poor residents)[5]

The full list of factors is included in addendum A.

Perhaps more powerful is local data developed from the EdHUB.[6] Table 10.1 displays the array of risk factors developed from the students and families discussed/serviced at the EdHUB meetings.

Poverty is the leading factor, but it serves as a root cause of other conditions such as homelessness, substance abuse, and various forms of violence.

This data is not just nice to know. We present it so that those in the community, including law enforcement, feel compelled to do something. It is our opinion that the EdHUB provides an effective approach to address children at risk and is a viable component of a community-based diversion strategy.

Table 10.1.

Risk Factors	Percent of Children
Basic needs/poverty	18.99
Substance use in family	11.17
Homelessness	9.50
Incarcerated loved one	8.94
History of trauma/victimization	8.38
Mental illness in family	7.26
Mental illness diagnosis	6.70
Truancy	6.15
Domestic violence	5.59
Intellectual or developmental disabilities	4.47
Criminal activity	4.47
History of abuse	3.91
Chronic illness/medical need	3.35
Runaway adolescent	0.56
Teen pregnancy	0.56
LGBTQ	0.00
Aging	0.00
Total	100.00

The EdHUB—Structure and Process

The Sequential Intercept Mode (SIM)[7] provides a framework for developing diversion strategies. The model identifies opportunities for diversion by identifying the interactions of various segments of the criminal justice system. For example, Intercept One identifies law enforcement and emergency services as the first opportunity to divert individuals in crisis from the criminal justice system and into treatment. Intercept Two and those that follow align with various interactions with the criminal justice system, namely:

- Intercept Two—Post Arrest: Initial detention and initial hearings
- Intercept Three—Post Initial Hearings: Jail courts, forensic evaluations, and forensic commitments
- Intercept Four—Reentry: Jails, prisons, and forensic hospitalization
- Intercept Five—Community: Corrections and community support

The SIM supports the evaluation of the interactions between the criminal justice system and other entities that influence diversion efforts. Linking the SIM to the diversion imperatives expands potential lines of inquiry. In other words, at each Intercept are processes supporting the imperatives for diversion that lead to key questions:

- Are systems operating at maximum financial efficiency?
- Are state-mandated regulations working properly?
- Are the public safety interests of the community protected?
- Are we in compliance with moral imperatives?

An opinion is emerging that intercepts prior to Intercept One, described as Intercept Zero, "align systems and services and connect individuals in need with treatment before a behavioral health crisis begins or at the earliest possible stage of system interaction."[8]

The EdHUB meets that alignment criteria.

To understand the EdHUB, we start with identifying interventions between a school district and its students. *Within* the school system normally are three levels of intervention:

1. Level One—Interaction between student and teacher
2. Level Two—Interaction between student and teacher/specialist (i.e., school psychologist, social worker, and so forth)
3. Level Three—Interaction between student and teacher/specialist/administrator

The EdHUB provides interventions beyond the capabilities of the educational system. This is not a failure of the system, but rather recognizes that the educational system cannot be all things to all students at all times.

The appropriate response is a community-based effort that we call the EdHUB. Figure 10.1 provides an overview of the EdHUB landscape and its component parts and influences.

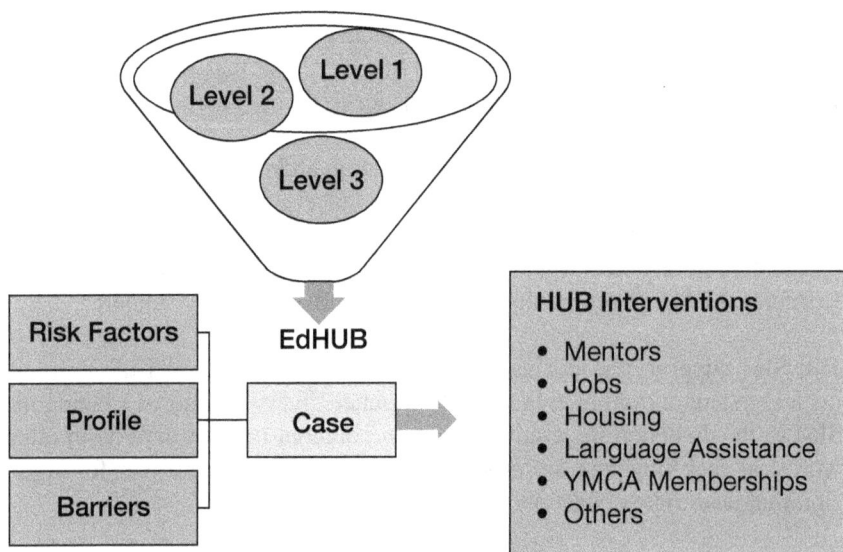

Figure 10.1.   The EdHUB Landscape

Interventions at any level may include parents, police, or outside social services and mental health agencies. The problem arises when the interventionist (school social worker, administrator), usually at level two or level three, exhausts all resources and options.

We believe that a viable approach to children at risk can be found in Phoenixville, Pennsylvania. Specifically, the Phoenixville Area School District (PASD) has a program called EdHUB, which is a modification of the hub concept used in communities in both the United States and Canada.

The PASD EdHUB is a resource when levels one through three have been exhausted. Each case represents a child or children in a family, at risk through a profile that identifies risk factors and barriers to an intervention. Representatives at the EdHUB facilitate or offer a range of resources to the child at risk.

As originally envisioned, a hub is a community-based group from an array of criminal justice, social services, and community-based organizations that embraces a preventive posture, addressing those with elevated risk to themselves or to the community.

The concept originated in Scotland, was developed in Canada, and is now being used in different parts of the United States, specifically in the neighboring community of Norristown, Pennsylvania. The hub originally was intended to address crime and primarily is driven by law enforcement.[9]

Dr. Chad Nilson from the University of Saskatchewan evaluated the hub in Prince Albert and offers this description:

> The hub is structured as a venue for human service professionals (hereafter referred to as discussants) from a variety of disciplines, to meet and collaborate on interventionist opportunities of addressing situations of acutely elevated risk.[10]

The hub seeks to:

- *reduce* crime rates;
- *reduce* the incidence of juvenile delinquencies and truancy; and
- *increase* diversion of those with mental illness out of the criminal justice system.

Drawing on the Norristown experience, Phoenixville established its own hub but with a unique twist: it addresses only at-risk students and is driven by the school district. To differentiate the Phoenixville program from the conventional hub model, we will use the term EdHUB (Ed referring to education).

To better understand the EdHUB, it is necessary to understand the Phoenixville community.

Located in suburban Philadelphia, the borough of Phoenixville is six square miles with a population of 16,658.[11] The white population is 81 percent, with a fairly even split between African Americans (8 percent) and Hispanics (7 percent).[12]

Beyond ethnicity, Phoenixville is diverse in many respects. A vibrant "main street" area has a growing number of restaurants that draw from the surrounding region. Immediately beyond that area are many row homes, moderately priced, which contributes to the feel of an urban setting. At the further reaches of the borough are expensive houses with a very suburban/rural feel.

To put the economic diversity of Phoenixville in perspective, as of June 17, 2019, eleven properties for sale were valued at more than $1 million each; at the same time, seven properties were for sale, each for less than $100,000.[13]

According to its website,[14] Phoenixville Borough was once the site of great iron and steel mills and manufacturing facilities. These mills all have closed, but in recent years the borough has undergone a renaissance. Events such as the Dogwood Festival, First Fridays, Blobfest, food festivals, and the farmer's market are popular throughout the area.

Phoenixville possesses a strong sense of community. It is home to a multitude of nonprofit social agencies, and at its core the Phoenixville Community Health Foundation provides both a forum and the funds to address a range of community issues.[15]

The Phoenixville Police Department is one of the few accredited police agencies in Chester County and one of three agencies within the geographic area of the PASD. The other two are in Schuylkill and East Pikeland Township.

The PASD enjoys a positive reputation in the community, the region, and the state. For example, 88 percent of its graduates pursue higher-level learning opportunities. In addition, the PSSA (Pennsylvania System of School Assessments) proficiency scores are materially higher than statewide averages.

Clearly, the Phoenixville Area School District is a high-performing district in a highly diverse community. In some respects, Phoenixville may be viewed as a microcosm of our society as a whole.

The program started in October 2016, and as of June 2019 the EdHUB group identified seventy-nine at-risk students, 53 percent male and 47 percent female. Addendum B contains a blank profile sheet used to introduce at-risk students to the EdHUB group. Addendum C shows the age profile of children introduced to the EdHUB.

Meetings are held every third week for ninety minutes (time limits are strictly enforced). Before their first meeting, participants sign a confidentiality agreement.

Case profiles are displayed on the screen (paper copy profiles are never shared with the group). The profile includes a brief problem description, applicable risk factors, and the identification of the initiating, lead, and support agencies. Each case is accepted or rejected for further action. Individual names are not included on the profile. Discussions may be taken off-line, when required, with appropriate parties. Such conversations may deal with sensitive issues, or where FERPA or HIPPA regulations may be compromised. The profile includes follow-up notes that may be addressed in subsequent meetings.

Attendees include representatives from the three local police departments and Chester County agencies, along with a cross-section of community organizations. In total, more than twenty-five nonprofit and for-profit agencies are part of the EdHUB.

An array of evidence supports the use of the EdHub concept in other districts, but casual conversation with some departments suggests a reluctance to engage in this process. Some cite a lack of need, perhaps that the school board or community would push back. We believe that this head-in-the-sand attitude reflects a need for self-protection, resulting in the failure to admit to problems. Unfortunately, drug and alcohol use, parental neglect, and school violence are pervasive in our society. What community can claim immunity from such issues? One police chief from a surrounding school district conveyed to us that the EdHub concept is a good idea, but it would never fly in his community because parents refuse to recognize the problems.

Expanding the EdHUB—HUB II

It's obvious that the EdHUB committee takes a great deal of personal satisfaction in cases where the community has contributed to meaningful intervention. However, the group is frustrated by regulation, bureaucracy, and some levels of indifference beyond the control of the committee.

As originally envisioned in Canada, a group aside from the Hub committee tackles the systemic deficiencies affecting the community. In Phoenixville, the EdHUB addresses individuals at risk. A separate group, called HUB II, addresses problems in the system.

In this book, we introduce the principle that data leads to collaboration, which, in turn, leads to innovation. With that in mind, Audubon Management Consultants conducted a survey in May 2019 of personnel in the PASD.

The survey measured, in part, the climate surrounding interaction between the educational system and other systems to address children at risk. The survey sought to measure partnership, confidence, and timeliness of service. It was administered to personnel at the Phoenixville Area School District. Survey results will help frame discussions with three critical systems: law enforcement, mental health, and social services.

Frank Mielke, Audubon Management Consultants, and school superintendent Dr. Alan Fegley served as project managers.

Survey participants responded to mostly declarative statements with both a positive and negative orientation, using a seven-point Likert scale (levels of agreement and disagreement).

The project followed strict confidentiality protocols:

• Confidentiality was assured in every communication.
• Only members of Audubon Management Consultants viewed individual responses.

The survey consisted of twenty-four core statements that draw on social science and management theories and research. The assessment is a product of more than twenty years of research based in large part on people-centered organization theory[16] developed by Dr. Miles Overholt. In addition, the survey team drew on the work of the American Institute of Chemical Engineers,[17] which identified a series of systemic or underlying problems that contributed to the outcomes of a series of catastrophic events.

District personnel were advised to communicate that participation was not mandatory, but to encourage participation in the interest of improving the response for students at risk. Participants were asked to identify a series of demographic factors including age, years of experience, and position.

The ability to analyze responses to the statements by demographic factor provides the opportunity to identify underlying systemic differences and the resulting influence on behaviors.

The process of analyzing data is driven by a series of scales, aggregate measures of responses around a common theme. The use of scales facilitates analysis and communication. The process provides the opportunity to dig down to individual statements and, if necessary, potential uniqueness by demographics.

The survey from 259 respondents framed the issue of alignment with three different providers of service, including the police, mental health, and social services systems. The EdHUB cannot solve the societal problems impacting our youth and depend upon these three entities for viable solutions.

The survey posed a series of declarative statements with seven response options ranging from very strongly agree to very strongly disagree. Three statements addressed each of the survey providers:

1. Our district works in partnership with <specific provider>
2. I have confidence in <specific provider>
3. I'm satisfied with the timeliness of service provided by <specific provider>

Table 10.2 provides the average weighted scores (ranging from a low of 1 to a high of 7) for partnership, confidence, and timeliness of service combined for each service provider.

Table 10.2.

Provider of Service	Average Weighted Score
Law enforcement (Police)	5.29
Mental health system (MH)	4.07
Local government social services providers (SS)	4.16

In general, scores in the mid-5 range and above are positive. Scores in the mid-4 to mid-5 range are satisfactory, and scores below the mid-4 range indicate problems.

Table 10.3 breaks down the detail by providing average weighted scores based on partnership, confidence, and timeliness of service measurements.

Table 10.3.

Measure	Police	MH	SS
Partnership	5.17	4.65	4.84
Confidence	5.52	3.92	3.88
Satisfaction with timeliness of service	5.17	3.57	3.69

It should not be surprising that the police score the highest among the three service providers. We believe several factors contribute to this result:

1. *Community Membership*—Both law enforcement and the school district reside in the same community. Often, the community name is present in both entities. The school district and the police department share common acquaintances, such as leaders in the community, businesses, and government. The police department readily supplies resources during high-profile events, including graduation and sporting events. It's clear that both the school district and the police department have a shared value that contributes to a strong sense of alignment.
2. *Joint Policies and Procedures*—Both the school district and the police department develop policies and procedures regarding school safety. Both entities conduct active-shooter exercises to help ensure the safety of students and school district personnel. In addition, the circumstances, roles, and responsibilities that require police assistance are defined.
3. *Police Visibility*—The police are often visible in the schools. Some superintendents make it a point to invite police officers to have lunch in the school cafeteria or make presentations on various subjects. Perhaps the most popular program involves school resource officers on-site at the school to be available when needed.

Although this intervention is popular and effective in many jurisdictions, care should be taken not to abuse the program. For example, the officer is not there to address bad behavior. The police can only intervene when the act or behavior qualifies for an arrest.

The mental health and social services systems are not provided like opportunities. Police respond when a threat is imminent, or danger exists. When mental health or social services entities are called into action, it should be with a sense of urgency, but their response does not rise to the level of immediacy associated with a police intervention.

It's certain that poor responsiveness scores (satisfaction with timeliness of service) contribute to poor scores for Partnership and Confidence.

TAKING THE NEXT STEPS

We propose a series of considerations and steps leading to the establishment of an EdHUB in your community. The considerations and steps are organized around a series of categories.

Contacts

The strengths of the EdHUB are contingent in large part around law enforcement contacts in the community. First and foremost is the nature of the relationship with school district personnel.

Being on a first-name basis with the superintendent and frequent interfaces demonstrates a solid foundation for moving forward. The superintendent should show a genuine interest in doing what's best for her students and be sufficiently inquisitive to learn about the EdHUB concept. Once that relationship is established and the agreement is to move forward, the law enforcement contact needs to gain the trust of other committee members.

Needs

Pursue documented evidence of the need for an EdHUB. Arrest records, incident reports, and similar types of data feed the law enforcement portion of the needs assessment. And solicit feedback from your frontline officers. They have a sense and feel of the community that should not be ignored.

School data rounds out the information that defines needs. Tardiness, absenteeism, and truancy may suggest the need for an intervention that an EdHUB can provide. Solicit input from school personnel who interface with parents, representatives of the criminal justice system, mental health, and social services agencies and others who may be involved with children at risk.

Organizations

Law enforcement, along with county mental health and social services organizations, are natural participants in an EdHUB. It's imperative to reach out to other organizations that have both an interest in and the capability to respond to children at risk.

Think about other organizations: YMCAs, for example. Reach out to all and, most important, allow those on the committee to keep reaching out to others. Developing an open door is important. You will be surprised who attends and who will provide the greatest amount of support.

Once established, several factors will be critical for success.

Leadership

Leadership is a critical feature of any organizational endeavor. Several characteristics distinguish the leader of an EdHUB. Because it is a community effort, the leader should enjoy the favor of the community. With the element of prestige, community leaders are more likely to attend meetings and offer advice and resources for children at risk. While being affable is a good quality, the process requires the leader to take control when time limits are exceeded or the participants continue to "beat a dead horse." Although it is not hard to imagine that this may be an unpopular decision, it is necessary. Such decisions are accepted when the leader commands the respect of those around the table.

The district superintendent happens to be the leader of the Phoenixville EdHUB. In other hubs, leaders come from law enforcement or social services agencies. More important than the leader's organization skills are the qualities presented above. Perhaps respect is most important.

Process

Dolores Winston (everyone calls her Dolly) is the community mobilizer for Phoenixville Communities That Care. She is a regular attendee at EdHUB meetings, and her contributions stem from her insights based on special relationships with many children in the community. On one occasion, she commented that she loves coming to these meetings (of the EdHUB) "because we get things done."

Things get done by design. The meeting starts promptly at 9 a.m. and ends at 10:30 a.m. sharp. Each year attendees sign a confidentiality agreement that extends to the end of the school year.

Cases are presented for consideration. A case is a response to one or more children at risk. A case may include siblings who, because of a family situation, are at risk. Contributing factors may include homelessness or the threat of homelessness.

Driving to the Root Cause

Teachers, counselors, and school psychologists mostly respond to signals suggesting deeper problems. Signals include truancy, fighting, and other antisocial behaviors. EdHUB committee members respond at two levels. First, consider the needs of the child at risk. After-school activities, mentors, and a variety of other options may or may not help. Committee members must address the second or root cause level. Often, the contributing factor resides in the household and the behaviors of parents or guardians.

Alcoholism, addiction, abuse, criminal activity, and neglect are among contributing factors. At times, the factors are less obvious. Consider the older adults (those in their seventies or eighties) serving as guardians to a sixteen-year-old. The committee recognized that a sixteen-year-old boy was at risk and addressed his needs. The committee also recognized the root cause and coordinated the development of a peer support group for the student's older guardians who, due to circumstances beyond their control, are raising children.

An EdHUB addresses the needs of children, but members must also pursue the underlying and root cause contributor(s) to the problem. It is at this level where the group can be highly frustrated.

Managing Frustration

Too often, EdHUB committee members are presented with children but are unable to provide viable solutions. In many cases, they are frustrated by the seeming inability of social services agencies to respond. Confronted with the challenges of dealing with children, the group operates against the background of alarming and depressing statistics. According to the Children's Society,[18] every year one hundred thousand children run away from home where they are at risk of serious harm, sexual exploitation, or physical abuse. As a result, they may resort to highly dangerous survival strategies such as stealing, begging, or staying with strangers.

Kristy McClure, who has more than twenty years' experience in the health and human services industry, identifies six challenges for the human services worker.[19]

At times, committee members see festering situations and turn to committee members from county departments charged with addressing children and

Table 10.4.

Factor	Comments
Low pay	Salaries are the most expensive budget item.
Compassion	Both apply especially when working in child welfare.
Fatigue/burnout/emotionally draining work	
Workloads	Staff numbers go down but work stays constant.
Scope of practice	The scope of practice is expanding to integrated care and whole health management. This shift requires a greater command of assessment and screening, interventions, best practices, and coordination of care with other providers.
Technology	The author views technological advancement as exciting, but like any advances, some are intimidated by a new way of doing things.
Well-informed patient or client	Some patients and their family members do research, believe they know what's best, and demand specific types of interventions.

families. Frustration was evident in the survey in which only 28.5 percent of respondents agree with the statement, "I have confidence in the social services system."

When these discussions arise, it's important to remember that the purpose of an EdHUB is to address the child at risk and deliver appropriate interventions. The EdHUB's charge is not to tackle system problems. To do so takes away from discussions where solutions are viable, causes frustration, and exceeds the intended scope of the committee.

Unfortunately, representatives from agencies that serve to protect children at risk often are the target of committee members' frustration. One county official said that her role is to listen, educate, and, at times, "bite my tongue." When listening, she can note situations where a child may be the victim of administrative failures. Although she cannot comment publicly on any of these situations, she has followed up with district personnel.

Committee member concerns revolve around regulations perceived not to be sufficiently responsive to children at risk. Changing regulations can be frustrating, time consuming, and clearly not within the scope of the EdHUB group. Recognize that many American regulatory agencies throughout the United States are underfunded and, as a result, lack sufficient manpower to meet demand.

Other frustrations arise. In some cases, parents appear to be unwilling or unable to take the necessary action to protect their children. David Ramsey, director of specialized programs and services, advises that attendees recognize the continuum of care process and theory of change. These popular concepts recognize that individuals at risk go through various levels of intensity of interventions and that the intervention should consider the individual's stage of change. These concepts also are applicable to parents and guardians. For example, parents and guardians, individuals critical to the welfare of the child, must first accept that a need is there, and that need may reflect the resistance to change from either the parent/guardian or child. Trying to force an intervention prematurely with a parent or guardian may result in total rejection of help.

Case Studies: Successes and Challenges

Not every case has a happy ending. The EdHUB group tried desperately to identify a motivator for one young lady. She indicated interest in being a hair stylist but rejected a part-time internship at a local beauty parlor. Community efforts to intervene with one boy were continually undermined by his alcoholic guardian, also his grandfather. One fourteen-year-old needed to be admitted to a mental health facility, but there wasn't one locally. Finally, she was transported three hundred miles away. The district was notified that she was released after a week to her parent. No other information was provided. The family moved immediately, and she has not been heard from since.

But there are good stories.

Too often, the group encounters children being raised by grandparents, so members took it on themselves to organize a "grandparent support group."

Frequently, the local YMCA offers free memberships to replace idle time with structured athletic activities and other programs. They were particularly helpful with a deaf family whose father had lost his job and faced the prospect of homelessness. The EdHUB assisted in finding housing, but in the meantime, the YMCA provided free use of its facilities—an effective diversion from pressures at home.

One young man, interested in pursuing a military career, frequently engaged in behaviors more serious than just mischievous. A local lawmaker made the offer of a scholarship to a local military school if he stayed out of trouble.

Failures are disappointing, and the unspoken words are palpable: "We failed." At times, systemic failures and the dark sides of our society seem insurmountable. But the quest to do right and respond to children at risk prevails. Successes are met with smiles, knocking on wood, and applause.

Propelled by the successes, coupled with a genuine interest in children, members of the Phoenixville Area School District EdHUB return every third week.

POTENTIAL IMPACT

A thorough vetting of the EdHUB concept goes beyond the scope of this book. Validating the EdHUB concept requires:

- comparisons with other school districts
- tracking individuals after graduation from high school
- more data and experience

These measures are yet to be completed. However, an abundance of positive anecdotal incidents and face-value validity justify the effort. We recognize that:

- the number of participants at EdHUB meetings has grown since its inception, and
- reports of success are met with applause and smiling faces.

CONCLUDING COMMENTS

We are constantly reminded by the medical community that early intervention is key to good health. Building on that advice, we recognize that if we attack the challenges of diversion at the earliest stage, we will increase the likelihood of success.

As a leader or potential leader in law enforcement in your community, you must make a decision: Do you believe in the EdHUB concept? Selling the concept to the local school superintendent might be the first challenge. It requires a careful consideration of the experience of schoolchildren using drugs or alcohol, and the level of school violence, truancy, and other outcomes recorded by the school district. It also requires careful consideration of the level, or the lack thereof, of positive parental influence.

Once the decision to move forward is made, it is necessary to engage community leaders who are instrumental to the process and recruit them, along with county officials from the behavioral health and social services departments. In this chapter, we provided the processes PASD uses, which can be modified immediately to fit the needs of the community.

If you are truly interested in diverting those with mental illness out of the criminal justice system and into treatment where appropriate, start early.

Addendum A

Risk Factors for the Perpetration of Youth Violence

Centers for Disease Control and Prevention

Research on youth violence has increased our understanding of factors that make some populations more vulnerable to victimization and perpetration. Risk factors increase the likelihood that a young person will become violent. However, risk factors are not direct causes of youth violence; instead, risk factors contribute to youth violence.

Research associates the following risk factors with perpetration of youth violence:

Individual Risk Factors

- History of violent victimization
- Attention deficits, hyperactivity, or learning disorders
- History of early aggressive behavior
- Involvement with drugs, alcohol, or tobacco
- Low IQ
- Poor behavioral control
- Deficits in social cognitive or information-processing abilities
- High emotional distress
- History of treatment for emotional problems
- Antisocial beliefs and attitudes
- Exposure to violence and conflict in the family

Family Risk Factors

- Authoritarian childrearing attitudes
- Harsh, lax, or inconsistent disciplinary practices
- Low parental involvement

- Low emotional attachment to parents or caregivers
- Low parental education and income
- Parental substance abuse or criminality
- Poor family functioning
- Poor monitoring and supervision of children

Peer and Social Risk Factors

- Association with delinquent peers
- Involvement in gangs
- Social rejection by peers
- Lack of involvement in conventional activities
- Poor academic performance
- Low commitment to school and school failure

Community Risk Factors

- Diminished economic opportunities
- High concentrations of poor residents
- High level of transiency
- High level of family disruption
- Low levels of community participation
- Socially disorganized neighborhoods

Addendum B

Case Profile Sheet

Case Number: Date:

Age: Gender:

Agency Initiating:

Risk Factors:

- ☐ Mental health diagnosis
- ☐ Chronic illness/medical need
- ☐ History of trauma/victimization
- ☐ Domestic violence
- ☐ LGBTQ
- ☐ History of abuse
- ☐ Substance use in family
- ☐ Mental illness in family
- ☐ Homelessness/transiency
- ☐ Incarcerated loved one
- ☐ Truancy
- ☐ Aging
- ☐ Basic needs/poverty
- ☐ Runaway adolescent
- ☐ Teen pregnancy
- ☐ Intellectual or developmental disability
- ☐ Criminal activity

Lead Agency:

Supporting Agencies:

Action:

Follow-up:

Addendum C

Distribution of At-Risk Students by Age

Table A.C.1.

Age	Percent Distribution
4	2.56
5	2.56
6	5.13
7	6.41
8	8.97
9	5.13
10	6.41
11	**10.26**
12	**15.38**
13	7.69
14	8.97
15	3.85
16	2.56
17	8.97
18	3.85
19	0.00
20	1.28
Total	100.00

Figure A.C.1 displays a graphic distribution by age. With more than 25 percent of this population, those age eleven to twelve are particularly vulnerable. There is another spike at age seventeen.

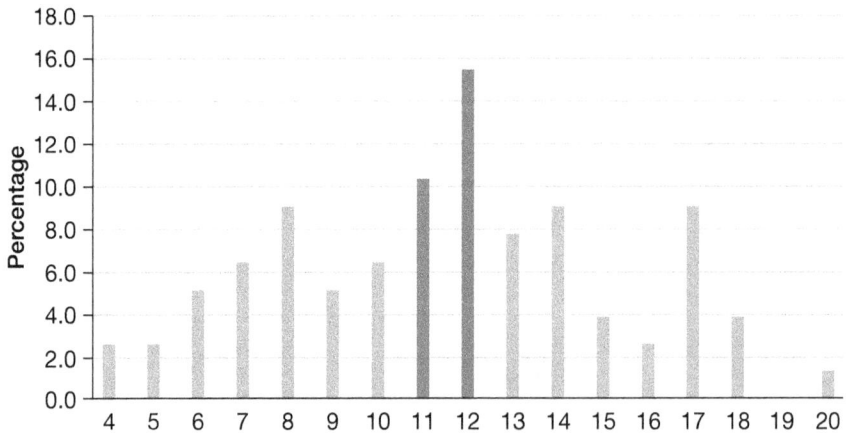

Figure A.C.1.

Addendum D

Assessing the Climate

Criminal Justice System and Mental Health System

Camden County	Montgomery County
Chester County	Philadelphia County

Frank Mielke
Audubon Management Consultants

Michelle Monzo
Montgomery County Emergency Service

William Mossman
East Coventry Police Department
May 15, 2019

CONTENTS

I. INTRODUCTION

A survey, titled Assessing the Climate, Diverting the Mentally Ill away from the Criminal Justice System and into Treatment, was conducted for select law enforcement agencies in Camden County, New Jersey; and Chester, Montgomery, and Philadelphia Counties, Pennsylvania.

The survey was conducted to support a book, being written by a larger team, titled *Changing Times: Transforming Culture and Behaviors for Law Enforcement.* The publisher is Rowman & Littlefield.

The survey team consisted of:

- Frank Mielke, Audubon Management Consultants (AMC)
- Michelle Monzo, Montgomery County Emergency Service (MCES)
- William Mossman, East Coventry Police Department and Audubon Management Consultants

Survey participants responded to mostly declarative statements with both a positive and negative orientation, using a seven-point Likert scale (levels of agreement and disagreement).

The project team followed strict confidentiality protocols:

- Confidentiality was assured in every communication.
- Only the project team viewed individual responses.

The survey consists of twenty-six core statements that draw on social science and management theories and research. The assessment is a product of more than twenty years of research based in large part on people-centered organization theory[1] developed by Dr. Miles Overholt. In addition, we draw on the work of the American Institute of Chemical Engineers,[2] which identified a series of systemic or underlying problems that contributed to the outcomes of a series of catastrophic events.

The police chiefs and department coordinators were advised to communicate that participation was not mandatory, but to encourage participation in the interest of improving the law enforcement/mental health climate. Participants also were asked to identify a series of demographic factors, including age, years of experience, and military experience.

The ability to analyze responses to the statements by demographic factor provides the opportunity to identify underlying systemic differences and the resulting influence on behaviors.

The process of analyzing data is driven by a series of scales, aggregate measures of responses around a common theme, as described in Section V: Scale Summary. The use of scales facilitates analysis and communication. The process provides the opportunity to dig down to individual statements and if necessary, potential uniqueness by demographics.

The 829 responses from this survey, coupled with data from other surveys, allows the team to do additional in-depth research. The result will be a series of white papers, with no references to specific departments, that will be in the public domain.

II. EXECUTIVE SUMMARY

This report contains the summary of responses from all participating departments in Camden County, New Jersey, and Chester, Montgomery, and Philadelphia Counties, Pennsylvania. This is a first in a series of reports; additional reports will follow, addressing specific issues. As a research project, it answers some questions and raises others. Some can be answered from the responses and others through cross-tabulation of response patterns by demographics, such as length of service, command staff versus line officers, military/combat experience, among others.

The survey was conducted to support a book, being written by a larger team, titled *Shifting Paradigms for Behavioral Health—Changing Law En-*

forcement Attitudes Culture and Behavior from a Reactive to a Proactive Approach. The publisher is Rowman & Littlefield.

Specific lines of inquiry are identified within the body of the report. To protect confidentiality, individual departments are not identified. Each participating department was advised individually of the findings for their department.

We provide findings in the executive summary around the following:

- mental health/law enforcement environment
- philosophy and crisis response
- training
- trauma
- culture and two-way communication

Mental Health/Law Enforcement Environment

The screaming headlines from the *Huffington Post* frames the environment: *Breaking Down the Silos—A Collaborative Answer to Mental Health.*[3] Some are loath to admit the problem to the extent that the term silo is stricken from verbal and written communication.

The silo mentality exists for those on the front line. The "least restrictive alternative" flies in the face of police practices regarding the use of restraints. Tension ensues that is counterproductive to diversion efforts. The consumer suffers.

Those with their heads in the sand (on the use of the term silos) need to understand law enforcement's perspective. Consider that only half of the respondents (51.6 percent) agree that law enforcement works in partnership with mental health providers. The larger problem revolves around the timeliness of services, where only 20 percent agree that they are satisfied.

The overall mental health landscape is complicated. The spheres of influence extend beyond just the responding crisis worker or police officer. Interested parties include an array of service providers and their funding sources; the health system, particularly emergency departments; the judicial system; private industry; and even the educational system. They all play a part and contribute to varying levels in the diversion effort.

Although the survey validated the obvious rift between law enforcement and the mental health system, the aggregated results mask a more detailed understanding of factors contributing to silos.

We gain greater insight, and possible segues to solutions, when we break down the results by parameter.

Philosophy and Crisis Response

An incident at a local hospital some years ago demonstrates the importance of a timely response to someone in crisis.

A 302 warrant (an order for an involuntary commitment) was issued for an individual. The responding police officers found the person barricaded. Rather than resort to force, they were able, with the help of his father, to coax him out into a peaceful resolution and deliver him to the emergency room for the required medical clearance. A successful resolution? Unfortunately, no. After several hours in a locked room at the hospital, waiting for placement in a mental health facility, the individual took matters into his own hands. He used the bed as a battering ram, destroying the security door and ripping out the overhead sprinklers, flooding the emergency room. The police had to return to quell the disturbance. The consequences: tens of thousands of dollars in damage, criminal charges, and very frustrated cops.

Some may cite the lack of beds at intake facilities as a cause, and they would be correct. Others may cite delegates, who are scarce given the demands. Still others may cite that the room contributed to the problem, or some combination thereof. Each of these observations contains some truth.

The situation was not resolved in a timely manner. The initial interaction by the police was peacefully resolved. The second interaction was violent and resulted in the individual's involvement in the criminal justice system.

A timely response to an individual in crisis is critical. It's hard to explain or reason with an individual in crisis. Uncertainty, and the presence of uniformed officers with guns, may exacerbate an already difficult situation.

Several years ago, a study found that the average wait time in the Phoenixville Hospital emergency room, for an individual in crisis, was almost seven and three-quarter hours.[4]

Scores for the timeliness of service, as registered by the respondents, were highly erratic and generally unsatisfactory. The statement was "I am satisfied with the timeliness of service provided by the mental health system." In response, the scores range from 1 to 7 matching options on a seven-point Likert scale, where the response options range from very highly agree to very highly disagree.

Consider the following scatter diagram in figure A.D.1 that shows scores by responding departments.

It's well known that Philadelphia has four Crisis Resource Centers and Montgomery County has Building 50, locations where the police can deliver those experiencing a mental illness crisis. The process in Chester County is

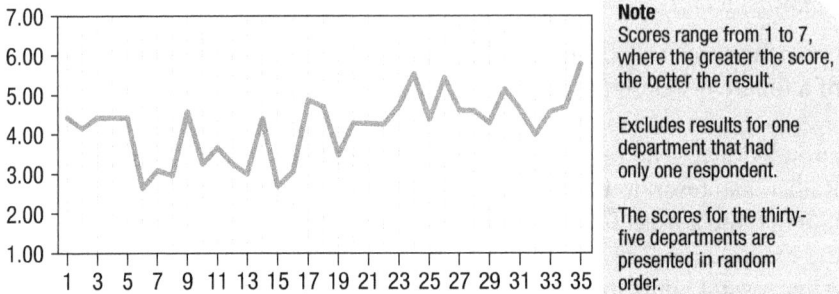

Figure A.D.1.

not as accommodating, much to the chagrin of Chester County police. For a variety of reasons, Chester County rejects the Montgomery County Emergency Service/Building 50 Model. It's not within the scope of this project to provide evidence of the efficacy of any model, but rather, profile the interactions of the police and the mental health system as a segue to collaboration and innovation as a path to diversion.

Chester and Montgomery County pursue different training strategies that may have differing levels of influence on culture and diversion.

Another dimension to crisis response occurs when a police officer is in crisis. The backdrop for this observation is the recognized higher rates of divorce, alcoholism, addiction, and suicide for law enforcement. Anecdotally, we believe that the critical incident stress management team (CISM) is more effective in Montgomery County, an observation that can be neither substantiated nor denied from the data in this survey.

Training

On the surface, training results appear positive. Respondents register satisfaction with training and confidence when intervening. However, a deeper analysis raises some questions. Examining results by specific disorder show weaknesses around autism and dementia. Further, scores for *understanding* specific disorders are lower than scores for *intervening* for those disorders. It raises a question: Can you intervene effectively without a commensurate understanding of the disorder?

The subject of training also raises questions about the influence of training on collaboration. Respondents identified their training credentials as either CIS (Montgomery County training model), CIT (Chester County training module), or Mental Health First Aid used in both counties.

Further analysis will determine whether there are correlations between training modules and measures of collaboration. That analysis will appear under separate cover.

Trauma

The trauma profiles, developed from self-measures as opposed to clinical definitions, show the exposure to one or more life-altering situations hovering just below 20 percent. When asked if management was supportive in the face of trauma, some 70 percent agree. Is this high enough? And are management attitudes sufficient to dispel the notion, as reported by 15 percent of responders, that they should handle trauma without the help of others? The 15 percent comprise a very vulnerable group.

An analysis of one of the larger participating departments in the survey demonstrates the obvious: the trauma profile becomes more severe as a police officer progresses through his career.

Additional analysis will explore the possible connections surrounding the vulnerable group including training, management attitudes, and demographic factors, such as length of experience and combat experience.

Anecdotally, we believe the relationship between law enforcement and the criminal justice system is stronger in Montgomery than Chester County. Again anecdotally, we believe the CISM team is more influential in Montgomery than Chester County.

On a related note, our project team, in conjunction with a private-sector strategic partner, currently is developing a "trauma-sensitive culture" model to assist dispelling the cultural notions of this vulnerable group.

We will communicate to all interested parties the results of this effort.

Culture and Two-Way Communication

A significant factor contributing to silos, which impede meaningful collaboration in the interest of diversion, is culture. Mental health thinks one way, whereas law enforcement see things differently. Breaking these and other barriers promotes horizontal alignment. Another dimension is vertical or internal alignment. Organizations that are aligned vertically think and behave in a consistent manner. Leaders strive for internal alignment through processes, procedures, and training. But it's not enough. Vertical alignment around attitudes and behaviors requires a new way of thinking about a new and emerging culture. Organizations must change.

A key statement in the survey tests the organizations' readiness for change. That statement and the results are listed in table A.D.2.

Table A.D.2.

| | Percent Responses | | | |
Statement	Agree	Uncertain	Disagree	Do Not Know
Members feel comfortable disagreeing with supervisor in circumstances other than a crisis.	46.8	21.7	26.9	4.6

The statement was structured to eliminate "red zone" situations where danger is imminent, requiring critical, often split-second decisions. Rather, the statement is intended for those situations where discussions, either formal or informal, address practices and policies. Healthy organizations create an environment of open, candid discussions where it's permissible to disagree. Leaders take such comments of disagreement as opportunities to explain. Often, the disagreement stems from a lack of complete understanding.

On the other hand, leaders are not always right, and open conversations provide the insights of those who must carry out the intended policy or procedure.

Two-way communication is one pillar of a *trauma-sensitive culture* and a skill learned from an effective training program.

Future Analysis (as identified in the body of the report)

We anticipate a series of follow-up analyses that will:

- Evaluate the three *major training options*—CIS, CIT, and Mental Health First Aid—to determine their impact, if any, on improving relations between the criminal justice and mental health systems.
- Compare the *results by county*, specifically Montgomery and Chester, because we have a sufficient number of participating departments in each county. This will enable us to compare the impact of their respective strategies regarding mental health.
- Explore various aspects of those at different levels of *trauma*. Specifically, is there an impact, and if so, what is the effect on the factors that contribute to diversion? In addition, is there an impact based on the organizational response to those experiencing trauma?
- Analyze *leadership effectiveness* by segmenting the group between those who develop strategy, essentially lieutenants and those of higher rank, and the remaining population, who execute strategy.
- Examine more closely how the leadership in this survey *interface with external organizations*.
- Leverage the insights gained from this survey and develop additional strategic partners to secure the resources necessary to continue the research.

We hope this report encourages more discussion on the subject of diversion. You may disagree with our assumptions or interpretation of the data, but the data is indisputable and represents the feedback of 829 men and women who operate in the real world. We are grateful to each and every one who participated.

III. PARTICIPATION

Thirty-six departments participated in the survey. The number of eligible participants in these departments was 1,291, and 829 responded for an overall participation rate of 64.2 percent. The number far exceeded expectations, especially because the survey was conducted during the holiday period November 2018 to January 2019.

A larger team currently is writing a book about diverting the mentally ill from the criminal justice system and into treatment where appropriate. Publication deadline was a significant and compelling reason for the timing of the survey.

Figure A.D.2 lays out participation rates for each of the thirty-six departments. To protect confidentiality, departments are identified by number only.

Exhibit 1

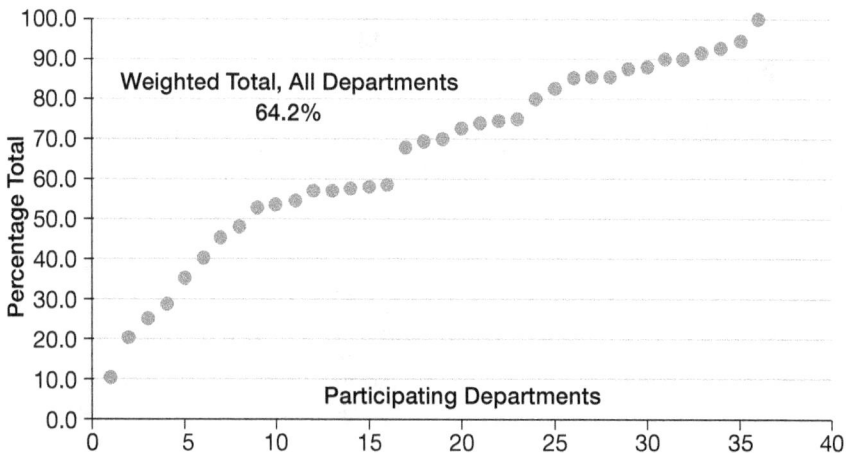

Figure A.D.2.

Addendum D

We attribute the success of the effort to two factors. First, those soliciting participation are highly regarded. Clearly, police chiefs responded to the requests of Michelle Monzo and Chief Bill Mossman based on their prominence in their respective counties. The second factor is the level of importance that participants attach to mental health issues.

Table A.D.3 shows the distribution by county.

Table A.D.3.

County	Number of Departments	Number of Participants	Percent Total, All Responses
Camden	1	54	6.52
Chester	16	200	24.03
Montgomery	18	381	46.01
Philadelphia	1	194	23.43
Total All Responses	**36**	**829**	**100.00**

Note:

The representation of Camden and Philadelphia Counties is limited to one department each. Comparing Chester and Montgomery Counties is potentially more revealing because they approach mental illness with remarkably different strategies.

FUTURE ANALYSIS

Compare scale scores, Chester versus Montgomery Counties, to explore the impact of strategy on the interface between the mental health and law enforcement systems.

IV. DEMOGRAPHIC PROFILE

The survey captures a series of demographic indicators that facilitate analysis that, at times, shows nuances not readily apparent to the casual observer.

In most organizations, varying attitudes and behaviors are associated with the demographic factors included in this survey. We reject the notion that any particular population is inherently bad or good. Rather, we recognize that diversity brings added perspective. It falls to the enlightened leader to maximize the strengths and to develop a strategy of accommodation where benefits accrue to both the individual and the organization. Further, the enlightened leader does not succumb to prejudices based on ignorance but approaches each individual as an individual.

The data from this profile facilitates cross-tabulation of survey findings by each of the demographic factors.

Following are a series of tables by demographic factor. Comments are included where the results are deemed noteworthy.

Age Profile

Table A.D.4.

Age	Number	Percent Total
18–21	5	0.66
22–25	44	5.82
26–30	144	19.05
31–35	133	17.59
36–40	110	14.55
41–50	214	28.31
51–60	93	12.30
Over 60	13	1.72
Total All Responses	**756**	**100.00**

Note:

This population is clearly "mature" where the percentage of those over the age of forty is 42.33 percent. Traditionally, we observe differences in responses to survey statements by age. Younger employees often are better educated and bring new values and behaviors to their organization. Older employees tend to cling to attitudes and behaviors reminiscent of "back in the day." This tension between the generations is not exclusive to law enforcement. For example, we all recognize this tension within our own families either from current (as a parent) or prior experiences (as a son or daughter).

The distribution leads to an examination of the Years of Experience profile.

Years of Experience Profile

Table A.D.5.

Years/Experience	Number	Percent Total
Less than 1	20	2.65
1–3	87	11.51
4–5	90	11.90
6–10	141	18.65
11–15	111	14.68
16–21	125	16.53
More than 22	182	24.07
Total All Responses	**756**	**100.00**

Note:

The distribution by Years of Experience mirrors the distribution by Age. The distribution of those with sixteen years or more of experience is just over 40 percent.

Anecdotal evidence indicates that attitudes change as police officers progress through their careers. Resistance to change remains where police officers, like most people, tend to cling to the way things were.

Because of their longevity on the job, we would expect a higher level of exposure to trauma and all of the associated consequences for this experienced group. This is a key consideration when we measure trauma.

FUTURE ANALYSIS

Break down and analyze the population at various increments based on years of service.

Job Profile

Table A.D.6.

Job	Number	Percent Total
Patrol/Corporal	498	67.39
Sergeant	103	13.94
Detective	64	8.66
Lieutenant	36	4.87
Captain	10	1.35
Chief/Superintendent	28	3.79
Total All Responses	**739**	**100.00**

Note:

The distribution of patrol officers, corporals, sergeants, and detectives is 90 percent versus 10 percent for lieutenants and those of higher rank. We make this distinction because the lieutenants and those of higher rank develop and enforce policies and procedures, whereas the remaining group executes policies and procedures. Usually the two populations have different response patterns, an area to be explored as a follow-up report.

FUTURE ANALYSIS

Develop measures of responses by those who develop and those who execute strategies.

Military Experience

Table A.D.7.

Military Experience	Number	Percent Total
None	617	82.05
Active Reserve	23	3.06
Discharged	112	14.89
Total All Responses	**752**	**100.00**

Combat Experience

Table A.D.8.

Combat Experience	Number	Percent Total
No	155	83.78
Yes	30	16.22
Total All Responses	**185**	**83.78**

Note:

Military and combat experience provide additional perspective on the trauma landscape. This data allows us to develop new insights into the consequences of trauma, including addiction, alcoholism, and suicide.

The analysis of Trauma is addressed in section XIV.

Training

Table A.D.9.

Training	Number of Times Selected	Percent Total
Crisis Intervention Specialist (CIS)	336	43.19
Crisis Intervention Training (CIT)	71	9.13
Mental Health First Aid (MHFA)	235	30.21
Adverse Childhood Experiences (ACEs)	34	4.37
Other	102	13.11
Total All Responses	**778**	**100.00**

Note:

The profile by county varies significantly. CIS has long been used in Montgomery County and is largely county funded; whereas Chester County has used CIT, through a grant, in in the past few years.

FUTURE ANALYSIS

Break down the population by training type to determine the impact on knowledge and comfort when dealing with mentally ill, and further, whether it has any impact on improving relations between the criminal justice and mental health systems.

V. SCALE SUMMARY

Scales are aggregate measures of results around a common theme. Six scales are included in this report, as indicated in table A.D.10.

Scales facilitate communication of survey results and serve as a segue to deeper analysis. You can drill down to individual questions that comprise the scale, then drill down further to the demographics.

Table A.D.10.

Scale	Total All Responses
Alignment	5.07
Leadership	5.23
Communication	5.20
External Alignment	4.73
Competencies—Interactions	4.97
Training	5.15

The data is compiled so that scores range from 1 to 7. Scores in the 5 to 7 range are viewed as generally positive and scores from 1 to 3 are viewed as problematic or potentially problematic. Scores in the 4 to 5 range from the marginal to the generally satisfactory.

The scoring follows response options that range from "Very strongly agree" to "Very strongly disagree" on a seven-point scale.

Leadership is the highest scoring scale; scores for External Alignment are marginal.

The following series of tables break down each scale by the weighted average by component statements that comprise the scale. Additional data includes:

- Highest reported average by a department
- Lowest reported average by a department
- Non-weighted average of the reporting departments
- Standard deviation

VI. ALIGNMENT

Organizational alignment is key to organizational efficiency and effectiveness. Law enforcement agencies are effective when patrol officers through senior leadership are all on the same page, all making decisions consistently and behaving in accordance with goals and objectives.

In an aligned organization, people know what to do and why they are doing it.

Signs of nonalignment include surprises and expressions of "I'm not sure why we are doing things this way."

Police departments, pursuing strategies of diversion and improving the overall process of dealing with the mentally ill, frequently find themselves going through a change of culture.

Alignment is particularly important for these organizations.

Table A.D.11.

Statement	Average
12. The behavior of the leadership team is consistent with my department's philosophy as I understand it.	5.07
14. I'm *aware* of our department's mental health policies.	5.23
15. I *agree* with our department's mental health policies.	5.20
16. Mental health policies in our department *influence my behavior*.	4.73
17. The philosophy reflected in mental health emergencies is consistent with my personal philosophy.	4.97
18. I feel comfortable that my department supports my decisions regarding mental health issues.	5.15
Total	**5.06**

Range of Averages by Statement

Table A.D.12.

Statement	Low	High	Average	Standard Deviation
12.	3.75	6.33	5.21	0.53
14.	4.13	5.77	5.32	0.38
15.	4.33	5.88	5.28	0.33
16.	3.71	5.75	4.79	0.41
17.	4.10	5.82	5.06	0.43
18.	4.00	6.00	5.27	0.45

Statements 14 (awareness), 15 (agreement), and 16 (influence behaviors) are key indicators of alignment. Normally, scores deteriorate going from statement 14 to statement 15 and to statement 16.

Perhaps the most important statement is 16, which reflects policy influence on behavior. The insights from this statement can be gleaned from a variety of influences such as Leadership, Communication, and Training, among others.

Overall alignment scores fall into the acceptable range except for Statement 16, which reflects policy influence on behavior. The gap between the high and low averages is material, suggesting a fairly wide response to this statement by department.

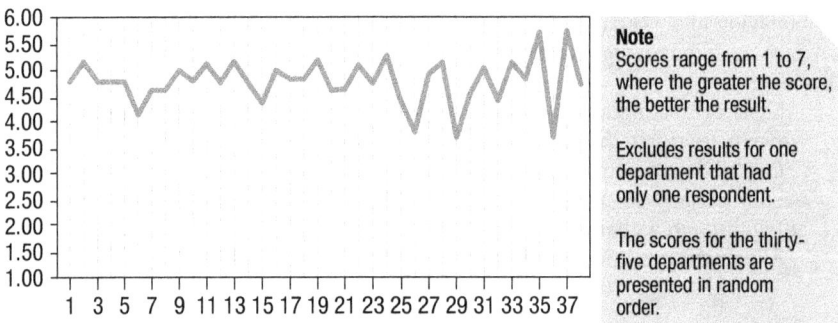

Note
Scores range from 1 to 7, where the greater the score, the better the result.

Excludes results for one department that had only one respondent.

The scores for the thirty-five departments are presented in random order.

Figure A.D.3.

Exhibit 2

Figure A.D.3 shows a general level of stability by participating police departments for departments 1 through 23, but is somewhat erratic for remaining departments. We will include the results of this statement as we analyze the potential influences such as training and others.

VII. LEADERSHIP

Management researchers and practitioners concur that the key to organizational effectiveness lies with its leaders.

Clearly, it's incumbent upon leadership to establish the mission and vision, and the supporting strategies, as well as to provide the necessary resources. But the key to the execution of strategy lies with those who interface directly with patrol officers, such as sergeants, in turn supported by those of higher rank, such as lieutenants and other command staff members.

This narrow focus on leadership factors is limited to two, albeit important components:

- "Supervisor has the information"
- Respondents "get the information"

Table A.D.13.

Statement	Average
9. My immediate supervisor has the information and knowledge I need to do my job.	5.46
10. I get the information I need to do my job from my supervisor.	5.14
Total	**5.30**

It is our experience that scores for Statement 9, "supervisor has the information," are consistently higher than those contained in Statement 10, where respondents "get the information" from the supervisor.

Table A.D.14.

Statement	Low	High	Average	Standard Deviation
9.	4.11	6.25	5.23	0.46
10.	3.00	6.00	4.98	0.70

The low–high gap for statement number 10 is significant, with a corresponding high standard deviation.

A logical link between Leadership and Communication is addressed in the next scale.

VIII. COMMUNICATION

Communication is the lifeblood of the organization. Ineffective communication systems impede living the mission and achieving the vision.

This scale addresses a series of obvious communication factors. Where communication deficiencies exist, the organization should examine other potential contributing factors, such as leadership qualities, length of service, and diversity, among others.

The communication scale serves as a segue to more detailed analysis.

Table A.D.15.

Statement	Average
11. I get the information I need to do my job from my peers and others within the department.	5.15
13. Members feel comfortable disagreeing with supervisor in circumstances other than a crisis.	4.25
Total	**4.70**

Table A.16.

Statement	Low	High	Average	Standard Deviation
11.	4.25	6.33	5.19	0.41
13.	3.71	5.33	4.50	0.36

The results from Statement 13 are consistent with virtually every organization we assess: namely, the ability, or inability, for individuals to disagree with supervisors.

For organizations going through cultural change, such as those associated with attitudes and behaviors regarding the mentally ill, it's important that members of the organization be given the opportunity to disagree. Often, the level of disagreement is based on lack of understanding of the strategy. Therefore, leaders should see these types of discussions as opportunities to clarify, reinforce, and promote, rather than as a personal affront.

This ability to disagree, reflected in statement 13, often characterized as Two-Way Communication, was cited by the American Institute of Chemical Engineers in its research on high-profile catastrophes such as Bhopal, Chernobyl, the Space Shuttle *Challenger*, among others.

In the case of the *Challenger* disaster, an engineer had voiced his concern to launch under certain atmospheric conditions. His comments were ignored, and a disaster of catastrophic proportions followed.

IX. EXTERNAL ALIGNMENT

Intuitively, we recognize that law enforcement alone cannot always effectively address an individual in crisis. Frequently, the situation requires support from a mental health specialist.

The following series of statements addresses how well law enforcement works with others who participate in an intervention with an individual in crisis. The level of cooperation at the point of contact significantly impacts the outcome; namely, does the individual go to jail or go to treatment?

Table A.D.17.

Statement	Average
6. I know whom I can contact to ensure that a detained individual will receive appropriate attention.	5.19
7. We work in partnership with mental health providers.	4.98
8. I have confidence in the mental health system as it relates to policing.	4.31
19. I'm satisfied with the timeliness of service provided by the mental health system.	4.19
Total	**4.67**

Table A.D.18.

Statement	Low	High	Average	Standard Deviation
6.	4.11	6.25	5.23	0.46
7.	3.00	6.00	4.98	0.70
8.	3.08	5.50	4.23	0.62
19.	2.63	5.75	4.14	0.81

The data supports the anecdotal evidence of the silos that exist between the mental health system and law enforcement. The timeliness of service is a frequent complaint, demonstrated in the data where the average for Statement 19, addressing timeliness, is the lowest in this scale.

The differences between low and high scores are particularly pronounced, and the standard deviations are somewhat higher than normal. Standard deviations, in particular, suggest a level of disparity that may be attributable to the differences that exist between Montgomery and Chester Counties.

We know that these counties have remarkably different philosophies regarding crisis intervention and the manner in which involuntary commitments (302s) are handled.

Under separate cover, we will provide a detailed comparison of the results for the two counties.

X. COMPETENCIES—INTERACTIONS

This scale measures a series of attitudes and behaviors surrounding the interaction between a law enforcement officer and someone in crisis. These measures serve as a natural segue to the issues of Training (section 11) and connects to Competencies by Type of Disorder (section 12).

Table A.D.19.

Statement	Average
2. I am comfortable that I can identify someone in crisis resulting from a mental health episode.	5.56
3. I can differentiate behaviors emanating from a mental versus a nonmental health episode.	5.26
4. I can adjust my response, depending on whether I'm dealing with a mental health or nonmental health issue.	5.61
5. I feel comfortable that I can influence the appropriate intervention when no danger is present, an arrest is not warranted, and mental health is an issue.	5.36
Total	**5.45**

Table A.D.20.

Statement	Low	High	Average	Standard Deviation
2.	5.00	6.08	5.56	0.26
3.	4.25	5.75	5.29	0.29
4.	5.20	6.09	5.64	0.24
5.	5.00	6.08	5.56	0.26

Overall scores are well within acceptable limits. The ability to differentiate behaviors emanating from a mental versus a nonmental health episode as seen in Statement 3 is the lowest.

Opportunities exist for improvement in understanding, recognizing, and intervening with specific disorders, covered in section XII.

Results of this scale, influenced by training, are covered in the following section.

XI. TRAINING

This scale measures training adequacy and application. One would expect consistency of scores. In other words, adequacy of training scores (Statement #1) would approximate comfort with intervention scores (Statement #5). However, care should be taken to recognize the potential influences of experience and common sense. In other words, an opinion may be that experience enables one to influence the appropriate intervention but "I always need more training."

Table A.D.21.

Statement	Average
1. I feel that I have been adequately trained in mental health issues.	5.11
5. I feel comfortable that I can influence the appropriate intervention when no danger is present, an arrest is not warranted, and mental health is an issue.	5.36
Total	**5.24**

Table A.D.22.

Statement	Low	High	Average	Standard Deviation
1.	4.00	5.91	5.11	0.44
5.	4.75	6.00	5.33	0.34

Like scores in section X (Competencies—Interactions), results are generally positive. It's interesting to note that training, specifically in Montgomery County, is provided by Montgomery County, while Chester County relies on grants, and until recently, funds from county commissioners. This raises a question: Is training a mechanism with the potential to bring both the mental health system and law enforcement together to reduce the silos?

In a study under separate cover, the influence of the three major training offerings will be analyzed to determine their effect on the alignment scores. The three major training offerings are Crisis Intervention Training (Memphis model), Crisis Intervention Specialists (Montgomery County Emergency Service model), and Mental Health First Aid.

XII. COMPETENCIES BY TYPE

Measuring competencies by disorder provides insights for developing mental health training for law enforcement officers. Clearly, different ways are needed to handle different disorders. For example, the individual who is depressed needs a hug, but don't treat someone who is autistic that way.

These statements raise three critical questions:

1. Do you *understand* the disorder?
2. Can you *recognize* the order?
3. Can you *intervene* in an appropriate manner?

Table A.D.23.

Disorder	Understand	Recognize	Intervene
A. Autism Spectrum Disorders	4.40	5.39	5.30
B. Bipolar Disease	4.60	5.19	5.27
C. Dementia	4.54	5.57	5.38
D. Intellectual Disabilities	4.61	5.35	5.24
E. Schizophrenia	4.56	5.24	5.24
F. Traumatic Brain Injuries	5.08	5.05	5.18

Overall, recognition and intervention scores are within acceptable ranges, but the data shows some slippage when it comes to understanding. However, the data does raise some questions.

For every disorder, the understanding scores are remarkably lower than the intervention scores. That given, can we expect an effective intervention without corresponding understanding of the disorder?

Table A.D.24 shows the difference between Understanding and Intervening with each disorder.

Table A.D.24.

Disorder	Understand	Intervene	Intervene—Understand
A. Autism Spectrum Disorders	4.40	5.30	.90
B. Bipolar Disease	4.60	5.27	.67
C. Dementia	4.54	5.38	.84
D. Intellectual Disabilities	4.61	5.24	.63
E. Schizophrenia	4.56	5.24	.68
F. Traumatic Brain Injuries	5.08	5.18	.10

The gap between intervening and understanding is particularly pronounced for the autism spectrum disorders and dementia. One may assume that these disorders are not particularly susceptible, but not exclusively, to a crisis requiring police intervention.

The unanswered question is, should training focus on some of these disorders?

XIII. EXTERNAL ALIGNMENT INTERFACES

This section continues the discussion of external alignment by characterizing the interfaces by frequency, and as either positive or negative.

We recognize that establishing strategic relationships mostly falls to the senior members of the department. This is an area for further exploration.

Table A.D.25 represents a view of the interactions between the police and various external entities.

Table A.D.25.

	Percent of Total, All Responses			
External Organization	*Infrequent*	*Frequent*		
External Entity	*No Need, Never, Infrequent*	*Negative*	*Varies*	*Positive*
Advocacy Groups	49.00	7.88	24.17	18.96
Business Community	21.99	1.68	35.96	40.36
Educational System	17.38	5.06	38.78	38.78
Faith-Based Organizations	41.72	4.30	24.77	29.20
Funders	61.43	4.29	22.60	11.69
General Public	18.55	2.33	47.21	31.91
Health System	18.76	6.47	51.49	23.29
Judicial System	10.91	3.90	52.34	32.86
Labor Unions	54.63	6.65	26.34	12.39
Mental Health Hospitals/Agencies	28.55	7.88	44.06	19.51
Politicians	50.26	6.88	31.43	11.43

Interactions will vary by position within the police department. For example, patrol officers and detectives are more likely to encounter the general public in their day-to-day activities than is the leadership within their department. Likewise, department leadership is more likely to interface with advocacy groups and politicians addressing more strategic issues.

Selection of labor unions as an external entity may require some clarification. A study by Columbia University[5] show the potential of engaging labor unions in mental health issues. Leaders in law enforcement and unions have a link: a union member, in crisis, needing help.

Because the nature of the interaction will vary between tactical and strategic issues, a more reasonable profile is to dissect the responses by job function. Therefore, we will show the level of interaction, patrol officers, sergeants, and detectives versus lieutenants and those of higher rank.

FUTURE ANALYSIS

Break down and analyze leadership interactions with external entities.

This issue will be pursued in a separate report.

XIV. TRAUMA

A growing body of evidence, supplemented by observations, suggests that stress and trauma are contributors to behaviors not aligned with organizational strategies and goals. For example, law enforcement incurs higher incidents of divorce, alcoholism, addiction, and suicide.

This problem cannot be ignored.

Dealing with an individual in crisis requires a sense of wellness by the interventionist.

The source of the stress and trauma goes beyond the workplace and includes past experiences, as well as the stress and trauma of dealing with everyday life. Unfortunately, individuals cannot forget such influences when they arrive on the job.

As a risk-intervention strategy, leaders must be in a position to identify and respond to those experiencing both stress and trauma. Dealing with such individuals is challenging. It requires the ability to identify when such factors may contribute to undesirable behaviors and then approach the individual in a very careful, caring manner.

Further, sergeants and above *must* know when any sort of intervention exceeds their capability, requiring the help of a professional.

The survey relies on self-described levels of trauma rather than any type of clinical evaluation. That type of evaluation goes well beyond the bounds of this survey.

Table A.D.26.

Trauma Experience	Number	Percent of Total, All Responses
No experience	30	3.82
Few experiences, non-traumatic	88	11.21
Many experiences, mostly non-traumatic	154	19.62
Few experiences, some traumatic	179	22.80
Many experiences, many traumatic	180	22.93
At least one life-altering experience	70	8.92
Many life-altering experiences	84	10.70
Total	**785**	**100.00**

Based on the analysis of individual departments, we know that the trauma profile varies by department. One department was pleased that its trauma profile was more favorable when compared to the total population. However, and we pointed this out, the impact of trauma is cumulative. In other words, the police officer with ten years of experience is likely to have a higher trauma profile than the police officer with two years of experience, all other things being equal.

This department recognized that its length of service profile was skewed toward newer employees and to expect its trauma profile to deteriorate.

In a follow-up report, we will analyze the trauma issue in detail. From available data, we will seek to validate our assumption that the trauma profile increases by length of service. We will also see whether an impact of trauma on other factors would support diversion. And finally, we will explore, in depth, responses to the next two statements.

Table A.D.27.

Statement	Average
21. Management is supportive when employees in our organization experience trauma.	5.03
22. Employees in our organization believe we should handle trauma we experience without the help of others (score logic reversed).	4.73

Table A.D.28.

Statement	Low	High	Average	Standard Deviation
21.	3.44	7.00[1]	5.28	0.66
22.	4.00	6.00	4.92	0.41

1. This is a perfect score from one small department, raising the question of departmental influence based on the size of the department. This will be considered in subsequent analysis.

The generally accepted average of 5.03 for Statement 21 is masked by the dispersion of responses. Note the significant difference between the low and high scores and a high standard deviation.

Figure A.D.4 demonstrates the erratic responses.

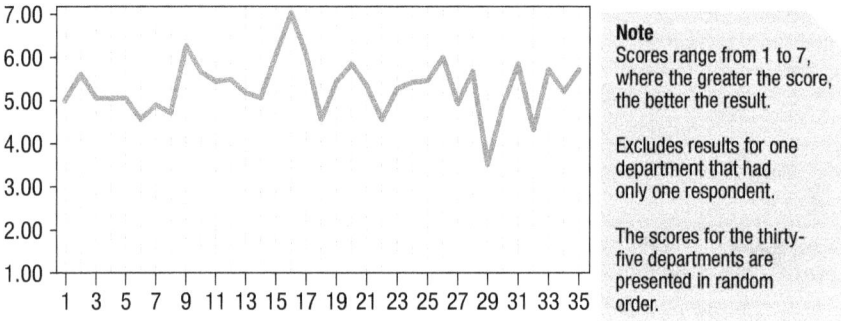

Note
Scores range from 1 to 7, where the greater the score, the better the result.

Excludes results for one department that had only one respondent.

The scores for the thirty-five departments are presented in random order.

Figure A.D.4.

Exhibit 3

We believe that a positive response to Statement 21 is critical for organizations with a high exposure to trauma, such as law enforcement. The positive response demonstrates the commitment of leadership to those who are exposed to traumatic events.

The scores are in contrast to statement 22, which has a significantly tighter standard deviation, indicating a prevailing belief that individuals should handle trauma by themselves.

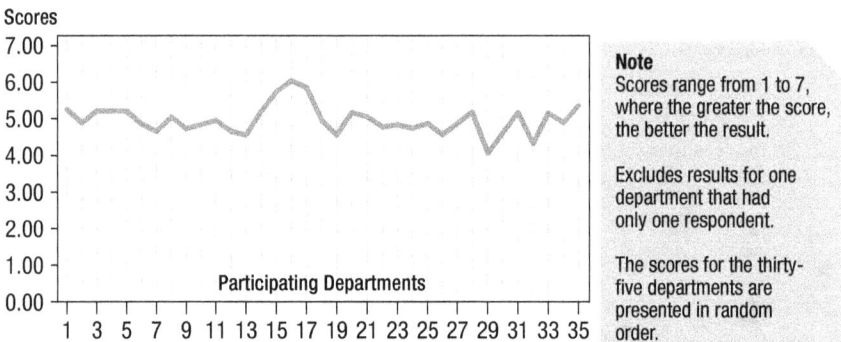

Note
Scores range from 1 to 7, where the greater the score, the better the result.

Excludes results for one department that had only one respondent.

The scores for the thirty-five departments are presented in random order.

Figure A.D.5.

The lack of volatility in figure A.D.5 demonstrates pervasiveness of police attitudes when dealing with their own crisis.

Statement 22 demonstrates individual beliefs about how trauma should be handled. Experts in crisis response and suicide prevention, along with enlightened leaders in law enforcement, believe that individuals experiencing problems due to exposure to traumatic events, shiftwork, and other disruptive occurrences should *not* try to handle these issues themselves.

The AMC/MCES partnership is exploring the development of a model, *trauma-sensitive culture*, that will help organizations navigate this challenging issue.

Notes

CHAPTER 1. RESPONSE TO A NEED

1. http://www.apa.org/helpcenter/data-behavioral-health.aspx.

2. http://mentalhealthandillness.com/systemstheory.html.

3. TriData Division, System Planning Corporation, *Mass Shootings at Virginia Tech Addendum to the Report of the Review Panel*, November 2009, 28.

4. Health Insurance Portability and Accountability Act, passed by Congress in 1996; a privacy act that protects individual's medical information.

5. https://www.nami.org/About-NAMI/NAMI-News/Understanding-What-HIPAA-Means-for-Mental-Illness.

6. https://www.nami.org/About-NAMI/NAMI-News/Understanding-What-HIPAA-Means-for-Mental-Illness.

7. CBC News, Montreal http://www.cbc.ca/news/canada/montreal/story/2013/01/31/montreal-police-mental-health-interventions.html.

8. https://www.integration.samhsa.gov/workforce/mental_disorders_and_medical_comorbidity.pdf.

9. Community hospitals are defined as all nonfederal, short-term general, and other special hospitals. Other special hospitals include obstetrics and gynecology; eye, ear, nose, and throat; rehabilitation; orthopedic; and other individually described specialty services. Community hospitals include academic medical centers or other teaching hospitals if they are nonfederal short-term hospitals. Excluded are hospitals not accessible by the general public, such as prison hospitals or college infirmaries.

10. Washington State Hospital Association Inpatient Mental Health: Community Hospitals in Crises.

11. Washington State Hospital Association Inpatient Mental Health: Community Hospitals in Crises.

12. Frank Mielke, Dr. Louis Becceria, and William Mossman, "Making a Difference—A Community Approach to Mental Illness," research paper, July 2013, 8.

13. http://www.c-span.org/History/Events/Experts-Testify-on-State-of-the-US-Mental-Health-System/10737437542/.

14. https://www.nami.org/Learn-More/Public-Policy/Jailing-People-with-Mental-Illness.

15. Substance Abuse and Mental Health Services Administration, Criminal and Juvenile Justice. Updated September 15, 2017.

16. https://newsone.com/2744141/prisons-mental-health-providers/.

17. https://www.nami.org/Learn-More/Public-Policy/Jailing-People-with-Mental-Illness.

18. Dr. Denise Malone, *Mental Health and Recidivism: A Comparison of the FY2009, FY2010, and FY2011 SR Release Cohorts*, Virginia Department of Corrections, Statistical Analysis & Forecast Unit, September 2015.

19. 106th Congress, 1st Session, 145 Cong Rec S 8295, vol. 145, no. 97.

20. David Hernandez and Richard Winton, "Fatal Shooting of Black Man by El Cajon Police Sparks Outrage, Protests." *Los Angeles Times*, September 28, 2016.

21. David A. Grahan, "The Murder of Miosotis Familia," *Atlantic*, July 5, 2017.

22. National Coalition for the Homeless, Mental Illness and Homelessness, July 2009.

23. Brian Stettin, Jeffrey Geller, Kristina Ragosta, Kathryn Cohen, and Jennay Ghowral, "Mental Health Commitment Laws A Survey of the States," Treatment Advocacy Center, February 2014.

24. Michael Rellahan, *Daily Local*, August 28, 2013.

25. Frank Mielke and William Mossman, "Making a Difference—Mental Health Crisis Processing, Police and Emergency Room Intervention." Research paper sponsored by the Chester County District Attorney's Office and the Phoenixville Community Health Foundation.

26. Maria Konnikova, "Is There a Link Between Mental Health and Gun Violence?" *New Yorker*, November 19, 2014.

27. Richard Friedman, "Violence and Mental Illness—How Strong is the Link?" *The New England Journal of Medicine*, 355 (2006): 2064–66.

28. Matt Shipman, "Study Shows Mentally Ill More Likely to Be Victims, Not Perpetrators, of Violence," *NC State News*, February 25, 2014.

29. gov/ https://www.samhsa disorders/co-occurring.

30. Daniel Yohanna MD, "Deinstitutionalization of People with Mental Illness: Causes and Consequences," *AMA Journal of Ethics®*, October 2013.

31. Miles Overholt, *Building Flexible Organizations: A People-Centered Approach* (Dubuque, Iowa: Kendall/Hunt, 1996).

32. Dr. Richard B. Jones, *Risk-Based Management: A Reliability-Centered Approach* (Houston, TX: Gulf Publishing, 1995).

CHAPTER 2. FRAMING THE ENVIRONMENT, UNDERSTANDING BEHAVIORAL HEALTH CRISES

1. T. Salvatore, *A Crisis Diversion Intercept Model: A Tool for Promoting Prevention and Recovery* (Norristown, PA: Montgomery County Emergency Service, 2012).

2. K. W. McDermott et al., "Trends in Hospital Inpatient Stays in the United States, 2005–2014" (Rockville, MD: Agency for Healthcare Research and Quality, June 2017).

3. H. Steadman et al., "Prevalence of Serious Mental Illness among Jail Inmates," *Psychiatric Services*, 60 (2009): 761, 764.

4. W. Anthony, "Recovery from Mental Illness: The Guiding Vision of the Mental Health Service System in the 1990s," *Psychosocial Rehabilitation Journal* 16, no. 4 (1993): 11–23.

5. S. Mead and D. Hilton, "Crisis and Connection," www.mentalhealthpeers.com/ (accessed March 27, 2012).

6. M. Copeland, *Action Planning for Prevention and Recovery*, Consumer Information Series, 10, HHS Pub. No.SMA-3720 (Rockville, MD: Substance Abuse and Mental Health Services Administration, 2002).

7. K. Kanel, *A Guide to Crisis Intervention*, 4th ed. (Belmont, CA: Thomson Brooks, Cole, 2012).

8. H. Parad, "Crisis Intervention," 196–202, in R. Morris, ed., *Encyclopedia of Social Work*, 16th ed. (New York: National Association of Social Work, 1971).

9. Technical Assistance Collaborative, Inc. (Boston, MA: Community-Based Comprehensive Crisis Response Service, 2005).

10. R. James, *Crisis Intervention Strategies* (Belmont, CA: Thomson Brooks, Cole, 2008).

11. G. Caplan, *Principles of Preventative Psychiatry* (New York: Basic Books, 1964).

12. G. Caplan and R. Caplan, "The Future of Primary Prevention," *Journal of Primary Prevention* (2000): 31–136.

13. S. Merson, P. Tyrer, S. Onyett, S. Lack, P. Birkett, S. Lynch, and T. Johnson, "Early Intervention in Psychiatric Emergencies: A Controlled Clinical Trial," *Lancet* (1992): 311–14.

14. G. Everly, "Five Principles of Crisis Intervention: Reducing the Risk of Premature Crisis Intervention," *International Journal of Emergency Mental Health* 2, no. 1 (2000): 1–4.

15. *Center for Mental Health Services Practice Guidelines: Core Elements for Responding to Mental Health Crises*, HHS Pub. No. SMA-09-4427 (Rockville, MD: Substance Abuse and Mental Health Services Administration, 2009).

16. B. Baldwin, "A Paradigm for the Classification of Emotional Crises: Implications for Crisis Intervention," *American Journal of Orthopsychiatry* 48, no. 3 (1978): 538–51.

17. A. Rosen, "Crisis Management in the Community," *Medical Journal of Australia*, 167 (1997): 633–38.

18. M. Allen, P. Forster, J. Zealberg, and G. Currier, *Report and Recommendations Regarding Psychiatric Emergency and Crisis Services* (Arlington, VA: American Psychiatric Association, 2002).

19. J. Ruiz and C. Miller, "An Exploratory Study of Pennsylvania Police Officers' Perceptions of Dangerousness and Their Ability to Manage Persons with Mental Illness," *Police Quarterly* 7, no. 3 (2004): 359–71.

20. J. Ball, P. Links, C. Strike, and K. Boydell, "It's Overwhelming . . . Everything Seems to Be Too Much": A Theory of Crisis for Individuals with Severe Persistent Mental Illness," *Psychiatric Rehabilitation Journal* 29, no. 1 (2005): 10–17.

21. M. Munetz and P. Griffin, "Use of the Sequential Intercept Model as an Approach to Decriminalization of People with Serious Mental Illness," *Psychiatric Services* 57, no. 4 (2006): 544–49.

22. M. Copeland, *Wellness Recovery Action Plan* (Brattleboro, VT: Peachtree Press, 1997).

23. Crisis Card: easy-to-read list of resources, carried by responders for distribution to those in need.

24. P. Solomon, "Peer Support/Peer Provided Services Underlying Processes, Benefits, and Critical Ingredients," *Psychiatric Rehabilitation Journal* 27, no. 4 (2004): 392–401.

25. L. Ashcroft, *Peer Services in a Crisis Setting: The Living Room* (Phoenix, AZ: Meta Services, 2006).

26. L. Ostrow and D. Fisher, *Peer-Run Crisis Respites* (Washington, DC: National Coalition for Mental Health Recovery, 2011).

27. S. Guo, D. Biegel, J. Johnsen, and H. Dyches, "Assessing the Impact of Community-Based Mobile Crisis Services on Preventing Hospitalization," *Psychiatric Services* 52, no. 2 (2001): 223–28.

28. M. Gould, L. Kalafat, J. Munfakh, and M. Kleinman, "An Evaluation of Crisis Hotline Outcomes Part 2: Suicidal Callers," *Suicide and Life-Threatening Behavior*, 37 (2007): 338–52.

29. R. Glick, J. Berlin, A. Fishkind, and S. Zeller, *Emergency Psychiatry: Principles and Practice* (Philadelphia: Lippincott Williams & Wilkins, 2008).

30. M. Boes and V. McDermott, "Crisis Intervention in the Emergency Room," 543–68, in A. Roberts, ed., *Crisis Intervention Handbook: Assessment, Treatment, and Research*, 3rd ed. (New York: Oxford University Press, 2005).

31. H. Steadman, K. Stainbrook, P. Griffin, J. Draine, R. Dupont, and C. Horey, "A Specialized Crisis Response Site as a Core Element of Police-Based Diversion Programs," *Psychiatric Services* 52, no. 2 (2001): 219–22.

32. V. Aldige and W. Wales, "Civil Commitment and Arrest," *Current Opinion in Psychiatry* 16, no. 50 (2003): 575–80.

33. Literally, a parent of the nation.

34. *Crisis Services: Effectiveness, Cost-Effectiveness, and Funding Strategies*, HHS Publication No. (SMA)-14-4848 (Rockville, MD: Substance Abuse and Mental Health Services Administration, 2014).

35. L. Joplin, *Mapping the Criminal Justice System to Connect Justice-Involved Individuals with Treatment and Health Care Under the Affordable Care Act* (Washington, DC: National Institute of Corrections, U.S. Department of Justice, 2014).

CHAPTER 3. DIVERTING SPECIAL NEEDS PERSONS FROM INAPPROPRIATE INCARCERATION

1. John Snook, "America's Crime Problems Being Fed by a Broken Mental Health System," 2019, https://www.american-in-justice.com/americas-crime-problems-being-fed-by-a-broken-mental-health-system/.

2. Mike Maciag, "The Daily Crisis Cops Aren't Trained to Handle," *Governing*, 55 (May 2016), http://www.governing.com/topics/public-justicesafety/gov-mental -health-crisis-training-police.html [http://perma.cc/Z6XM-FBFB].

3. Linda Chafetz, Harold Goldman, and Carl Taube, "Deinstitutionalization in the United States," *International Journal of Mental Health* 11, no. 4 (Winter 1982): 48–63.

4. L. L. Anderson, K. C. Lakin, T. W. Mangan, and R. W. Prouty, "State Institutions: Thirty Years of Depopulation and Closure," *Mental Retardation* 36, no. 6 (December 1998): 431–43.

5. Richard Lamb, and Leona Bachrach, "Some Perspectives on Deinstitutionalization," *Psychiatric Services* 52, no. 4 (August 2001): 1039–45. https://doi .org/10.1176/appi.ps.52.8.1039.

6. *Mental Health, United States, 2010*, HHS Publication No. (SMA) 12-4681 (Rockville, MD: Substance Abuse and Mental Health Services Administration, 2012).

7. T. Lutterman, A. Berhane, B. Phelan, R. Shaw, and V. Rana, *Funding and Characteristics of State Mental Health Agencies*, HHS Pub. No. (SMA) 094424 (Rockville, MD: Center for Mental Health Services, Substance Abuse and Mental Health Services Administration, 2009).

8. Daniel Yohanna, "Deinstitutionalization of People with Mental Illness: Causes and Consequences," *American Medical Association Journal of Ethics* 15, no. 10 (October 2013): 886–89.

9. Ashley Primeau, Thomas Bowers, Marisa Harrison, and Xu Xu, "Deinstitutionalization of the Mentally Ill: Evidence of Transinstitutionalization from Psychiatric Hospitals to Penal Institutions," *Comprehensive Psychology* 2, no. 2 (2013): 1–10, https://doi.org/10.1377/hlthaff.28.3.676.

10. Eric Wright, William Gronfein, and Timothy Owens, "Deinstitutionalization, Social Rejection, and Self-image of Former Mental Patients," *Journal of Health and Social Behavior*, 4 (March 2000): 68–90.

11. A. Loch, "Discharged from a Mental Health Admission Ward: Is It Safe to Go Home? A Review on the Negative Outcomes of Psychiatric Hospitalization," *Psychology Research and Behavior Management*, 7 (2014): 137–45.

12. H. Lamb and D. Shaner, "When There Are Almost No State Hospital Beds Left," *Hospital and Community Psychiatry* 44, no. 10 (1993): 973–76.

13. Lamb and Shaner, "When There Are Almost No State Hospital Beds Left."

14. C. Mowbray, K. Grazier, and M. Holder, "Managed Behavioral Health Care in the Public Sector: Will It Become the Third Shame of the States?" *Psychiatric Services* 53, no. 2, (2002): 157–70.

15. E. Fuller Torrey, *Out of the Shadows: Confronting America's Mental Illness Crisis* (New York: John Wiley & Sons, 1997).

16. K. Heslin and A. Weiss, *Hospital Readmissions Involving Psychiatric Disorders, 2012*, HCUP Statistical Brief #189 (Rockville, MD: Agency for Healthcare Research and Quality, 2015).

17. Doris Fuller, Elizabeth Sinclair, and John Snook, *Released, Relapsed, Rehospitalized: Length of Stay and Readmission Rates in State Hospitals* (Arlington, VA: Treatment Advocacy Center, 2016), https://www.treatmentadvocacycenter.org/stor age/documents/released-relapsed-rehospitalized.pdf.

18. Ellen Hochstedler Steury, "Specifying Criminalization of the Mentally Disordered Misdemeanant," *Journal of Criminal Law & Criminology* 82, no. 2 (1991): 334–59.

19. Risdon Slate, Jacqueline Buffington-Vellum, and W. Wesley Johnson, *The Criminalization of Mental Illness: Crisis and Opportunity for the Criminal Justice System*, 2nd ed. (Durham, NC: Carolina Academic Press, 2013).

20. Milton Mack, *Decriminalization of Mental Illness: Fixing a Broken System*, Conference of State Court Administrators, 2016-17 Policy Paper, 2016, https://cosca.ncsc.org/~/media/Microsites/Files/COSCA/Policy%20Papers/2016-2017-Decriminalization-of-Mental-Illness-Fixing-a-Broken-System.ashx.

21. R. Slovenko, "The Transinstitutionalization of the Mentally Ill," *Ohio Northern University Law Review* 29, no. 3 (2003): 641–60.

22. Steven Raphael and Michael Stoll, "Assessing the Contribution of the Deinstitutionalization of the Mentally Ill to Growth in the U.S. Incarceration Rate," *Journal of Legal Studies* 42, no. 1 (2013): 187–222.

23. K. Reiter and T. Blair, "Punishing Mental Illness: Trans-institutionalization and Solitary Confinement in the United States," 177–96, in K. Reiter and A. Koenig, eds., *Extreme Punishment: Palgrave Studies in Prisons and Penology* (London: Palgrave Macmillan, 2015).

24. Domenic Sisti, Andrea Segal, and Emanuel Esekiel, "Improving Long-Term Psychiatric Care: Bring Back the Asylum," *Journal of the American Medical Association* 313, no. 3 (2015): 243–44.

25. Sisti, Segal, and Eskiel, "Improving Long-Term Psychiatric Care."

26. Mark Pogrebin and Eric Poole, "Deinstitutionalization and Increased Arrest Rates among the Mentally Disordered," *Journal of Psychiatry and Law* 15, no. 1 (1987): 117–27.

27. Interdepartmental Serious Mental Illness Coordinating Committee. *The Way Forward: Federal Action for a System That Works for All People Living with SMI and SED and Their Families and Caregivers* (Rockville, MD: Substance Abuse and Mental Health Services Administration, 2017).

28. *Mentally Ill Offenders in the Criminal Justice System: An Analysis and Prescription* (Washington, DC: The Sentencing Project, 2002).

29. H. Steadman, F. Osher, P. Robbins, B. Case, and S. Samuels, "Prevalence of Serious Mental Illness among Jail Inmates," *Psychiatric Services*, 60 (2009): 761–65.

30. Michael McGill, "What Is Psychosis?" *Medical News Today*, 2017, https://www.medicalnewstoday.com/articles/248159.ph.

31. McGill, "What Is Psychosis?"

32. Paul Appelbaum, Pamela Robbins, and John Monahan, "Violence and Delusions: Data from the MacArthur Violence Risk Assessment Study," *American Journal of Psychiatry*, 157 (2000): 566–72.

33. A. Lurigio and D. Lewis, *Toward a Taxonomy of Criminal Mental Patients* (Evanston, IL: Center for Urban Affairs and Policy Research, Northwestern University, 1987).

34. J. Merrick, E. Merrick, Y. Lunsky, and I. Kandel, "Suicidal Behavior in Persons with Intellectual Disability," *Scientific World Journal*, 5 (2005): 729–35.

35. *The Diagnostic and Statistical Manual of Mental Disorders*, 5th ed. (Washington, DC: American Psychiatric Association, 2013).

36. R. Schalock, S. Borthwick-Duffy, V. Bradley, W. Buntinx, D. Coulter, E. Craig, S. Gomez, Y. Lachapelle, R. Luckasson, et al., *Intellectual Disability: Definition, Classification, and Systems of Support*, 11th ed. (Washington, DC: American Association of Intellectual and Developmental Disabilities, 2010).

37. S. Horowitz, B. Kerker, P. Owens, and E. Zigler, *The Health Status of Individuals with Mental Retardation* (New Haven, CT: Department of Epidemiology and Public Health, Yale University School of Medicine, 2000).

38. J. Jones, "Persons with Intellectual Disabilities in the Criminal Justice System: Review of Issues," *International Journal of Offender Therapy and Comparative Criminology* 51, no. 6 (2007): 723–33.

39. Leigh Ann Davis, "People with Intellectual Disability in the Criminal Justice System: Victims and Suspects," The Arc, 2009, https://www.thearc.org/sslpage.aspx?pid=2458.

40. *Suspects with Developmental Disabilities and the Criminal Justice System: The Developmentally Disabled Offenders Program* (Livingston, NJ: Arc of New Jersey, n.d.).

41. *Suspects with Developmental Disabilities.*

42. L. Douglas and M. Cuskelly, "A Focus Group Study of Police Officers' Recognition of Individuals with Intellectual Disability," *Psychiatry, Psychology and Law* 19, no. 1 (2012): 35–44.

43. Arc of the United States, "10 Facts Law Enforcement Needs to Know When Serving and Protecting People with Intellectually and Developmental Disabilities," 2015, https://www.thearc.org/file/documents_initiatives_nccjd/NCCJDTipSheet_LE-FINAL.pdf.

44. Arthur Bowker, "Handle with Care: Dealing with Offenders Who Are Mentally Retarded," *FBI Law Enforcement Bulletin* (July 1994): 12–16.

45. *Suspects with Developmental Disabilities.*

46. National Institute of Mental Health, "Autism Spectrum Disorder," https://www.nimh.nih.gov/health/topics/autism-spectrum-disorders-asd/index.shtml.

47. Centers for Disease Control and Prevention, "Autism Spectrum Disorder: Data and Statistics," 2015, http://www.cdc.gov/ncbddd/autism/data.html.

48. L. Spencer, C. Lyketsos, E. Samstad, A. Dokey, D. Rostov, and M. Chisolm, "A Suicidal Adult in Crisis: An Unexpected Diagnosis of Autism Spectrum Disorder," *American Journal of Psychiatry* 168, no. 9 (2011): 890–92.

49. *Diagnostic and Statistical Manual of Mental Disorders: DSM-5* (Washington, DC: American Psychiatric Association, 2013).

50. E. Rydén and S. Bejerot, "Autism Spectrum Disorder in an Adult Psychiatric Population. A Naturalistic Cross-Sectional Controlled Study," *Clinical Neuropsychiatry* 5, no. 1 (2008): 13–21.

51. Dennis Debbaudt and Darla Rothman, "Contact with Individuals with Autism: Effective Resolutions," *FBI Law Enforcement Bulletin* (April 2001): 20–24.

52. M. Raja, A. Azzoni, and A. Frustaci, "Autism Spectrum Disorders and Suicidality," *Clinical Practice and Epidemiology in Mental Health* 30, no. 7 (2011): 97–105.

53. E. Müller, A. Schuler, and G. Yates, "Social Challenges and Supports from the Perspective of Individuals with Asperger Syndrome and Other Autism Spectrum Disabilities," *Autism: International Journal of Research and Practice* 12, no. 2 (2008): 173–90.

54. Dennis Debbaudt, "Autism Spectrum and Law Enforcement Training," Organization for Autism Research, 2006, https://researchautism.org/autism-spectrum-and-law-enforcement-training/.

55. Debbaudt and Rothman, "Contact with Individuals with Autism."

56. Debbaudt, "Autism Spectrum and Law Enforcement Training."

57. Debbaudt and Rothman, "Contact with Individuals with Autism."

58. Diane Fast and Julianne Conry, "The Challenge of Fetal Alcohol Syndrome in the Criminal Justice System," *Addiction Biology* 9, no. 2 (2006): 164–65.

59. Jerrod Brown, Anthony Long-McGie Wartnik, Pamela Oberoi, Janina Wresh, et al., "Fetal Alcohol Spectrum Disorders in the Criminal Justice System: A Review," *Journal of Law Enforcement* 3, no. 6 (2014), https://jghcs.info/index.php/l/article/view/309.

60. Jerrod Brown, "FASD: A Guide for Mental Health Professionals," *Counseling Today*, 2017, https://ct.counseling.org/2017/07/fasd-guide-mental-health-professionals/.

61. Brown, "FASD: A Guide for Mental Health Professionals."

62. Erin Watts and Jerrod Brown, "Interrogative Suggestibility in People with Fetal Alcohol Syndrome Disorder," *Forensic Scholars Today* 1, no. 4 (2016), https://online.csp.edu/blog/forensic-scholars-today/interrogative-suggestibility-in-people-with-fetal-alcohol-spectrum-disorder.

63. Karen Smith-Theil, Nora Baladerian, Katherine Boyce, Olegario Cantos, Leigh-Ann Davis, et al., "Fetal Alcohol Spectrum Disorders and Victimization: Implications for Families, Educators, Social Services, Law Enforcement, and the Judicial System," *Journal of Psychiatry & Law*, 39 (Spring 2011): 121–57.

64. Centers for Disease Control and Prevention, "TBI: Get the Facts," 2017, https://www.cdc.gov/traumaticbraininjury/get_the_facts.html.

65. T. Ashman, W. Gordon, J. Cantor, and M. Hibberd, "Neurobehavioral Consequences of Traumatic Brain Injury," *Mount Sinai Journal of Medicine* 73, no. 7 (2006): 999–1005.

66. J. Langlois, W. Rutland-Brown, and M. Wald, "The Epidemiology and Impact of Traumatic Brain Injury: A Brief Overview," *Journal of Head Trauma Rehabilitation* 21, no. 5 (2006): 375–78.

67. M. Oquendo, J. Friedman, M. Grunebaum, A. Burke, J. Silver, et al., "Suicidal Behavior and Mild Traumatic Brain Injury in Major Depression," *Journal of Nervous and Mental Disease* 192, no. 6 (2004): 430–34.

68. Jerrod Brown, Brooke Luckhardt, Diane Harr, Thomas Poser, and Amanda Fenrich, "Traumatic Brain Injury (TBI): A Guide for Probation Officers," *Journal of Trauma & Treatment* 7, no. 1 (2018): 714–25.

69. D. Admire and A. Mitchell, "Brain Abnormalities in the Criminal Justice System: United Public Policy and Scientific Knowledge," *International Journal of Interdisciplinary Social Sciences*, 5 (2010): 343–55.

70. A. Piccolino and K. Solberg, "The Impact of Traumatic Brain Injury on Prison Health Services and Offender Management," *Journal of Correctional Health Care*, 20 (2014): 203–12.

71. Brown, Luckhardt, Harr, Poser, and Fenrich, "Traumatic Brain Injury (TBI)."

72. Brown, Luckhardt, Harr, Poser, and Fenrich, "Traumatic Brain Injury (TBI)."

73. For example, see "Centers for Disease Control and Prevention, Traumatic Brain Injury in Prisons and Jails: An Unrecognized Problem," https://www.cdc.gov/traumaticbraininjury/pdf/prisoner_tbi_prof-a.pdf.

74. Jeffrey Draine and Phyllis Solomon, "Describing and Evaluating Jail Diversion Services for Persons with Serious Mental Illness," *Psychiatric Services* 50, no. 1 (1999): 56–55; Henry Steadman, "A Model Prison Diversions Program: The Criminal Justice Outreach Department of the Montgomery County Emergency Service, Norristown, Pennsylvania," *Psychiatric Services* 51, no. 11 (2000): 1440–43; Kristin Stainbrook, Patricia Griffin, Jeffrey Draine, Randy Dupont, and Cathy Horey, "A Specialized Crisis Response Site as a Core Element of Police-Based Diversion Programs," *Psychiatric Services* 52, no. 2 (2001): 219–22.

75. Tony Salvatore, "Montgomery County Emergency Service—A Model Provider-Based Diversion Strategy," *CIT in Action (National Alliance for Mental Illness)* 3, no. 2 (February 2008): 13–14.

CHAPTER 4. ALIGNMENT WITHIN ORGANIZATIONS

1. Fred Kofman and Peter Senge, *Communities of Commitment: The Heart of Learning Organizations* (Boston: Massachusetts Institute of Technology, Organizational Learning Center, 1994).

2. http://www.wbrz.com/news/officer-involved-shootings-linked-to-suspects-with-mental-illness-d-a-says-in-report.

3. Marti Hause and Ari Melber, "Half of People Killed by Police Have a Disability: Report," NBC News, March 14, 2016.

4. Bruce Barge and John Carlson, *The Executive's Guide to Controlling Healthcare and Disability Costs* (New York: John Wiley and Son, 1993).

5. http://www.businessdictionary.com/definition/management-theory.html.

6. Jeff Boss, "A Simple Flow to Think about Organizational Alignment," *Forbes*, January 21, 2018.

7. Treatment Advocacy Center, "Serious Mental Illness Prevalence in Jails and Prisons," September 2016.

8. https://www.nimh.nih.gov/health/statistics/mental-illness.shtml.

9. Miles Overholt, *Building Flexible Organizations: A People-Centered Approach* (Dubuque, IA: Kendall/Hunt, 1996).

10. Richard Morin, Ken Parker, Renee Stepler, and Andrew Mercer, "Behind the Badge," Pew Research Center, January 11, 2017.

11. Overholt, *Building Flexible Organizations*, 15.

12. Dr. Richard B. Jones, *Risk-Based Management: A Reliability-Centered Approach* (Houston, TX: Gulf Publishing, 1995).

CHAPTER 6. BUILDING EMOTIONAL MUSCLE MEMORY

1. President's Task Force on 21st Century Policing, *Final Report of the President's Task Force on 21st Century Policing* (Washington, DC: Office of Community-Oriented Policing Services, 2015).

2. Blue H.E.L.P, https://bluehelp.org (accessed July 22, 2019).

3. For additional information about the CISM Police School, see "'The Police School': A Crisis Intervention School for Law Enforcement and Criminal Justice Personnel," Montgomery County Emergency Service, 2017.

4. J. T. Mitchell and G. S. Everly, *Critical Incident Stress Management (CISM): Group Crisis Intervention*, 3rd ed., rev. (Ellicott City, MD: International Critical Incident Foundation, 2003).

5. J. T. Mitchell, *Group Crisis Intervention* (Ellicott City, MD: International Critical Incident Stress Foundation, 2015).

6. J. P. Woods, "Prioritizing Emotional and Mental Health through Peer Support Officer Safety Corner," *Police Chief*, 81 (June 2014): 10–11.

7. Kim Colegrove, "My Husband's Suicide: Recognizing Predictors of Police Suicide," *Public Safety*, August 2018.

CHAPTER 7. RESILIENCY

1. See, for example, Federal Emergency Management Agency "Crisis Response and Disaster Resilience 2030: Forging Strategic Action in an Age of Uncertainty," pp. 6–11 in U.S. Department of Homeland Security, ed., *The Strategic Foresight Initiative* (Washington, DC: USDHS; International Association of Chiefs of Police, 2013); "Breaking the Silence on Law Enforcement Suicides," National Symposium on Law Enforcement Officer Suicide and Mental Health, Office of Community-Oriented Policing Services, 2014.

2. President's Task Force on 21st Century Policing, *Final Report of the President's Task Force on 21st Century Policing* (Washington, DC: Office of Community-Oriented Policing Services, 2015).

3. International Association of Chiefs of Police, "Breaking the Silence on Law Enforcement Suicides" (Washington, DC: National Symposium on Law Enforcement Officer Suicide and Mental Health, Office of Community Oriented Policing Services, 2014).

4. A. Houser, B. Jackson, B. Bartis, and D. Peterson, *Emergency Responder Injuries and Fatalities: An Analysis of Surveillance Data* (Santa Monica, CA: RAND, 2010).

5. Blue H.E.L.P. is a not-for-profit group of active and retired police officers and their families, along with health and treatment providers, who advocate for the mental health and against stigma for law enforcement officers. It offers support, resources, education, and outreach. To learn more, visit https://bluehelp.org.

6. G. S. Everly and J. T. Mitchell, *Critical Incident Stress Management* (Ellicott City, MD: Chevron, 1999); J. M. Violanti, ed., *Dying for the Job: Police Work Exposure and Health* (Springfield, IL: Charles C. Thomas, 2014).

7. M. H. Chae and D. J. Boyle, "Police Suicide: Prevalence, Risk, and Protective Factors," *Policing: An International Journal of Police Strategies & Management* 36, no. 1 (2013): 91–118; P. M. Griffin, "Resilience in Police: Opioid Use and the Double-Edge Sword" (unpublished doctoral dissertation) (Philadelphia: Temple University, 2017); J. Gunderson, M. Grill, P. Callahan, and M. Marks, "Responder Resilience: Evidence-Based Program Improves and Sustains First-Responder Behavioral Health," *Journal of Emergency Medical Services* (March 2014): 57–61; J. Horn, "The New NFFF Initiative 13 Works to Change Traumatic Incident Response Stigma," *Journal of Emergency Medical Services* (July 11, 2014), www.jems.com/articles/print/volume-39/issue-7/health-and-safety/new-nfff-initiative-13-works-change-trau .html; J. J Hurrell, A. Pate, R. Kliesmet, R., Bowers, S. Lee, and J. Burg, *Stress among Police Officers* (Cincinnati, OH: National Institute of Officer Safety and Health, 1984); E. Kirschman, *I Love a Cop: What Police Families Need to Know*, rev. ed. (New York: Guilford Press, 2006); E. Kirschman, M. Kamena, and J. Fay, *Counseling Cops: What Clinicians Need to Know* (New York: Guilford Press, 2014); V. Lindsay, "Police Officers and Their Alcohol Consumption: Should We Be Concerned?" *Police Quarterly* 11, no. 1 (2008): 74–87; A. T. Matsakis, *In Harm's Way: Help for the Wives of Military Men, Police, EMTs, and Firefighters* (Oakland, CA: New Harbinger Publications, 2005); P. L. Obst, J. D. Davey, and M. C. Sheehan, "Does Joining the Police Service Drive You to Drink? A Longitudinal Study of the Drinking Habits of Police Recruits," *Drugs: Education, Prevention and Policy* 8, no. 4 (2001): 347–57; M. Swatt, C. L. Gibson, and N. L. Piquero, "Exploring the Utility of General Strain Theory in Exposing Problematic Alcohol Consumption by Police Officers," *Journal of Criminal Justice*, 35 (2007): 596–611; J. M. Violanti, "Police Trauma: Psychological Impact of Civilian Combat," 5–9, in J. M. Violanti and D. Paton, eds., *Police Trauma: Psychological Aftermath of Civilian Combat* (Springfield, IL: Charles C. Thomas, 1999); R. H. Woody, "The Police Culture: Research Implications for Psychological Services," *Professional Psychology: Research and Practice* 36, no. 5 (2005): 525–29.

8. E. Levy-Gigi, G. Richter-Levin, and S. Keri, "The Hidden Price of Repeated Traumatic Exposure: Different Cognitive Deficits in Different First-Responders," *Frontiers in Behavioral Neuroscience*, 8 (August 2014): 1–10.

9. *Substance Abuse Prevention, Education and Outreach for First Responders* (Bensalem, PA: Livengrin Foundation, 2014).

10. J. Janik and H. M. Kravitz, "Linking Work and Domestic Problems with Police Suicide," *Suicide and Life-Threatening Behavior*, 24 (1994): 267–74; L. B. Johnson, M. Todd, and G. Subramanian, "Violence in Police Families: Work-Family Spillover," *Journal of Family Violence* 20, no. 1 (2005): 3–12; Woody, "The Police Culture."

11. M. Morash, R. Haarr, and D. H. Kwak, "Multilevel Influences on Police Stress," *Journal of Contemporary Criminal Justice* 22, no. 1 (2006): 26–43; J. B. Stinchcomb, "Searching for Stress in All the Wrong Places: Combating Chronic Organizational Stressors in Policing," *Police Practice and Research*, 5 (2004): 3; Woody, "The Police Culture."

12. Chae and Boyle, "Police Suicide"; J. Davey, P. L. Obst, and M. C. Sheehan, "It Goes with the Job: Officers' Insights into the Impact of Stress and Culture on Al-

cohol Consumption within the Policing Occupation," *Drugs: Education, Prevention and Policy*, 8 (2001): 141–49; Gunderson, Grill, Callahan, and Marks, "Responder Resilience"; Horn, "The New NFFF Initiative 13"; Hurrell, Pate, Kliesmet, Bowers, Lee, and Burg, *Stress among Police Officers*; Kirschman, *I Love a Cop;* Kirschman, Kamena, and Fay, *Counseling Cops*; Lindsay, "Police Officers and Their Alcohol Consumption"; Matsakis, *"In Harm's Way"*; Swatt, Gibson, and Piquero, "Exploring the Utility of General Strain Theory"; Violanti, "Police Trauma."

13. Violanti, *Dying for the Job*.

14. B. A. Chopko, P. A. Palmieri, and R. E. Adams, "Associations between Police Stress and Alcohol Use: Implications for Practice," *Journal of Loss and Trauma*, 18 (2013): 482–97.

15. Chopko, Palmieri, and Adams, "Associations between Police Stress and Alcohol Use."

16. R. W. Balch, "Police Personality: Fact or Fiction," *Journal of Criminal Law and Criminology* 63, no. 1 (1972): 106–19; Bennett and Greenstein, "The Police Personality: A Test of the Predispositional Model," *Journal of Police Science and Administration*, 3 (1975): 439–45; J. P. Crank, *Understanding Police Culture* (Cincinnati, OH: Anderson, 1998); P. K. Manning, *Police Work: The Social Organization of Policing*, 2nd ed. (Prospect Heights, IL: Waveland Press, 1997); Jerome H. Skolnick, *Justice without Trial: Law Enforcement in Democratic Society* (New York, Wiley; Twersky-Glasner, 2005); "Police Personality: What Is It and Why Are They Like That?," *Journal of Police and Criminal Psychology* 20, no. 1: 56–67.

17. Woody, "The Police Culture."

18. Reiner, *The Politics of the Police* (New York: Oxford University, 1986).

19. K. Tausinga, January 3, 2015. Grieving behind the Badge, http://grievingbehindthebadgeblog.net.

20. J. Tucker, "What Shapes Police Officer Willingness to Use Stress Intervention Services? An Empirical Study of Current Factors in Pennsylvania" (unpublished PhD dissertation) (Philadelphia: Temple University, 2012).

21. B. Lansdowne, presentation before the Police Executive Research Forum, San Diego, CA, 2012.

22. N. Trautman, *Police Code of Silence: Facts Revealed*, proceedings from the Annual Conference of the International Association of Chiefs of Police (San Diego: CA, 2000).

23. A. Callaghan, "Pain Medication Addiction," *Peace Officer* (Philadelphia: Lodge 5, 2012), 153–54.

24. J. H. Wineman, "Personal Resilience in Law Enforcement," *Nebraska Trooper Magazine*, (n.d.).

25. D. Paton, J. M. Violanti, P. Johnston, K. J. Burke, J. Clarke, and D. Keenan, "Stress Shield: A Model of Police Resilience, *Journal of Emergency Mental Health* 10, no. 2 (2008): 95–107.

26. M. Fischer, "A Guide to U.S. Military Casualty Statistics: Operation New Dawn, Operation Iraqi Freedom and Operation Enduring Freedom," *Congressional Report No. RS22452* (Washington, DC: Library of Congress Congressional Research Services, 2014).

27. D. Grossman, *On Killing: The Psychological Cost of Learning to Kill in War and Society* (New York: Back Bay Books, 2009).

28. L. S. Meredith, C. D. Sherbourne, S. Gaillot, L. Hansell, H. V. Ritschard, A. M. Parker, and G. Wrenn, *Promoting Psychological Resilience in the U.S. Military* (Santa Monica, CA: RAND, 2011).

29. Bandura, "Self-Efficacy: Toward a Unifying Theory of Behavioral Change," *Psychology Review*, 84 (1977): 191–215.

30. Horn, "The New NFFF Initiative"; Paton, Violanti, Johnston, Burke, Clarke, and Keenan, "Stress Shield."

31. G. Pietrantoni and L. Prati, "Optimism, Social Support, and Coping Strategies as Factors Contributing to Posttraumatic Growth: A Meta-Analysis," *Journal of Loss and Trauma: International Perspectives on Stress & Coping* 14, no. 5 (2008): 364–88.

32. M. A. Meyer, "Social Capital and Collective Efficacy for Disaster Resilience: Connecting Individuals with Communities and Vulnerability with Resilience in Hurricane-Prone Communities in Florida" (unpublished doctoral dissertation) (Fort Collins: Colorado State University, 2013).

33. Griffin, "Resilience in Police."

34. H. M. Tiebout, "The Act of Surrender in the Therapeutic Process with Special Reference to Alcoholism," *Journal of Studies on Alcohol and Drugs* 10, no. 1 (1949): 48–58.

35. N. Colier, "When It's Time to Let Go of Control . . . and Surrender!" *Psychology Today*, May 4, 2016 (accessed March 3, 2019).

36. S. Satel, B. Becker, and E. Dan, "Reducing Obstacles to Affiliation with Alcholics Anonymous among Veterans with PTSD and Alcoholism," *Hospital & Community Psychiatry* 44, no. 11 (1993): 1061–5. doi: 10.1176/ps.44.11.1061.

37. D. Maclurcan, *The Power of Asset-Based Approaches*, 2014, http://postgrowth .org/the-power-of-asset-based-approaches/; M. Zimmerman, "Resiliency Theory: A Strengths-Based Approach to Research and Practice for Adolescent Health," *Health Education Behavior* 40, no. 4 (2013): 381–83. doi: 10.1177/1090198113493782.

38. Griffin, "Resilience in Police."

39. Chopko, Palmieri, and Adams, "Associations between Police Stress and Alcohol Use."

CHAPTER 9. PROMISING PRACTICES AND PROGRAMS

1. https://www.ptsd.va.gov/understand/common/common_veterans.asp.

2. http://www.ptsdunited.org/ptsd-statistics-2/.

3. John S. Hollywood, Dulani Woods, Sean E. Goodison, Andrew Lauland, Lisa Wagner, Thomas J. Wilson, and Brian A. Jackson, *Fostering Innovation in U.S. Law Enforcement: Identifying High-Priority Technology and Other Needs for Improving Law Enforcement Operations and Outcomes* (Santa Monica, CA: RAND Corporation, 2017). https://www.rand.org/pubs/research_reports/RR1814.html. Also available in print form.

4. I. Janis, *Victims of Groupthink: A Psychological Study of Foreign-Policy Decisions and Fiascoes* (Boston: Houghton Mifflin, 1972).

5. https://www.pantagraph.com/lifestyles/health-med-fit/mclean-county-to-open -mental-health-triage-center/article_cae0a9ef-c818-5fd4-9df8-a05771acee91.html.

6. Steven R. Pliska, Bruce Adams, Sally Taylor, and Dawn Velligan, "Mental Health Crisis in Bexar County a 'New Normal?' *Express-News*, August 13, 2016.

7. https://www.bostonglobe.com/metro/2016/12/10/the-san-antonio-way-how -one-texas-city-took-mental-health-community-and-became-national-model/08 HLKSq1JdXSTZppaECk2K/story.html.

8. http://www.sandhillscenter.org/partnership-to-bring-new-behavioral-health -crisis-centers-to-guilford-county/.

9. https://www.conehealth.com/news/news-search/2018-news-releases/inte grated-mental-health-center-coming-to-guilford-county/.

10. "Guide for Consumers, Providers and Unions," The Workplace Center, Columbia University, and the New York Work Exchange, The Coalition of Voluntary Mental Health Agencies, Inc., September 2002.

11. https://stepuptogether.org/people/boston-police-ride-along-2.

12. https://www.nrtoday.com/news/health/roseburg-police-and-compass-behav ioral-health-team-up-for-ride/article_2239350a-08a3-5d33-b9e9-d16774362769.html.

13. https://www.coloradoan.com/story/news/2018/01/06/colorado-pairing-police -officers-mental-health-experts/1009854001/.

14. Gary Puleo, "Norristown Police and School District Team up for Children's HUB," *Times Herald*, May 29, 2019.

15. https://www.stocktoninformationdirectory.org/kb5/stockton/directory/service .page?id=1N2_WMAtp_Q.

16. https://nypost.com/2019/08/13/nypd-chief-admits-city-has-poor-mental -health-care-in-wake-of-cop-suicides/
https://www.nbcnews.com/news/us-news/chicago-s-cluster-police-suicides-raises -alarms-heroes-need-saving-n954386.

17. https://www.northjersey.com/story/news/new-jersey/2019/08/06/new-jersey -ag-announces-plan-stop-rise-police-suicides/1925941001/.

18. https://www.njspotlight.com/stories/17/04/04/addressing-specific-needs-of -first-responders-struggling-with-addiction/.

CHAPTER 10. THE PHOENIXVILLE EDHUB

1. Caitlin Curley, "Juveniles Tried as Adults: What Happens When Children Go to Prison," www.genfkd.org/juveniles-tried-adults-happens-children-go-prison.

2. Liji Thomas, *News—Medical*, one in thirteen children affected by PTSD, according to landmark study, February 2019.

3. Centers for Disease Control and Prevention, https://www.cdc.gov/violencepre vention/childabuseandneglect/fastfact.html.

4. Centers for Disease Control and Prevention, "Youth Violence, Facts at a Glance," 2016, https://www.cdc.gov/violenceprevention/pdf/yv-datasheet.pdf.

5. Centers for Disease Control and Prevention, "Youth Violence: Risk and Protective Factors," https://www.cdc.gov/violenceprevention/youthviolence/riskprotective factors.html.

6. Cite the dates of the data.

7. Mark Munetz and Patricia Griffin, "Use of the Sequential Intercept Model as an Approach to Decriminalization of People with Serious Mental Illness," *Psychiatric Services*, April 1, 2006.

8. Policy Research Associates, https://www.prainc.com/wp-content/uploads/2016/11/Intercept-0-Infographic-2.pdf.

9. Dale R. McFee and Norman E. Taylor, "The Prince Albert Hub and the Emergence of Collaborative Risk-Driven Community Safety," *Canadian Police College Discussion Paper Series*, 2014.

10. Dr. Chad Nilson, "Risk-Driven Collaborative Intervention: A Preliminary Impact Assessment of Community Mobilization Prince Albert's Hub Model" (Centre for Forensic Behavioural Science and Justice Studies University of Saskatchewan).

11. https://suburbanstats.org/population/pennsylvania/how-many-people-live-in-phoenixville-borough.

12. https://suburbanstats.org/population/pennsylvania/how-many-people-live-in-phoenixville-borough.

13. http://www.homes.com/for-sale/phoenixville-pa/p13/?order_by percent5B0 percent5D=price_desc.

14. www.phoenixville.org.

15. http://www.pchfl.org/.

16. Miles Overholt, *Building Flexible Organizations: A People-Centered Approach* (Dubuque, IA: Kendall/Hunt, 1996).

17. Dr. Richard B. Jones, *Risk-Based Management: A Reliability-Centered Approach* (Houston, TX: Gulf Publishing, 1995).

18. https://www.childrenssociety.org.uk/what-we-do/policy-and-lobbying/children-risk.

19. https://www.relias.com/blog/6-challenges-of-the-human-services-worker.

ADDENDUM D. ASSESSING THE CLIMATE

1. Miles Overholt, *Building Flexible Organizations: A People-Centered Approach* (Dubuque, IA: Kendall/Hunt, 1996).

2. Dr. Richard B. Jones, *Risk-Based Management: A Reliability-Centered Approach* (Houston, TX: Gulf Publishing, 1995).

3. Carolyn Reinach Wolf, "Breaking down the Silos—A Collaborative Answer to Mental Health," *Huffington Post*, March 12, 2014.

4. Frank J. Mielke and William Mossman, *Mental Health Crisis Processing, Police and Emergency Room Intervention*. Sponsored by the Phoenixville Community Health Foundation, District Attorney's Office, and Audubon Management Consultants. August 2014, 5.

5. Sheila Akabas, Lauren Gates, and Lori Bikson, *Unions Helping Workers with Mental Health Conditions: A Guide for Consumers, Providers and Union Representatives* (New York: The Workplace Center, Columbia University, September 30, 2002).

Index

About the Authors and Editors

The authors and editors of this book comprise a cross-section of disciplines that collectively mirror the participants of those required to successfully divert the mentally ill out of the criminal justice system and into treatment.

They are in the classroom preparing their students for a career in criminal justice. As law enforcement officers and mental health specialists, they possess hands-on experience dealing with those in crisis. They are leaders in the community shaping the lives of our children or promoting philanthropic programs in the interest of diversion. They participate in research in the quest for gaining knowledge and promoting collaboration in the interest of developing new and innovative approaches to diversion.

This diverse team is linked together in a common cause: to do right for those suffering from mental illness.

Louis J. Beccaria, PhD, is a 1967 BA graduate in social science-education of LaSalle College. He earned his MEd in social science education from the University of Delaware in 1969, as well as his MA (1975) and PhD in urban affairs and public policy from the University of Delaware in 1979. Dr. Beccaria has more than forty-seven years of experience in criminal justice, higher education, health and human services, twenty-nine of them in philanthropy.

Alan Fegley, EdD, is superintendent of the Phoenixville Area School District. Previously, he was superintendent of the Haddonfield, New Jersey, School District; a special educator at Children's Hospital of Philadelphia; and a consultant in the Office of Special Master, Federal District Court. Dr. Fegley received his EdD in educational leadership from the University of Delaware.

Patricia Griffin, PhD, is assistant professor of criminal justice and director of graduate criminal justice at Holy Family University. She is also a senior research consultant for the United Nations Office of Drugs and Crime in East Africa, tasked to assess alcohol and substance use by police and develop workplace policies that support officer wellness. She served as research associate and community coordinator, substance abuse prevention, education, and outreach for first responders for the Livengrin Foundation. Previously, she was a special agent for the U.S. Department of Labor, Office of the Inspector General, Office of Organized Crime and Labor Racketeering. Dr. Griffin received her PhD in criminal justice from Temple University.

Charles Kocher, EdD, is professor of justice studies at Cumberland Community College and affiliate professor at Saint Joseph's University. He is the author of *Camden Police: In Defense of Law and Order* and numerous articles. He worked for the Camden Police Department for twenty-seven years, most recently as deputy police chief. He is affiliated with the International Chiefs of Police administration committee, Academy of Criminal Justice Sciences Eastern Conference of the ACJS, the American Society of Criminology (ASC), among others. He received his EdD from Saint Joseph's University, Philadelphia.

Frank Mielke, as president of Audubon Management Consultants, blends his understanding of organizations and experience from his public safety teaching, research, and consulting. He previously was on the faculty of Saint Joseph's Institute for Criminal Justice and Public Safety. He is the author of *Management Processes—A Guide for Leaders in Public and Industrial Safety*, and he has conducted research on and consulted to fire, police, emergency dispatch, and public safety organizations. Frank received his BBA from Saint Francis College, Brooklyn, and his MBA from Temple University, Philadelphia. He currently directs research programs to broaden the cross-discipline influences on diversion and responses to members dealing with trauma.

Michelle Monzo has been with MCES for twenty-five years and currently is a nationwide instructor for the MCES Crisis Intervention Specialist police school. Ms. Monzo also provides crisis intervention training to community agencies, universities, schools, and numerous other organizations. She is a member of the Mobile Crisis Intervention team, certified in Critical Incident Stress Management (CISM) and Peer Support for first responders. As a trained specialist for the FBI, New York Police Department, and Homeland Security, she serves on the board of the Delaware Valley regional negotiators.

She was the 2016 recipient of the NAMI Criminal Justice Award. Ms. Monzo received her degree in psychology from West Virginia University.

William Mossman has twenty-eight years of police service and currently is chief of the East Coventry, Pennsylvania, Police Department. He received his BS in criminal justice and MS in public safety management from Saint Joseph's University, Philadelphia. He holds an array of certificates from the FBI National Academy, Penn State University, and the University of North Florida. Bill is president of the Chester County Police Chiefs Association and serves as liaison between the association and the county's Department of Mental Health/Intellectual and Development Disabilities. He is also an executive board member of the Chester County Regional Emergency Response Team.

Anthony Salvatore is director of development and suicide prevention at Montgomery County Emergency Service, Norristown, Pennsylvania. He earned his MA from Temple University. In addition to writing many articles on a variety of mental health issues, he has conducted numerous training sessions for police officers and other emergency responders on suicide prevention and postvention. He is very experienced in assisting police officers dealing with mental health emergencies.

Darren K. Stocker is a professor and program coordinator of criminal justice at Cape Cod Community College. He has spoken throughout the United States and internationally on issues of criminal justice, policing, and vicarious trauma. He earned a BS from West Chester University and graduate degrees from Saint Joseph's University and the University of Massachusetts. He has authored and coauthored numerous articles for trade publications, peer journals, and book chapters.

www.ingramcontent.com/pod-product-compliance
Lightning Source LLC
Chambersburg PA
CBHW071854270326
41929CB00013B/2230